Success Studybooks

Success in
OFFICE
PRACTICE

Penny Hackett, M.A., M.I.P.M.

John Murray

© Penny Hackett 1984

First published 1984
by John Murray (Publishers) Ltd
50 Albemarle Street, London W1X 4BD

Typeset by Butler & Tanner, Frome

Printed and bound in Hong Kong by
Wing King Tong Co Ltd

British Library Cataloguing in Publication Data
Hackett, Penny
  Success in office practice
  1. Office practice
  I. Title
  651   HF5547.5

ISBN 0-7195-3923-4

Foreword

As countries develop and grow, the needs of their people change; in particular, their needs for specific types of work change. In modern societies, diminishing numbers work on farms and in factories, while on the other hand there is increased emphasis on the provision of services and information. Job opportunities therefore exist for office workers rather than for farm or factory hands— but those seeking employment in offices need to be thoroughly trained, both in basic skills and in new techniques.

This book aims to give you the essentials of such training. It starts by answering some questions about the world of work and the place of the office within it. Each of the skills you will need is then discussed in a logical order, with the emphasis on how you can improve your practical ability. Office machines, including word-processors, computers, facsimile text transmission, view-data, and the whole range of reprographic equipment are explained and their use discussed. To help you understand the different procedures and documentation you will meet in various departments of the organization, a Unit is devoted to each. And to help you to get an office job where you can use your skills, the final Unit gives advice on where to learn about, and how to apply for, a position.

At the end of each Unit you will find some Quick Questions, to test your recall. There are also two Short Exercises per Unit. These are to help you to carry out a more detailed review of the topic. They can be tackled individually, or, in some cases, on a group basis. At the end of the text are some longer Assignments, several of which are taken from past examination papers. These may call for you to bring together work from more than one Unit. All can be handled by the student working alone, though some may require you to talk to colleagues or people you know who have an office job. Some can also be dealt with as group assignments.

If you are studying for an Office Practice examination, you will find that the book is suitable for BTEC General, RSA (Stage I), LCCI (Elementary) and Pitman (Elementary and Intermediate) courses. It is also recommended if you are taking a pre-vocational course such as CSE. The self-study format will help you to gain and test the knowledge and practical skills that are needed for a successful office career.

P.J.H.

Acknowledgments

Many people have given unstintingly of their time and expertise to help with the preparation of this text. In particular, I owe a great deal to Mrs Margaret Jones for her constructive criticism and professional advice, and to Dr Jean Macqueen for her expert editing. Mrs Sheila May, Mrs Judy Vegh, Mrs Mary Sturt, Miss E. M. Ramsay, Miss Diana K. Jones, Mr Roger Logan and Mr R. A. D. Foster advised at various stages in the preparation of the text. I should also like to thank Tom and Freda Duncan and my husband, Dave, for their help and encouragement throughout.

I am grateful to the following for their kind assistance with illustrations: Acco International Ltd, Apple Computers Ltd, British Olivetti Limited, British Telecom, Business Aids Ltd, Copeland Chatterson Co Ltd, Dictaphone Co Ltd, Elite Manufacturing Co Ltd, Esselte Dymo Ltd, Facit Business Systems Division, Gestetner International Limited, Hasler (Great Britain) Limited, W. H. Hayden & Co Ltd, IBM United Kingdom Limited, Kalle Infotec Ltd, Kardex Systems (UK) Ltd, Kodak Ltd, Myers (Office Equipment) Ltd, National Girobank, National Westminster Bank PLC, Olympia Business Machines Co Ltd, Philips Business Systems, Pitney Bowes PLC, Portable Factory Equipment Ltd, Postal Marketing Department of the Post Office, Ryman Contract Stationery, Spicers Ltd, Standard Telephones & Cables PLC, Supreme Equipment & Systems (Europe) Ltd, Westra Office Equipment Ltd, Whitaker's *British Books in Print*.

Assignments are reproduced by permission of the Royal Society of Arts (Units 3, 8, 12 and 20) and the Business and Technician Education Council (Unit 11). Extracts from Crown copyright material (Tax Tables A and B—Figs. 20.1 and 20.2) are reproduced with the permission of the Controller of Her Majesty's Stationery Office.

P.J.H.

Contents

x Contents

xii Contents

Unit One

The Office and the Organization

1.1 Introduction

If you could hover in a helicopter above the City of London at the start of a working day, you would see the streets below you packed with thousands of people, hurrying along on foot or in their cars, all on their way into the towering buildings around them. Many, perhaps most, of these people are office workers. And the scene is repeated in every great city of the world, and on a smaller scale in every town as well. In hospitals, courts of law and schools, on farms and in football clubs, in factories, hotels and shops, office workers play a vital part.

In this book we shall look at their role, its importance and the many ways in which it is carried out. But if you have never worked in an office, you may not have much idea of what happens there, or what purpose an office serves within the wider organization of which it is a part. In this first Unit, we shall answer some of the general questions you may have in mind, and in later Units we will discuss the range of duties that office workers are asked to carry out.

1.2 What is an Office?

Every organization needs a certain amount of *information* in order to function properly. The office is the place where this information is recorded, copied, stored, retrieved and passed on.

The information may be about people, such as customers and clients, suppliers and employees. It may be about things—goods and services bought and sold by the organization. Much of it is about the money which the organization receives or pays out in exchange for goods and services.

An office may be very small—just a desk and a filing cabinet in the corner of a workshop. Or it may be very large—a multi-storey office block in the business quarter of a city.

1.3 What is the Purpose of an Office?

The information passing through an office each day has five main purposes.

(a) To Provide a Basis for Future Decisions

If a lecturer does not know how many students enter the college each year, he does not know how many copies of a particular textbook he should order for each class. The college office records the admission of all students to the college, and can give him the information he needs.

(b) To Allow a Situation to be Watched and Kept under Control

If a store fashion buyer does not keep track of (or *monitor*) the difference between the number of size 12 dresses sold and the number of size 22, the store may well run out of the more popular size, and end the season with a stockroom full of outsized remnants. The stock control clerk, who records the details of dresses coming into and going out of the department, can provide this information.

(c) To Ensure that the Business is Financially Sound

If managers spend money that their firm does not have, the organization will go out of business. All payments into and out of the organization are recorded in the accounts office, whose staff can tell the managers how much money is available, or *budgeted*, for particular purposes. They also know how much money the business owes to other people, and how much is owed to it.

(d) To Ensure that the Organization Operates Legally

If an organization does not keep records of the amount of income tax deducted from employees' wages, it cannot prove that it is obeying the law that says that tax must be deducted. The wages office, where all payments to employees are calculated, can provide the necessary proof.

(e) To Set Activities and Projects in Motion

If a business has no one to answer the telephone when people ring in to order goods, it cannot sell much of what it produces. The sales office staff can put through an order, telling the production manager what the customer wants, and when he wants it.

1.4 What Do Office Staff Do?

Work which is done in an office is generally described as *clerical* work. (The word 'clerical' was once used to describe scholars and clergymen, but now has a much broader meaning.) This description distinguishes office work from the other main kinds of work activity, such as manual work, which is done with the hands, management, which involves co-ordinating the work of others, and the work of the professions (doctor, teacher, architect). Table 1.1 shows that clerical work can take many forms.

Office work has six main elements. All involve the handling of information.

(a) Storing and Retrieving Information

One of the most important tasks in a traditional office is *filing*. The filing clerk's main function is to collect documents from various sources, and to make sure that they are stored where they can be found when they are next wanted.

(b) Passing on Information

The facts and figures kept in the office must often be communicated to other people. Sometimes this is done by means of the spoken word, either face to face or over the telephone. Sometimes it is done in writing. Inter-office memoranda may be sent by internal messenger, to ask for or give information to other

Table 1.1 Some clerical occupations

Audit clerk	Ledger clerk
Bank/counter/office cashier	Post office counter clerk
Book-keeper	Press-cuttings clerk
Cash desk clerk	Progress clerk
Chartering clerk	Purchasing clerk
Checker (goods/raw materials)	Receptionist
Control clerk (data-processing)	Records clerk
Conveyancing clerk	Reservations clerk
Correspondence clerk	Sales order clerk
Cost clerk	Statistical clerk
Dispatch clerk	Stockbroker's clerk
Filing clerk	Stock-control clerk
Foreign exchange clerk	Stock-taker
Freight clerk	Telephone sales order clerk
General clerk	Time clerk
Information clerk	Traffic dispatcher
Insurance broker's clerk	Wages clerk
Invoice clerk	

departments. Letters, forms and reports may be sent by post to people outside the organization.

(c) Recording Information

Sometimes information is just copied, as when the copy typist prepares a typed document from a handwritten report. Sometimes the information must be gathered together from several different sources, as when details of sales are taken from a series of orders and entered on an invoice (see Unit 17.2(f)). Either way, the information must be recorded accurately and legibly, whether by hand or by using a typewriter, a word-processor or a computer.

(d) Handling Money

Every organization spends and receives money. Where the sums concerned are very large, a purely 'paper' transaction takes place, using the services of the banking system. But there is also often a need for small amounts of ready cash— to buy stamps, for example, or to pay taxi fares. Office staff make and record all such payments.

(e) Processing Information and Making Calculations

Much of the information dealt with in offices comes in the form of figures, and the clerk in an accounts department, for instance, may find that the figures on an accounts sheet have to be added, subtracted, or adjusted in some way, perhaps by the addition of VAT (see Unit 19.5). Various forms of accounting equipment are available to help with tasks like these, ranging from pocket calculators to computers.

(f) Providing Administrative Support

Some clerical workers have a more general, servicing role. A secretary, for instance, transcribes (types back) information dictated by the manager, and files copies of letters and reports. But a secretary also makes appointments, keeps the diary, makes travelling arrangements, arranges meetings and acts, to some degree, in the manager's stead when he or she is away from the office. This sort of work requires special training, and we will not discuss it in detail in this book.

1.5 What are the Career Prospects?

In most offices, there are five main steps on the promotion ladder.

(a) Junior Clerk

If you are leaving school or college, probably with CSE, O-level, BTEC or parallel qualifications, you can expect to come into an office at this level. Fig. 1.1 shows a job description for a junior clerk in an insurance company, listing the sort of duties you might be asked to carry out. To these may be added running errands and making tea and coffee for visitors and staff.

(b) Clerk or Clerical Assistant

After a year or two as a junior clerk, you may move on to the full range of clerical duties. Or you may join the organization at this level if you have a higher standard of general education—several O levels or an office practice qualification. The work could involve any or all of the aspects discussed in Unit 1.4. And you will probably still have to make the tea from time to time.

(c) Senior Clerk/Team or Section Leader

When you have enough knowledge of office procedures and of the requirements of the business, you may be promoted to co-ordinate the work of a small group of clerks. As a team leader, you may have to assign work among members of the group, train newcomers and handle queries, as well as carrying out normal clerical duties.

(d) Supervisor

The next step on the ladder is the job of supervisor, who is responsible for the day-to-day smooth running of the department. This means:

    (i) assigning work among team leaders;

    (ii) dealing with queries and complaints that cannot be resolved by the staff directly concerned;

    (iii) liaising with other departments of the organization to make sure that work coming in flows through smoothly and can be dealt with as required;

    (iv) introducing and training new staff;

    (v) planning to ensure that there are always enough staff available in the

JOB DESCRIPTION

Job title: Junior clerk

Department: Insurance claims

Responsible to: Claims manager

Responsible for: not applicable

No. in this position: 1

Main purpose: To provide a mail collection and delivery
service between claims department and the company's
post room and to provide a file storage and retrieval
service for claims clerks.
Duties:
  (i) to collect claims department mail from post room
rack by 8.50 a.m. each day
  (ii) to open all mail except that marked 'personal'
and 'confidential'
  (iii) to check references on incoming mail and marry up
with appropriate files
  (iv) to distribute letters and files to claims clerks'
in-trays, as appropriate
  (v) to fetch other files for clerks (from filing room or
archives) as requested, orally or in requisitions, by
claims clerks
  (vi) to empty out-trays of all claims clerks at intervals
during day
  (vii) to file additional documents as directed by senior
filing clerk
  (viii) to replace files in correct (numerical reference)
order in filing room
  (ix) to ensure that all out-going mail is collected from
clerks by 4.00 p.m. each day
  (x) to insert all out-going mail in envelopes as supplied by
clerks, seal and deliver to post room by 4.45 p.m.
  (xi) to maintain diary card system, under supervision of
senior filing clerk
  (xii) to distribute inter-departmental mail by hand from
claims department
  (xiii) to carry verbal or written messages for the department
manager and assistant manager
  (xiv) such other duties as may from time to time be requested
by the senior filing clerk, assistant manager or manager.

Fig. 1.1 Job description for a junior clerk

office: it is very frustrating for a user of office services to find that all the staff who could help him have gone off to lunch or are away on holiday;

(vi) making sure that all staff are giving of their best and are keeping to the rules of behaviour and standards of work set down by the manager.

(e) Manager

At the top of the office career ladder in a large organization is the post of office manager. (In smaller businesses the supervisor may report direct to the owner or manager.) The office manager must ensure that the department as a whole does its job in the way that best serves the needs of the organization of which it forms a part. This means:

(i) *planning* the people, the work and the time schedule;

(ii) *organizing* the people, the systems and the jobs;

(iii) *staffing*—getting, training, rewarding, disciplining and keeping the people the office needs;

(iv) *directing*—explaining what is required and publicizing standard procedures;

(v) *controlling*—to make sure that financial and other targets will be met;

(vi) *co-ordinating* all these activities.

1.6 Who Owns the Organizations?

For business organizations, whether large or small and whether they supply goods (like food or furniture) or services (like banking facilities or health care), there are two main forms of ownership. Some organizations are *privately* owned. That means that a private individual, alone or with a group of others, has raised the money to start and operate the business.

Other organizations are *publicly* owned. That means that the government of the country has been involved in setting them up and has made arrangements for them to be financed.

(a) Private Sector

Private sector firms are of four main types. The chief differences between them lie in the way in which *capital* (money and other resources) is obtained for the business, the number of people who have a share in the *ownership* and *control* of the business, and the extent of their *liability* for the debts of the business (that is, the extent to which they must use their own money to settle with those to whom the business is in debt). We shall look at these types of firm in turn.

(i) **Sole traders.** If you walk down the high street, or glance at the classified (trade) advertisements of your local newspaper, you will see that many small retail shops operate as one-man bands. So do many tradesmen, like plumbers and electricians. The proprietor may be helped by his family or some hired employees, but in terms of providing capital and ownership and control, the proprietor *is* the business.

The retail sole trader, for instance, rents or buys his own shop, buys the stock, pays the suppliers of the goods offered for sale in the shop and of the other services used—heating, lighting and so on—out of the money coming in from sales. He lives off the money left over—the *net profit* of the business.

If the business gets into debt, with stock not paid for and the rent in arrears, the sole trader may have to raise money by selling his car, his personal possessions or even his house. He has *unlimited liability* for the debts of the business.

(ii) **Partnerships.** A sole trader can share the worries, responsibilities and rewards of the business, and bring in new finance, without any complex legal arrangements. A *partnership* can be formed by two or more people agreeing together to share the firm's profits and losses.

For most types of partnership there is a maximum of twenty partners, but there is no upper limit for professional partnerships, such as accountancy firms. The firm can operate under the joint names of the partners—Messrs Smith, Smith and Brown, for instance; if the partners wish to choose another name, they must register it (in the United Kingdom) with the Registrar of Business Names in London.

Like sole traders, members of a partnership put some of their own money into the firm and usually have unlimited liability for its debts.

(iii) **Limited companies.** A trader can avoid unlimited liability by forming a company with limited liability—a *limited company*. Limited companies are registered with the Registrar of Companies and, in the United Kingdom, their behaviour is regulated by several Acts of Parliament, the Companies Acts.

Limited companies are financed mainly by the issue of *shares*. People with money to invest buy shares in the business. They thus become part-owners of it, and are entitled to a share in its profits, called a *dividend*.

The formation of a limited company means that the company is set up as a separate legal entity. This in turn means that the business, rather than individual shareholders, can itself be sued by people with complaints against the company. The resources of the company, not those of the shareholders, are all that can be called upon to settle debts.

Limited companies may themselves be either private or public. The shares of a *private limited company* may not be offered for sale to the general public. The word 'Limited' or the abbreviation 'Ltd' must appear after the name of the company.

The shares of a *public limited company*, on the other hand, are available to the general public and to other institutions, like pension funds. They may be bought and sold, and their prices may be quoted on the London Stock Exchange. A public limited company must use the words 'public limited company', or the abbreviation 'p.l.c.', after its name.

(iv) **Co-operative societies.** It is possible for a business to be jointly owned by a group of people who run it for their mutual benefit. Each member has a limited number of shares in the organization, and has a say in how it is run. In some co-operatives the members actually work for the business, providing goods and services. In others, the members are customers of the co-operative and purchase goods and services from it at favourable prices. The retail co-operative movement, the 'Co-op', is the best-known British example.

You will find more details about all these types of company, and about methods of financing companies, in a companion volume to this book, *Success in Commerce*.

(*b*) **Public Sector**
In the public sector there are three main types of organization.

(i) **Public corporations** (nationalized industries). Many large organizations are owned by the state, rather than by groups of private individuals. In the United Kingdom, an organization cannot be taken into public ownership without an Act of Parliament.
   These organizations have no shareholders and pay no dividends. Their aim is to provide something which is of use to the community, while meeting the financial targets laid down for them by the government. In the United Kingdom their products and services range from electrical power (the electricity generating boards) to shipbuilding (British Shipbuilders) and from television and radio (the BBC) to travel (British Rail).
   Public corporations are financed partly by government and partly by the users of their services. The BBC, for instance, relies on the revenue raised by the sale of television and radio licences.

(ii) **Central government departments.** Most countries have both a *legislature*, where laws are made, and an *executive*, which carries them out. In Britain 650 Members of Parliament are elected to help frame the laws of the country, while several hundred thousand civil servants ensure that these laws are properly executed. The administrative and other services they provide are paid for out of taxation.

(iii) **Local government.** The teachers at state schools, some of the dustmen who collect your rubbish, the firemen, and the keepers of your town's parks, libraries and museums, are among the two million or so people who work for the local authorities in the British Isles.
   Some local authority services are paid for directly by those who use them: the fares charged to passengers, for instance, finance local bus services, in part at least. Others are paid for indirectly through the *rates*, the local taxes paid by the people living in the area. Rates are assessed in relation to the size and type of house occupied by the householder, and these payments, together with a grant from central government, are important sources of local government finance.

1.7 Who Runs Them?

The business of a sole trader or partnership is often small enough to be run
personally by the owner or owners. As it expands, perhaps by taking over
another shop or workshop, some help begins to be necessary. So the trader may
ask someone else to manage one of the shops, on a day-to-day basis. The
proprietor may continue to manage the other shop, keeping overall responsibility for and control over both.

The ownership of a limited company is much more widespread, and the
shareholders elect a *board of directors*, headed by a managing director, to
manage the business for them. These directors are answerable to the shareholders for the profitability and general conduct of the business. We will
discuss their obligations to them more fully in Unit 1.8.

Some directors are full-time or *executive* directors. This means that they take
charge of a particular aspect of the business, for which they are answerable to
the managing director.

A company may also have *non-executive directors*, who advise their fellow
board-members, but do not have anyone inside the company reporting directly
to them.

Below the board of directors, the business may be organized in different ways.
The larger it is, the more difficult it will be for everyone to be concerned in all
aspects, and the more likely it is that the business will have to be split into
different *divisions* and/or *departments*.

The business may be split geographically, perhaps with a northern division
and a southern division. Or it may be split by products: some motor vehicle
manufacturers, for example, have a car division and a bus and truck division.
Yet others organize themselves in relation to the types of customer with whom
they are dealing, and have an industrial division, a commercial division and a
consumer division.

One of the most common ways of subdividing the company is to organize
according to function or activity. There may thus be a production division to
produce goods and services, a sales and marketing division to sell them, a
finance division to obtain and monitor the money the business needs, a personnel division to make sure there are enough people to operate all the other
divisions effectively, and so on. (We will discuss each of these functions in Units
16 to 22.)

The organization chart in Fig. 1.2 shows a possible organization structure for
a manufacturing concern. Each function is headed by an executive director,
who has two or more managers reporting to him or her. At the bottom of the
chart are shown the individual departments, each headed by a department
manager.

The department manager plans and organizes the work of a department. The
divisional manager or director, on the other hand, must consider the work of
the division as a whole, and his or her decisions affect a much larger portion of
the organization, may involve more money and more people, take longer to put
into operation, and be more far-reaching in their effects.

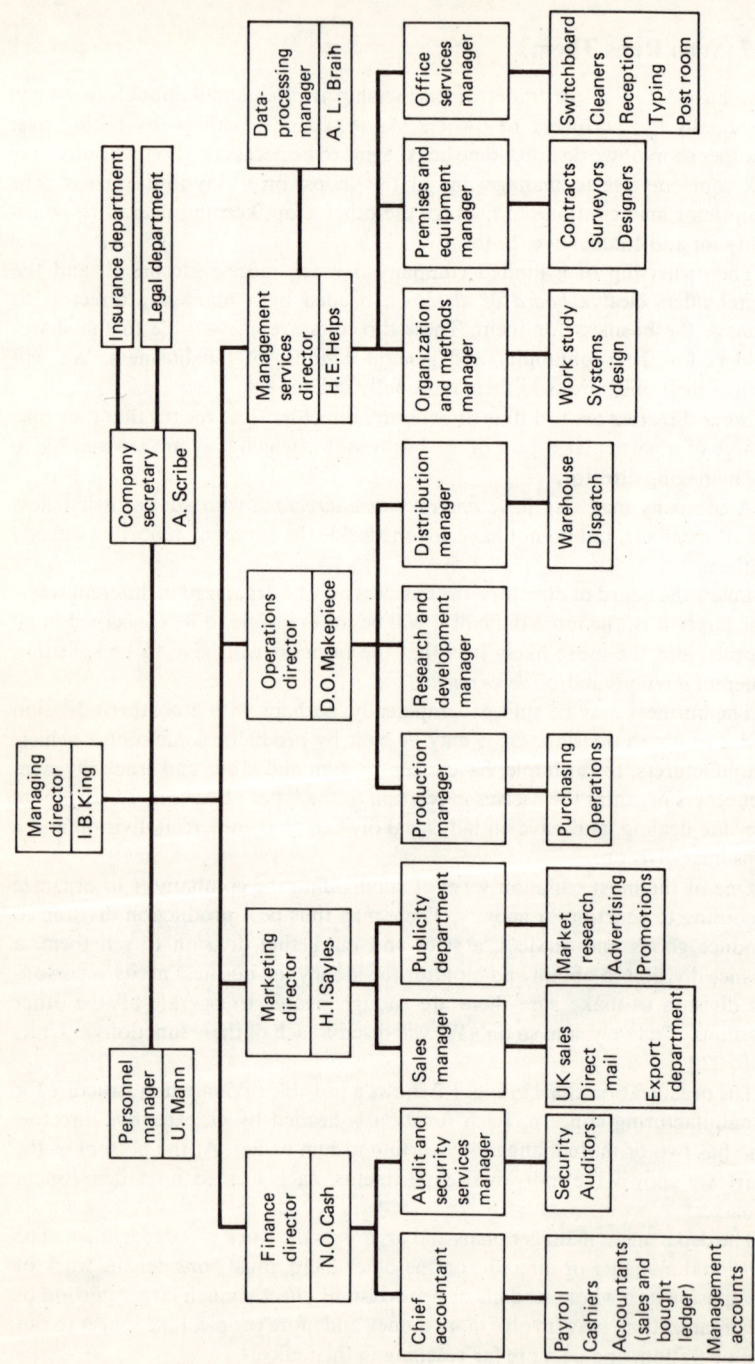

Fig. 1.2   An organization chart

1.8 Business Relationships and Obligations

No organization can exist in isolation. Unless people want the products or services it produces, it will go out of business. So businesses need *customers*.

But businesses also need materials from which to make their products, equipment for the office and the factory, stationery for the office, food for the canteen, and so on. The organization must find reliable *suppliers* to provide all these things.

As we have seen, limited companies also need to attract investment in the business. They need *shareholders* willing to buy shares in the firm.

And when the work becomes too much for one person, all organizations need to recruit and keep *employees* who will devote time and skill to working for the organization.

In addition to these specific relationships, all organizations are part of a much wider community, and indeed of the *world at large*.

If the organization is to remain on reasonably good terms with its customers, suppliers, shareholders, employees and the world at large, there are certain obligations it should meet. Some are determined by law, others are common sense.

(*a*) Obligations to Customers

An organization which values its customers tries to establish a good reputation. It charges fair prices, provides prompt and efficient services and delivers on time. It also ensures that its products and services are well made and safe to use. This is how customer loyalty is built up and maintained.

In addition, all business organizations must abide by the laws regulating trade in the countries in which they operate. In the United Kingdom these requirements include:

(i) Selling goods that are fit for the purposes for which they are sold, and that live up to the supplier's description of them.

(ii) Selling goods in standard measures and making sure that each packet, case or item really does weigh or measure the stated amount.

(iii) Ensuring that edible items are manufactured and sold under safe and hygienic conditions.

(iv) Supplying household goods which are safe to use.

(v) Delivering goods in accordance with the terms of the *contract of sale*, that is, the agreement whereby the supplier offers to deliver certain goods in a certain place on a certain date, and in return the customer promises to pay an agreed amount.

(vi) Supplying goods under proper credit arrangements. If a customer arranges to pay by instalments over a period of time, that is, *on credit*, he or she should be advised of the total cost of buying on credit, compared with the cost of paying cash. (Sales on credit usually cost more because the customer is, in effect, borrowing money from the supplier.) The rate at which the extra charge is calculated (the true *interest* rate) must also be quoted to the customer.

(b) Obligations to Suppliers

When buying goods or services from another organization, it is good business practice for the buying organization, who is now the customer, to treat the supplier in the same way as it would like to be treated by its own customers.

This means sticking to the terms of the contract of sale agreed between the two organizations, without last-minute changes of delivery dates or places or of the size of the order.

It also means giving clear instructions as to what is required, and allowing the supplier reasonable time to carry out his side of the bargain.

And if every large business organization paid its debts to its suppliers promptly, there would be a lot fewer small companies with financial problems.

(c) Obligations to Shareholders

A limited company is owned by those who have invested their money in the organization's shares. The board of directors has certain specific obligations to both big and small investors. In the United Kingdom these are laid down in a series of Companies Acts, and include:

(i) Registering the company with the Registrar of Companies. Various documents are needed for this, including a *memorandum of association*, which gives the name and purpose of the organization, its address and a statement limiting the liability of the shareholders, and the *articles of association*, which are the rules for the management of the company.

(ii) Holding meetings and providing information for shareholders. An *Annual General Meeting* (AGM) must be held at least once every calendar year. The directors must report the company's financial position and various other matters. *Extraordinary General Meetings* (EGMs) may also be called from time to time, to resolve specific issues.

(iii) Keeping statutory books. The directors must make a number of records available for inspection at the organization's registered offices. These include *registers* of shareholders and directors, the *minutes* (reports) of general meetings, and certain accounting records—the balance sheet, the profit and loss account, the directors' report and an auditor's report. These must show the true financial position of the organization.

(d) Obligations to Employees

The relationship between the organization (the employer) and the employee is a two-way affair. When you start work for a business you enter into a contract with it, which imposes duties and obligations on both you and your employer.

You, as an employee, have a duty to work hard for your employer. You are expected to be competent in your work, attend regularly and obey instructions. You must not give away the employer's trade secrets to outsiders. And you must make certain you don't risk your own safety or that of other people—for instance, by interfering with safety equipment or disregarding safety instructions.

Your employer also has obligations to you. The main ones, which in the United Kingdom can be enforced by law, are:

(i) To give you a *contract of employment*, or a written statement of your terms and conditions of employment, within thirteen weeks of your starting work;

(ii) To pay you and to give you holidays and sick leave in accordance with the terms of your contract;

(iii) Not to dismiss you without the period of notice which is written into your contract (in the United Kingdom the minimum is one week's notice after one month's service);

(iv) Not to dismiss you for incompetence or misconduct without warning and without giving you a chance to improve. If you are guilty of gross misconduct, though, like fighting or stealing, you can be sacked on the spot;

(v) Not to dismiss you without compensation if the employer has to end your contract because the business needs fewer people or can't afford to keep you on. If your job has thus become *redundant*, you should receive a payment related to your age and length of service, provided you have worked for the employer for at least two years. You are entitled to half a week's pay for each year of your service between the ages of 18 and 21, and the amount increases as you get older;

(vi) Not to discriminate against you because of your sex, marital status or race. In the United Kingdom you have the right to complain to a special *industrial tribunal* if you feel you have been turned down for a job or denied training or promotion chances because of your sex or race. Men and women doing the same work must also be paid the same;

(vii) To make sure, so far as is reasonably possible, that you are not exposed to risk of injury or disease while at work;

(viii) In certain circumstances, to negotiate with your *trade union* (see Unit 20.1(a)(vii)) about rates of pay, hours, pensions, holidays, working conditions, and so on. Procedures for dealing with employee complaints and disputes, and to enable the employer to discipline unsatisfactory employees, may also be agreed with the union and the employer should abide by these.

(e) Obligations to the World at Large

The prosperity of a whole community can be affected by the actions of a major employer. If, for instance, a firm declares a large number of redundancies at once, unemployment in the district will rise and there will be less money about to be spent on the goods and services offered by other organizations.

In other ways, too, the organization's operations can have a considerable impact, for better or worse, on the quality of life in the neighbourhood. Its obligations include:

(i) Avoiding atmospheric pollution;

(ii) Preserving the character and appearance of its surroundings, for instance, making sure its buildings blend in with their neighbours and are properly and safely constructed;

(iii) Avoiding risks to the health and safety of people, other than employees, who may be affected by the operation of the business.

Now that you have a basic grasp of the activities of offices and organizations, we will move on to consider the skills that you must develop if you are to succeed in office practice.

1.9 Quick Questions

1. List five purposes of office work.
2. What are the six main elements of office activity?
3. List six activities of the supervisor.
4. What are the six main elements of the manager's job?
5. List three forms of ownership for business organizations.
6. What do the letters 'p.l.c.' stand for?

1.10 Short Exercises

1. Discuss, or write down a list of, the essential qualities and qualifications required by (*a*) a general clerk, (*b*) a supervisor, and (*c*) a manager.
2. Discuss, or write down a list of, the ways in which the activities of the office can influence the overall success of a business.

Unit Two

Spoken Communication

2.1 Introduction

As we saw in Unit 1, the work of every office revolves around the information which flows through it. But information is of no use unless it is given to the people who need it, in a form they can understand. This is the art of *communication.*

Communication may be either written or spoken. In Unit 4 we will consider the main forms of written communication. Here we are concerned with the spoken word.

Interviews, training sessions, meetings and general conversation all use *oral* (spoken) communication. During any one day in the office, you could find yourself taking part in all these. And you may be expected to exchange information with a wide range of people, from your own colleagues and supervisor to the organization's customers, suppliers and other business contacts.

You will need two basic skills: *talking* and *listening.* You must learn to do both well if you are to communicate effectively.

2.2 Talking

You must think *what to say*, and *how best to say it.*

(a) What to Say

When you are asked to provide information, there are several points to bear in mind:

(i) Decide which are the most important facts.

(ii) Communicate those facts first. Most business people prefer to get the answers to their questions in the first few minutes of a conversation. Details and examples can be added later if necessary.

(iii) Place these additional but less important points in a logical order, so that the listener is led through step by step. This is particularly important if you are trying to support an argument or a recommendation where you want the other person to agree with your own conclusions.

(iv) Choose words that the other person can understand. Unnecessarily long words, particularly if used wrongly, can create confusion. Initials and abbreviations can speed up communication between people who know, say, that a Form K21 is the firm's stationery requisition form. They bewilder anyone who does not.

(v) Check that you and the other person have really understood each other.

Ask if it would be useful if you repeated any points, or if they repeated information back to you. Where it is important that instructions have been clearly communicated, you can question your listeners to make sure they have understood.

On the other hand:

(i) Don't clutter up your communications with irrelevant facts or personal opinions for which the other person has not asked.

(ii) Don't assume that the other person will always interpret information the way you intended. Vague words—like *big*, *good*, *quite*, *very early*, *a lot*, *plenty*, *average*—are interpreted differently by different people. People's past experience may have made them uncertain whether you mean what you say. So a promise to 'get on with it right away' could be interpreted as meaning you may make a start next week.

(iii) Don't forget to use the English language correctly. Confusion can arise through the use of pronouns like he, she, it, they, this, that. Used properly, pronouns save repetition of the nouns they are replacing. Used unthinkingly, the listener can become hopelessly lost trying to understand sentences like: 'So then he gave him some more work to do; when he had finished he gave it back to him and he told him he would go home if he had nothing else for him to do.'

(iv) Don't use slang expressions. Although most offices are a good deal less formal than they used to be, all organizations still expect their employees to be courteous and use an appropriate amount of decorum. While you may greet your own friends with 'Hi, sunshine', this is not a form of address to use in the office, and, like all slang, is ambiguous in its meaning. A foreigner might think you were talking about the weather.

(v) Don't be too familiar with colleagues, your boss, clients or other contacts. Always address people by name when you can—it is much more polite. But notice what people normally call each other in your office. Some firms are quite formal, with the staff always addressing and referring to each other and the boss as Mr, Mrs or Miss. Customers and strangers are usually 'Sir' or 'Madam'; this may be extended to cover anyone more senior than yourself.

Other organizations are much less formal in their internal relations, using first names even to senior people. (Some family firms, where several managers and directors have the same surname, refer to these people as, say, Mr David, Mr George or Mr John rather than calling them all Mr Smith or whatever the family surname happens to be.) If in doubt, always err on the side of formality.

(vi) Don't use words that add nothing to your meaning. Think about the words you are using and try to make sure that each one is contributing to or clarifying the information you are communicating. Try underlining all the unnecessary words in the next paragraph.

'I got this order, right. And, um, you see, I didn't altogether quite know properly what to do with it for the best, you see. So I put it in the file, you see. And the customer came in, right, and he said he wanted to make a complaint like, you see. So I sort of got a bit anxious and worried like, and so I told him, I said it wasn't nothing to do with me and so he wants to see you, you see.'

(vii) Don't rely on memory. Check any complex or important facts carefully before passing them on, making a note to make sure you don't forget or get anything wrong. Don't forget, either, that you may have to justify what you said at a later date, so it is a good idea to keep a written record of how you came to pass on the information you did.

(viii) Don't blame other people if things go wrong. Effective communication requires effort both from the person giving the information and from the person receiving it. But it is the sender's responsibility to make sure that information has been received and understood correctly, rather than the receiver's.

(*b*) **How to Say It**
When you speak to someone face to face rather than by telephone, you use *non-verbal* as well as verbal communication. That is, your tone of voice, the expression on your face, the position of your body, the movements of your hands, the look in your eyes, your clothes, indeed everything about you, affects the information you are trying to communicate.

It should help other people to understand and take note of what you say if you follow these guidelines:

(i) Sit or stand straight.

(ii) Look interested in the other person.

(iii) Look directly at the other person, not over his head or to the side.

(iv) Keep your hands fairly still (but not in your pockets) using them only to emphasize particular points.

(v) Keep your feet still. If you are standing, don't shift from one leg to the other too often—it makes you appear uneasy. If you are sitting, don't keep crossing and uncrossing your legs.

(vi) Wear clothes that are business-like and conform to the organization's standards of dress.

(vii) Speak at a reasonable speed. If you speak very slowly, people will get tired of waiting for you to say what you have to say and may not be listening when you finally get to the point. If you talk very fast, people may not be able to keep up with you.

(viii) Speak at an appropriate volume. Don't talk loudly to one or two people in a closed room as if you were addressing a crowd of thousands without a microphone: you cannot improve people's understanding simply by shouting. But don't whisper either. Think how annoying it is when your radio suddenly fades and you can't quite catch what is being said. Spare other people the same frustration.

(ix) Speak clearly, starting and ending each word properly. 'Thereawas sittinin thoffice, thinkinuvsendin thisorder, whenin e came' is hardly intelligible and sounds slovenly. To communicate, you must be understood.

2.3 Listening

The points in Unit 2.2 can help you to pass information on to other people effectively. But it is equally important that you learn how to respond to information when other people are talking to you.

(*a*) Concentrate—don't let your mind wander away from the subject.

(*b*) Make a note of the main points.

(*c*) Watch for signals that may throw fresh light on what the speaker really means—head-shaking, smiles, impatient gestures.

(*d*) Ask for clarification if you are not sure you have understood correctly.

(*e*) If you are being given instructions, assess the urgency of what you are being asked to do. If you are in any doubt at all, say something like 'When would you like it done by?'

(*f*) If the information is complex, or if the communicator has not bothered to give you the facts in a logical order, make a list of *matters arising*. You can do this by sorting through your notes of the points you have made and organizing them in a way that shows clearly what needs to be done, by whom and in what order.

2.4 Meetings

Any discussion between two people can be described as a meeting. Often, more people are present and the proceedings are more formal than the encounters we have considered so far. The most formal meetings you are likely to encounter are company board meetings or, if you work in the public sector, committee and council meetings. At the other end of the scale, meetings held about a specific subject, perhaps at short notice—*ad hoc* meetings—are relatively informal and unstructured.

(*a*) Documentation for Formal Meetings

Certain documents must be prepared, before, during and after a formal meeting.

(i) **Notice of the meeting.** This must be circulated to all who are eligible to attend. If the meeting is an Annual General Meeting or an Extraordinary General Meeting all the company's shareholders are notified individually and an announcement also appears in the press.

(ii) **Agenda.** At formal meetings items for discussion are generally taken in a set order (Fig. 2.1). The names of the people who have said that they cannot attend are first read out, the minutes (see (v) below) of the previous meeting are then read and agreed as a true record of proceedings and signed by the chairman, and any matters arising from them are discussed. If, for instance, a member of the board or committee was to take action on a particular point, he or she can now let fellow-members know the outcome. Next follows the business for which today's meeting was called. Finally, members are given the chance to raise other issues which they want to discuss at this meeting and which have arisen since

```
COSTALOT LTD


MEETING OF THE SPORTS AND SOCIAL CLUB COMMITTEE, TO BE HELD AT 5.30 p.m.

ON MONDAY 5 JULY 19.. IN THE SOCIAL CLUB, HOMETOWN


Agenda


1. Apologies for absence

2. Minutes of the meeting held on 4 February 19..

3. Matters arising

4. Proposed sports programme for 19../.. (Schedule I attached)

5. Proposed social events programme for 19../.. (Schedule II attached)

6. Proposal to form a special-purpose committee to deal with arrangements

   pertaining to Christmas dinner dance

7. Any other business



K.R.BIDEMAN
Secretary
```

Fig. 2.1   Agenda for a committee meeting

the agenda was circulated. The agenda is sent out to members well in advance of the meeting, so that they can consider their views on the topics to be discussed. A special copy of the agenda is prepared for the chairman, to include details which will help him to conduct the meeting, and space for his notes. Fig. 2.2 shows an agenda for an Annual General Meeting.

(iii) **Supplementary papers.** Often an item on the agenda will be the subject of a paper submitted by those particularly interested in the topic. Two such papers are referred to in Fig. 2.1.

(iv) **Attendance record.** The secretary must record the names of all those present at a formal meeting. Members can be asked to sign a register or sheet of paper as they arrive or at the start of the meeting.

(v) **Minutes of resolution.** The minutes are a summary of the main points discussed in the meeting (Fig. 2.3). They are always written in the third person, past tense. If a member makes (or *proposes*) a formal *motion* (see (*b*) below), which is usually introduced by the words 'I move that' or 'I propose that', his

```
COSTALOT LIMITED

ANNUAL GENERAL MEETING


The company's Annual General Meeting will take place at 2.30p.m. on
WEDNESDAY 15 JUNE 19.. at COSTALOT HOUSE, TOURTOWN


AGENDA

1.  Minutes of the last Annual General Meeting, held on 5 May 19..

2.  Matters arising from the minutes

3.  Chairman's report for the year ended 31 March 19..

4.  Financial accounts for the year ended 31 March 19..

5.  Election of two directors on the retirement of Mr H.E.Helps and Mrs
    J. Wilson.  Mrs Wilson is willing to stand for re-election

6.  Formation of a subsidiary company to develop foreign exchange banking
    facilities

7.  Sale of freight forwarding subsidiary


A. SCRIBE
Secretary
```

Fig. 2.2   Agenda for an Annual General Meeting

words must be taken down *verbatim* (word for word). The name of the proposer of a motion, that of the person proposing any amendment (or *addendum*) to it and the exact wording of the amendment, and the name of the seconder of the motion must appear in the minutes. If a vote is taken the result should be recorded as a resolution made by the committee to either reject or accept the proposal.

(b) Procedure for Formal Meetings

Formal meetings always have a *chairman*. Those present must address the chair when they speak, by beginning their remarks with 'Mr Chairman' or 'Madam Chairman'. It is bad practice for members to talk among themselves during the meeting; all comments should be made *through the chair*. There must also be a *secretary* to the meeting who will arrange for the proceedings to be recorded.

The other people present at the meeting may be elected representatives of the owners (as in the case of board meetings). At a committee meeting, they will be members of a group elected or appointed for a particular purpose. Some of

```
COSTALOT LTD


MINUTES OF THE MEETING OF THE SPORTS AND SOCIAL CLUB COMMITTEE, HELD AT
THE SOCIAL CLUB, HOMETOWN, ON 5 JULY 19..
```

Present	J.P.Bradley (Chairman)
	K.R.Bideman
	R.B.Frost
	P.L.Roberts
	H.I.Sayles
	P.D.Watson
	U.Mann

Apologies for absence were received from G.Buxton and M.Cotgrove.

25/.. MINUTES OF MEETING HELD ON 4 FEBRUARY	The minutes of the previous meeting were read, approved and signed as correct, with the exception that the name in Item 22/.., Jones, should be replaced with James.
26/.. MATTERS ARISING	Mr Bideman advised that the committee's nominations for the UK Travel Sports Committee had been forwarded and a reply was awaited.
27/.. SPORTS AND SOCIAL PROGRAMMES FOR 19../..	These two items were taken together. Mr Frost tabled the proposed programmes and explained the general theme of 'total staff involvement'. A wide range of activities had been included, to appeal to all sections and age groups. All dates have been confirmed as available by the other clubs and organizations involved. Mr Sayles expressed some concern that only three evenings appeared to have been allocated for the Costalot Scrabble Tournament. Mr Frost advised that, under the rules agreed last year (minute 55/.. refers), the initial knockout rounds would be arranged by contestants independently. Mr Frost then moved that the committee approve the proposed programme so that arrangements could be finalized and the programme published to all staff.
	The motion was seconded by Mr Mann and carried nem con.
28/.. ARRANGEMENTS FOR THE APPOINTMENT OF A DINNER DANCE SPECIAL PURPOSE COMMITTEE	Mr Roberts circulated a list of names, attached as Appendix One, of those who had expressed interest in the formation of a special purpose committee. Mr Watson congratulated Mr Roberts on his efforts.
	It was AGREED that a special open meeting be held in the near future so that those whom Mr Roberts had contacted could discuss the matter with the full committee.

There being no other business, the meeting closed at 6.30 p.m.

J.P.Bradley

Chairman
5 August 19..

Fig. 2.3   Minutes of a committee meeting

these members will in fact be officers of the committee—secretary, treasurer and so on.

Before the business of the meeting can start the chairman must be satisfied that he has a *quorum*—a sufficient number of people to conduct the business of the meeting. This figure is laid down in the Regulations of the board or committee, or in its constitution. If too few people are present, the chairman cannot declare the meeting open, and it must be postponed. If the meeting is postponed without a date for the new meeting being fixed, it is said to be *postponed sine die* ('without a day').

The formal meeting proceeds through a series of *motions*. A motion is a proposal, like the proposed programme of sports and social activities in Fig. 2.1, and is normally written out and given to the secretary or chairman before the meeting. Each motion is debated and the proposer or *mover* of the motion is asked to speak to it, putting forward his point of view and justifying it, if necessary, to his fellow members. Before the *question*, as the motion is called while it is under discussion, can be put to the vote, it must be *seconded*. If there is no seconder for the motion, the motion is *dropped* and is not discussed further.

When there has been sufficient debate on a question, the chairman *puts the question* to the meeting by announcing 'the question before the meeting is . . .'

When the question is put to the *vote*, those *in favour* (those who agree with the motion) raise their hands and are counted by a *teller*. Those *against* then do the same. Those who have voted neither for nor against (*abstained* from voting) are asked to identify themselves too.

When the votes have been counted, the result is announced. There are several possibilities.

(i) If all the members have voted in favour of the motion, the *resolution*, as a motion that has been approved is called, is said to have been passed *unanimously*.

(ii) If all the votes cast were in favour of the motion, but some members abstained from voting, the resolution is said to have been passed *nem con*, which means no one contradicting, or *nem diss*, no one dissenting.

(iii) If there are more votes in favour than against, the resolution may be *carried by a majority*. The organization's constitution will specify whether a simple majority (more than half the votes) is needed to carry a resolution, or whether a larger proportion of the votes—perhaps two-thirds—is required.

(iv) If there are equal numbers of votes for and against the motion, the chairman may, under the constitution, have a *casting vote*, which will decide the issue one way or the other.

(v) If there are more votes against the motion than there are in favour, the motion will not be carried.

2.5 Quick Questions

1. List five 'do's' and 'don'ts' of spoken communication.

2. List three ways in which you can improve your listening skill.

3. What is an 'ad hoc' meeting?

4. List five documents which must be prepared before or after a formal meeting.

5. What does 'nem con' mean?

6. Who usually has the casting vote at a formal meeting?

2.6 Short Exercises

1. Discuss, or write down a list of, some expressions which you use every day but which might not be acceptable in business.

2. Discuss, or write down a list of, the things that the chairman of a sports and social club committee should know before calling his or her first committee meeting.

Unit Three

Telecommunications

3.1 Introduction

In the United Kingdom there are more than 25 million telephones—approximately one for every two people. These telephones, and the network of telephone lines, exchanges and operators which enable telephones to be used for both local and *trunk* (long-distance) calls, are operated mainly by British Telecom, a public corporation. Other countries have their own telecommunications companies, some publicly and some privately owned.

The people who rent telephones from the telephone companies are called *subscribers*. Private subscribers are people who have rented sets for use in their own homes. Business subscribers are organizations which have telephones installed in their offices.

In addition to a main telephone with a direct line to a public exchange, most businesses need one or more telephone *extensions*, connected to the main telephone, so that calls can be made and received in more than one part of the building. Calls coming into the business can be intercepted at a central point and passed on to the person best able to deal with them.

A very small business may find it sufficient to have one main telephone in the reception office (see Unit 22.2) linked to several numbered extensions in other offices. For a business requiring a dozen or more telephones, however, some kind of switchboard (*private branch exchange*) is needed. One or more company telephonists answers incoming calls and relays them to extensions in various departments (see Unit 3.3). Small additional extension circuits can then be used to provide a link between the switchboard on one hand and a manager and his or her secretary on the other.

When you start work in an office, the ringing of a telephone might be among the first sounds you hear. This may be a call on an *internal* line (calls from other people in the same organization) or on an *external* line (calls from people outside the organization, phoning from anywhere in the world).

Before you pick up the handset to answer the call, you should be familiar both with the equipment itself and with good telephone procedure. The traditional telephone, with its dial and receiver or *handset*, is a very familiar piece of equipment. More streamlined versions,with pushbuttons instead of a dial, are even easier to use. But if you are answering a telephone that is an extension of either another telephone or your organization's switchboard, there are some points to watch to ensure that you deal with all calls in the most efficient manner.

3.2 Telephone Extensions

When one telephone is linked to another, it is all too easy to 'lose' the call between the two. To prevent this, you need to know how to transfer a call from one extension to another, or back to the switchboard. Several different systems are available (Figs. 3.1 to 3.5), each with its own method of operation (and new systems are being developed all the time); sometimes combinations are used to good effect. When you start work in an office, find out what the system is, and how it works, before—and not after—you need to use the telephone.

3.3 The Switchboard

If you look up the telephone number of a large organization you will probably find only one telephone number listed in the directory, even though the organization employs hundreds of people and is divided into many different departments. If you dial the number given, you will be answered by the switchboard *operator*. The switchboard acts as a main telephone, and all the other telephone sets in the building are numbered extensions connected to it, rather than to the public exchange.

Company switchboards are properly called *private branch exchanges* or PBX, to distinguish them from public exchanges. The PBX consists of a board or *console*, manned by the company telephone operator or telephonist, together with electrical equipment or *switching gear*. This is normally housed in special cabinets or units close to the switchboard; its maintenance is not the responsibility of the switchboard operator.

There are three main types of PBX.

(i) **Private Manual Branch Exchanges (PMBX).** These are the oldest kind of switchboard and are no longer widely used. All calls into or out of the organization must be routed through the switchboard. If you want to make a call, you lift your receiver and, when the telephone switchboard operator answers, you ask for the telephone number of the person you wish to contact. The operator will either connect you to the number itself or give you an outside line—that is, connect you to the public telephone circuit—in which case you can dial the number yourself as soon as you hear the dialling tone.

Figs. 3.6 and 3.7 show two types of manual switchboard.

(ii) **Private Automatic Branch Exchanges (PABX).** With this type of switchboard, you can make calls from one extension to another, and external calls, without contacting the switchboard. To call a colleague in another office, you simply pick up the receiver and dial the extension number you want. For external calls you dial 9, followed by the telephone code and number. Incoming calls come through the operator: when your telephone bell rings and you pick up the receiver, the outside caller is on the line.

Some PBX equipment can also carry *camp on busy* facilities, which means that the switchboard continues to call an engaged extension until it is free. Some

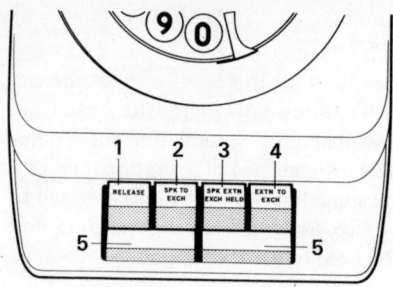

Fig. 3.1 Plan 107 telephone system: key arrangement of main telephone. 1. Self-restoring key, which is pressed when an extension user has completed a call. 2. Key for connecting the main telephone to the switchboard or exchange—it can then be used as an ordinary telephone. 3. Key enabling a call from the exchange to be held while the users of the main telephone and the extension confer; a red lamp glows meanwhile. 4. Key connecting the extension directly with the exchange; a white lamp glows. 5. Bars used to call the extensions

Fig. 3.2 Keymaster 1+5 telephone system. 1. Telephone dial. 2. Handset. 3. 'Bell off' button: if this is pressed down, the bell will not ring except on the main telephone. 4. Exchange button: this must be pressed down to enable you to make an external call. 5. Lamp: this glows red while any extension is connected via the exchange line. 6. Lamp: this glows white while any internal line is in use. 7. Numbered 'stations': to call station 1, lift the handset and press button '1'; if you then press another button or buttons, the corresponding stations can join in the conversation

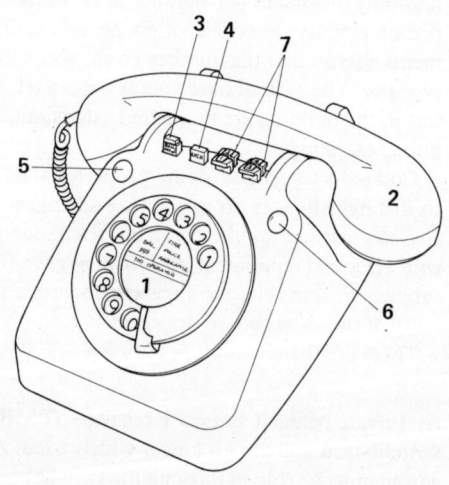

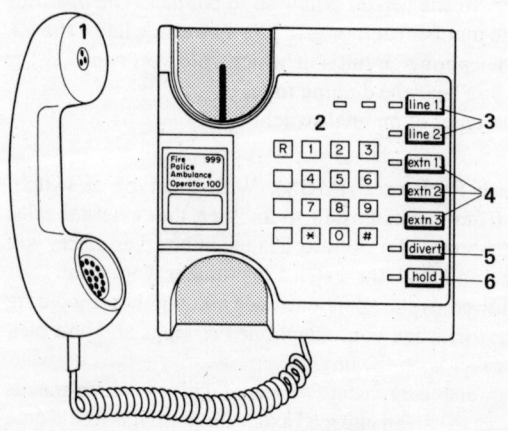

Fig. 3.3 Ambassador electronic switching system. 1. Handset. 2. Pushbutton dialling. 3. Exchange lines. 4. Extensions are contacted by pressing the appropriate button. 5. This button allows incoming calls to be diverted to another extension. 6. Exchange line calls can be held while an enquiry is made

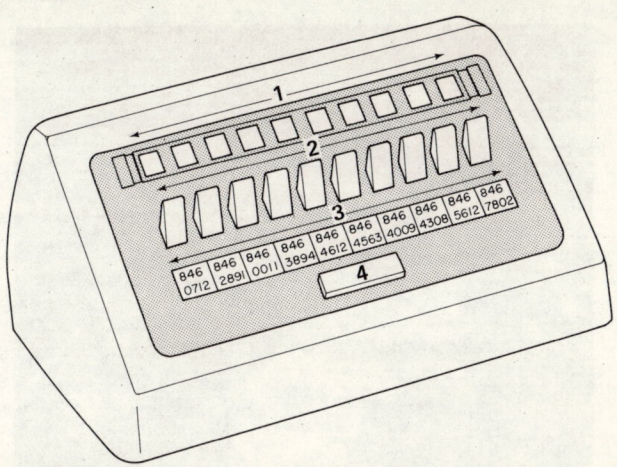

Fig. 3.4 Key and lamp unit. 1. Lights: a flashing light indicates that there is an incoming call waiting to be answered, while a continuously glowing light indicates that the line is engaged. 2. Position keys: up = normal, centre = hold, down = line connected. 3. Line numbers. 4. Recall buzzer

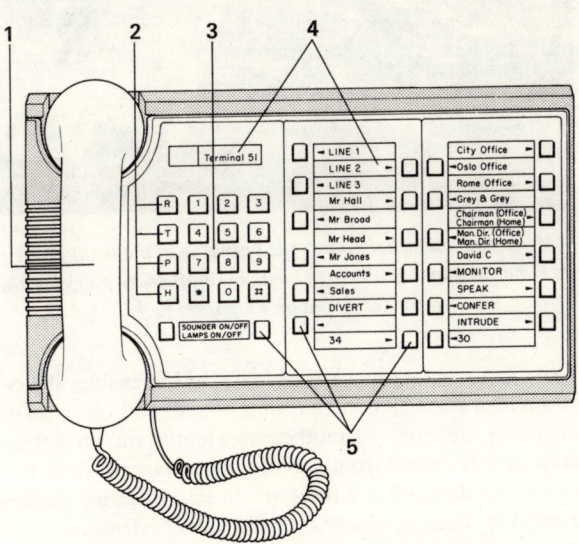

Fig. 3.5 Herald system. 1. Handset (a direct speech loudspeaker or a headset can be supplied). 2. Buttons for recall, transmit, program and hold. 3. Keypad. 4. Some of the label areas. 5. Some of the programmable buttons, with lamps for exchange lines, intercom etc, allowing each telephone in the system to be programmed to suit the user's requirements

Fig. 3.6   PMBX manual switchboard: the operator in the front of the picture has several calls connected and is about to connect another by plugging the cord into a socket called an extension jack

have a *priority cut-in* or *trunk offering* service, which enables the switchboard operator to sound a warning note (a ticking sound) and cut in on one conversation to announce the arrival of another more important call. Some extensions can be automatically *barred* from making international, trunk or even local calls, so preventing their unauthorized use. Special *metering equipment* can be connected either to the switchboard or to individual extensions, to measure the time taken on outgoing calls and enable the firm to keep track of its telephone costs rather than waiting for the quarterly account from the telephone company.

Some boards have special arrangements for the switchboard when it is unattended at night. Incoming calls can be answered from any extension in the building by dialling, say, 8.

One of British Telecom's **PABX** switchboards is shown in Fig. 3.8 (page 30).

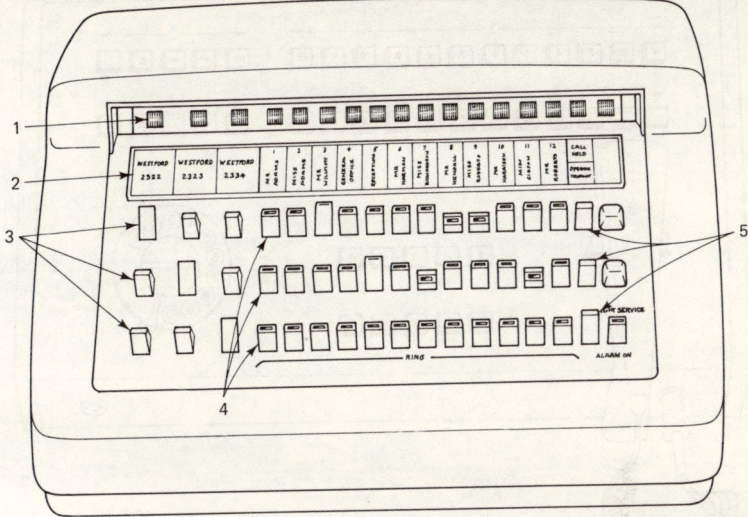

Fig. 3.7   PMBX 3 + 12 cordless console. 1. Lamps. 2. Labels. 3. Exchange line keys. 4. Extension line keys. 5. Operator's line keys. In this diagram exchange line 1 is connected to extension 3; extension 8 is connected to extension 9; exchange line 2 is connected to extension 5; extension 7 is connected to extension 11; and the operator is dealing with a call on exchange line 3

(iii) **Private Electronic/Digital Exchanges (EBX/PDX).** These automatic exchanges rely on advanced electronic technology and are likely to be an important feature of the office of the future. The Philips EBX 8000 (Fig. 3.9, page 31) has the full range of facilities available on the traditional PABX, and can deal with up to 8000 extensions and 850 exchange lines; it also has a *follow me* facility. This means that when you are leaving your desk you can dial a special code and automatically direct incoming calls to another extension. It can also store regularly used telephone numbers in its 'memory' in shortened form. A fifteen-figure number can be coded into three digits. When you want the number, you dial just the three code digits and the equipment does the rest.

3.4 Operating the Switchboard

If you are to operate a switchboard, you will need careful training in its use from an experienced operator. The switchboard operator's voice and manner is an important part of a firm's 'shop window', so the job is a vital one: an incompetent operator gives a very poor impression of an organization and can lose business for it.

   (i) Find out the style of telephone answering that your organization prefers, and use it. 'Good morning, Costa!ot Travel Limited' sounds welcoming and lets the caller know the name of the company straight away.

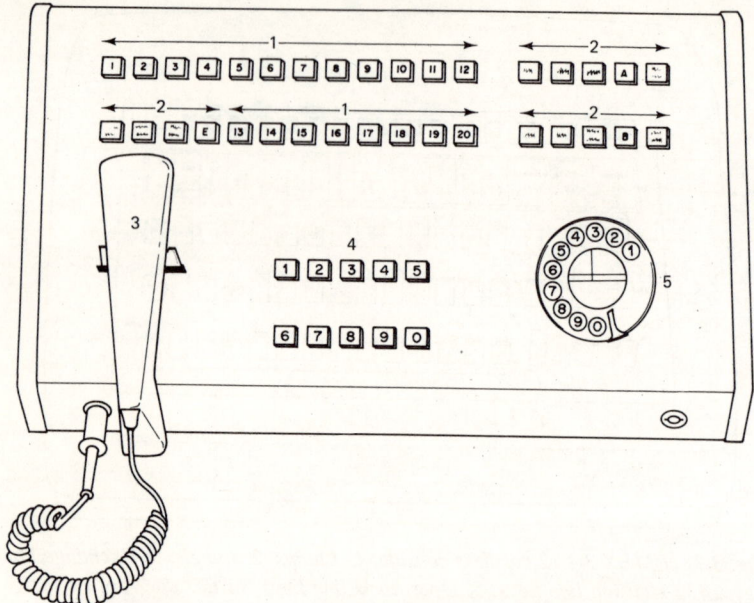

Fig. 3.8   PABX 7 cordless console. 1. Exchange lines: lights glow while lines are in use. 2. Special functions, including night service. 3. Handset. 4. Keypad, for connecting up to 100 extensions (numbered from 200 to 299). 5. Dial

(ii) Greet all callers, external and internal, courteously and by name if possible. 'Yes, Mr Kingsley, I'll put you through to the accounts department' tells Mr Kingsley that you have recognized him as an individual, and he will respond positively. (Such courtesy can even take the edge off his annoyance if he has rung up to complain!)

(iii) Memorize the extension numbers of people and departments who regularly receive calls. This will save time for you and for callers as well.

(iv) Keep callers informed about the progress of their calls. If a busy customer is kept waiting in silence for a connection, he will become impatient and angry. Tell the caller you are trying to connect him and, if you cannot make the connection, go back on his line and ask whether he would like to wait, to give you a message, or to call back later. If he decides to wait, keep trying to connect him and say, every thirty seconds or so, 'I'm sorry to keep you' or 'I'm still trying to connect you', so that he knows he is not forgotten.

(v) If an extension proves difficult to contact, suggest other people who may be able to deal with the call. For instance, 'I'm sorry, Miss Porter's line is still engaged. Would you like to speak to Mr Harris?' If you don't know who could help, ask someone who might know, such as a secretary in a related office.

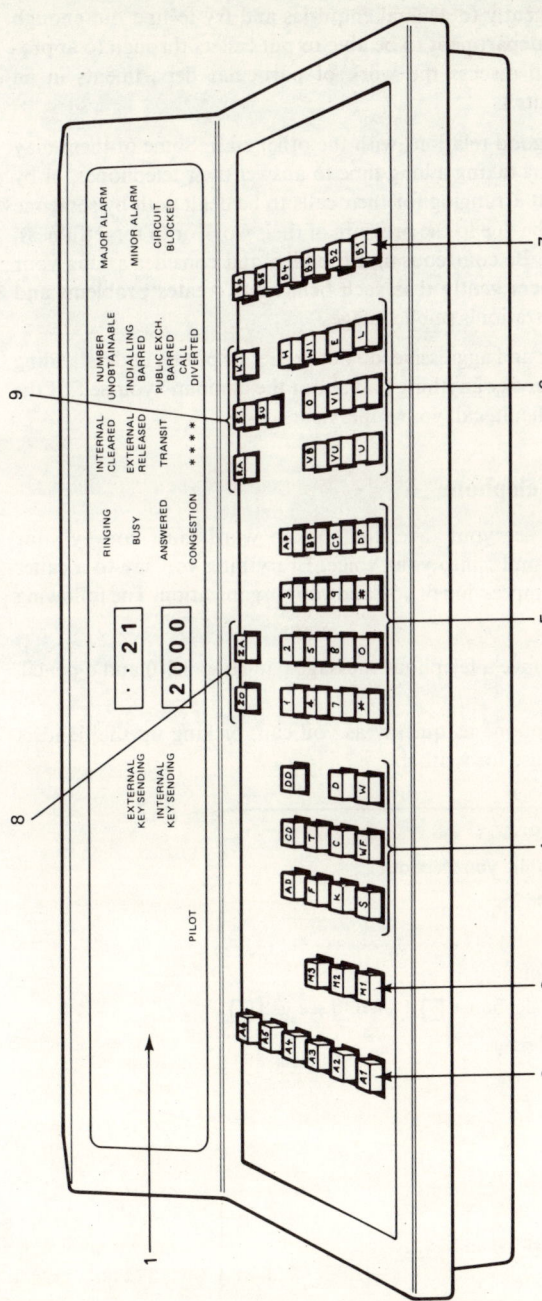

Fig. 3.9 EBX 8000 electronic console. 1. Illuminated visual display, informing the operator about calls connected through the board. 2. Pushbuttons that light up to indicate incoming calls. 3. Keys that light up when extensions require assistance. 4. Pushbuttons indicating special facilities, including 'camp on busy', available through the switchboard. 5. Operator's keypad, enabling quick and easy 'dialling' of external and internal numbers. 6. Pushbuttons enabling the operator to monitor or to break into calls. 7. Pushbuttons enabling the operator to obtain an outside line. 8. Pushbuttons controlling audible signals for attracting the operator's attention. 9. Keys for bringing into use special facilities such as metering the number of units used, or calling several numbers in sequence

(vi) Respond intelligently to general enquiries and try to find out enough about the work of each department to be able to put callers through to appropriate people. (We shall discuss the work of particular departments in an organization in later Units.)

(vii) Try to develop good relations with the other staff. Some of them may make your job difficult by taking a long time to answer their telephones, or by leaving the office without arranging for their calls to be dealt with by someone else. But this is likely to be due to the pressure of their work or to forgetfulness, not malice towards you. Be courteous and friendly, and consider asking your supervisor to remind them gently that such behaviour creates problems and could damage the organization's public image.

(viii) If a caller is rude and aggressive, do not argue. Be polite, understanding and apologetic, and never say anything bad about the company yourself. If the caller becomes really difficult, call your supervisor.

3.5 Answering the Telephone

Since the caller cannot see your face, the spoken word must convey your meaning clearly. Put a 'smile' into your voice. Everything you say to a caller contributes to his or her impression of you and your organization. The following points will help you:

(i) Make sure you have a telephone message pad (Fig. 3.10) and a pencil, close to the telephone.

(ii) Answer the telephone as quickly as you can, picking up the handset with the hand you *don't* use for writing.

To. . . . .
While you were out
Mr/Ms . . . .
of . . . .
Tel: . . . .
Telephoned ☐ Called to see you ☐
Message

Call taken by: . . . .
Date : . . . . Time : . . . .

Fig. 3.10 Telephone message pad

(iii) If the call is an external one put through from the company switch-board, the telephonist will already have told the caller that he or she is connected to Costalot Travel Limited, so you can pick up the receiver and say 'Good morning, Reservations Department'. If, on the other hand, you know the call is coming in direct on an outside line, you should say, 'Good morning, Costalot Travel Limited, Reservations Department'. This saves time: the caller knows that he is through to the right place and can go ahead to ask for the person he wants, or tell you what he is phoning about.

(iv) Listen carefully to what the caller says, writing down his or her name, company, telephone number and other key facts on your pad. If necessary, ask the caller to spell names and addresses. Some letters, like F and S, M and N, P and T, can sound alike over the telephone. Using the telephone alphabet—'F for Freddie', 'S for Samuel', 'M for Mary', and so on—can help you clarify anything you may have misheard. Read back names, addresses, telephone numbers and figures, to make sure you have got them right.

(v) If you don't know the answers to the caller's questions, say so, and offer either to fetch someone who can help, or to find the answer and ring back. Most callers are quite happy with this and a positive response is always far better than a vague 'Well, I don't really know, but I suppose it might be'.

(vi) The person on the other end of the line is usually paying for the call, so never leave the telephone while you search for information without giving some indication of how long this will take and offering to ring back when you've found it.

(vii) Keep your side of the conversation brisk and businesslike, but cour-teous.

(viii) If you don't catch the caller's name, company and telephone number at the beginning of the conversation, always ask for them before you ring off, in order that he or she may be easily contacted again if necessary.

3.6 Making a Call

When you first start work, you will be told by your manager or team leader whom to telephone, and when calls should be made. Later, as you get to know the job, the decision of whether to telephone or not may be left to you.

Table 3.1 shows how your decision can be arrived at, in the light of particular circumstances. First choose the descriptions in the left-hand column which apply to the information you wish to pass on. Now look across the chart to see which of the methods of communication (*media*) have a tick against your chosen features. If none matches up precisely, you may need to use more than one medium—a telephone call with the main points confirmed later by letter, for example. (Written communication is discussed in Unit 4, facsimile text trans-mission in Unit 9.6 and telex in Unit 3.9(*b*).)

Table 3.1 Choosing a medium for communication

	Personal visit	Telephone	Telex	Telemessage	Letter	Facsimile text transmission
Speed is important (i.e. minutes or hours, not days)	√ If close at hand	√	√	√ Delivery next working day		√
A written record is required			√ If copy kept by sender	√	√ If copy kept by sender	√
A personal explanation will help	√	√				
It's important to check other person has understood immediately	√	√				

	Expensive equipment but cost of transmission less than postal rate	Cost of postage + paper + typing must be compared with cost of telephone call	Where the conversation is kept brief, especially for local calls at standard or cheap rate	Only if this will not take any more time than a telephone call	Not usually (but see Unit 3.7)
Message is brief	√				
Message is long and complex	√	√			
Cost is to be kept to a minimum	√	√	√		
Other person may be absent when you wish to communicate		√		√	
Other person has no receiving equipment		√	√		√

(a) Decide the Purpose of the Call

Get out relevant letters and documents and check on the present situation. Sort out in your mind the purpose of the call and the points you want to make. Write these down so that you can refer to them as you speak and check you haven't missed anything. Have a pad ready to write down key points that emerge from the conversation.

(b) Find the Number

There are several ways in which you can do this. You can check the letter heading on letters received from the person you want to telephone, or you can consult the office telephone index (see Unit 6.6). Or you can look up the number in the appropriate telephone directory. There are over eighty of these in Britain, including nine for the London area. Subscribers receive the directory for their own area free of charge, and can buy directories for other areas. The entries in the directory are arranged alphabetically, in accordance with the rules of alphabetical filing discussed in Unit 7.2.

If you do not have the right directory, dial 'Directory Enquiries'. You will find the number listed under 'Inland Telephone Services—operator and fault repair services' near the front of your local directory. Tell the operator which town you want to telephone and, when asked, the name, initials and address of the person whose number you want. Write down the name of the exchange and the number you are given, and repeat them back to the operator to check you have got them right. Then enter the number in the office telephone index for future reference.

(c) Choose the Best Time

Telephone calls in the United Kingdom are charged according to the distance of the call (local calls being the cheapest), the duration of the call and the time of day. *Peak rate* (the most expensive) is between 9 a.m. and 1 p.m., *standard rate* between 8 a.m. and 9 a.m. and again between 1 p.m. and 6 p.m., and *cheap rate* between 6 p.m. and 8 a.m. on Monday to Friday and all day on Saturday and Sunday.

(d) Dial Direct where Possible

The telephone network is organized through a series of public exchanges. If you are telephoning someone whose telephone is connected to a different public exchange from your own, it is not enough just to dial the number of the other subscriber's telephone. You must first obtain a connection to his or her local exchange.

Although you can dial 100 and ask your own public exchange operator to connect you, it is much cheaper and quicker to dial direct.

(i) **Subscriber Trunk Dialling (STD).** Subscribers in most parts of the British Isles can be dialled direct by subscribers in other parts of the country, using an all-figure STD code. All the current STD codes are listed in your local British Telecom booklet *Telephone Dialling Codes*.

Look up the name of the exchange you want in the alphabetical listing. Make a note of the number shown, alongside the telephone number of the person you are calling.

(ii) **International Direct Dialling (IDD).** If you live in the United Kingdom and your town has this facility, you can dial direct to more than four-fifths of all the telephones in the world. The appropriate codes are listed in the *International Telephone Guide*. To call one of them, you begin by dialling 010, which is the international code, followed first by the code for the country you are calling, then the area code for the particular part of the country you want (if there is one), and finally the telephone number of the person you are trying to contact. If you have a business contact in Wagga Wagga, Australia, on Wagga Wagga 2222, you would therefore dial

010	61	69	2222
International code	Country code for Australia	Wagga Wagga area code	Telephone number

If you cannot use the IDD facility, you will need to dial the international operator. This usually costs about twice as much as dialling direct.

Even with direct dialling, international calls are very expensive. A cheap-rate call to Europe costs many times as much as a peak-rate local call.

(*e*) **Dial**

(i) If your office telephone is connected to a private manual branch exchange (see Unit 3.3(i)) you will need to lift the receiver (or dial 0) and ask the telephonist for a line to the public network. Then you can dial the exchange and number you want.

If your organization has an automatic branch exchange, your office telephone can be used to call other parts of the building as well as other subscribers. So when you want to make an external call you must first obtain an outside line, usually by dialling 9. You can dial as soon as you hear the *dialling tone* - in the United Kingdom this is a continuous purring noise, but it is different in other parts of the world. You can get a free demonstration of what telephone tones sound like: details of this service are to be found in the *Telephone Dialling Codes* booklet.

If your telephone is a direct line to the public exchange, you are automatically connected to the public network and will normally hear the dialling tone as soon as you lift the receiver. If you don't hear it, replace the receiver and try again.

(ii) Dial carefully. Although some telephones are now pushbutton-operated, most still have a round disc or dial at the front, with the numbers from 0 to 1 arranged round it. Rotate the dial firmly and don't pause too long between digits, especially on overseas calls.

(iii) When you have finished dialling, wait for the *ringing tone*, which is a repeated 'burr-burr' in the United Kingdom, but different in other parts of the world. You may have to wait up to 15 seconds before you hear the ringing tone, and on overseas calls for up to a minute.

(iv) If, instead of the ringing tone, you hear either the *engaged* tone (a repeated single note in the United Kingdom, a medium tone repeated at short intervals in Europe and North America) or the *number unobtainable* signal (a steady note in the United Kingdom, three rapid pips in ascending pitch on overseas calls), replace the receiver and try again later. If you still get the 'unobtainable' signal, call the operator.

(*f*) When your Call is Answered

(i) Listen carefully to make sure you have got the right number and the right person or company. If the answering voice doesn't identify itself clearly, ask (for instance): 'Is that Bradshaw and Company?' If it is not, and you have a wrong number, apologize, replace the receiver and start again.

(ii) If you are through to the right place, go ahead and ask for the person you wish to speak to.

(iii) Keep your conversation factual and resist the temptation to chat or pass the time of day at the company's expense. Make notes of the key points and, if agreement has been reached on certain issues, repeat them in summary at the end of the call so that you're both quite certain of what has been agreed.

(iv) When you have finished talking, replace your receiver carefully. If you don't, the telephone company could continue to charge your organization for the call long after you have stopped speaking.

(v) Take the action promised on the telephone and consider whether the points made are sufficiently important to warrant written confirmation. If so, compile a letter following the guidelines given in Unit 4.3. If not, it may still be useful to place a note of your conversation on the relevant file, so that you and others concerned know what has been said.

3.7 Answering Devices

An unanswered telephone always gives a bad impression. But there may be occasions, particularly in the smaller firm, when the office is unmanned for a while and there is no one to answer the telephone. This is where an answering device can be invaluable. These are of two main types.

(*a*) Answering Sets

These machines enable you to tape-record a message, apologizing for your absence and saying where you can be contacted or when you will be back. When a call comes in, the equipment will play the recorded message to the caller. Although the caller cannot communicate with you or leave his own message on this type of machine, he at least has some positive information, not the frustration of an unanswered telephone.

(*b*) Telephone Answering and Recording Machines

Like the answering set, the telephone answering machine will answer an unmanned telephone and play a tape-recorded message. Unlike the answering set, it can then record a message from the caller on another tape. When you return to your office a red light shows you there has been a call and you can play back the tape and listen to the caller's message. You can then ring back or take whatever action is needed.

Answering machines are essential to many businesses and professional people, and most callers are now used to the process of recording a message giving name, number and the gist of what it is about. Some trading companies or service companies have 24-hour answering services, so anyone can phone at any time, including the middle of the night, and place an order or make a request.

An answering machine may even be used during office hours, so economizing in time and staff. Wherever a business receives routine requests such as 'Could you send me details of the range of kitchen equipment advertised in today's *Sunday Trumpeter*?' or 'Can you deliver five tonnes of coke, COD [cash on delivery] next Tuesday?', the machine can record them all and enable the sales department staff to act on them without being constantly interrupted by the telephone. If there are queries about an order later, the tape provides a record of what the customer did, or did not, ask for. The answering machine is, in effect, being used as an automatic order-taker.

3.8 Telephone Services

Besides the familiar links between telephone subscribers, telecommunications companies provide other services that can either save an organization money or increase its efficiency, as well as the emergency services available to everybody. You will find details of the United Kingdom services in the *British Telecom Guide*. Here is a brief review of some of them.

(a) Emergency Services
You can contact the emergency services operator by dialling 999 from any telephone in the United Kingdom. Tell the operator which service you want (Fire, Police, Ambulance, Coastguard, Lifeboat, Rescue) and give your exchange (or code) and number. The operator will immediately connect you to the service requested, and you should give your name, the full address where help is required, and brief details of what has happened.

(b) Fixed-time Calls
If you have an important call that must be made at a specific time, you can book this in advance through the operator. At the appointed time the operator will make the connection and call you back.

(c) Transferred-charge Calls
If a caller wishes your organization to pay for a call, he or she can dial 100 and ask the operator to make the connection and transfer the charge to the organization's account. The operator will ring through and ask whether the organization will accept the charge. The caller is only put through if the subscriber agrees.

Find out what is your organization's policy on accepting transferred-charge calls. Often acceptance must be authorized by a senior member of staff.

(d) Credit Card Service

Employees who regularly have to telephone from outside the office can be issued with credit cards. They can then use any telephone for calls to other parts of the country and overseas. Newer telephone kiosks have been designed so that credit card calls can be dialled direct, but most older installations require such calls to be made via the British Telecom operator. Where authorized staff are issued with credit cards, the organization's switchboard operator can be instructed not to accept any transferred-charge calls.

(e) Freefone Arrangements

Another way in which a company can pay for incoming telephone calls is by joining the British Telecom Freefone service. Callers dial 100 to contact the British Telecom operator and ask for 'Freefone', followed by the Freefone number issued to the organization by British Telecom. The cost of the call is added to the organization's account. This service is used to encourage people to telephone for information or to place orders. It can be an excellent bait to attract business.

(f) Advice of Duration and Charge (ADC)

Sometimes it is necessary to find out straight away how much a phone call has cost. On operator-connected calls, the caller can ask the operator for an ADC on the call. At the end of the call, the operator will ring the caller with details of how long the call lasted (the *duration*) and what it cost (the *charge*).

(g) Telephone Information Services

British Telecom 'Guidelines' provide information on a range of topics. The Timeline, popularly known as Tim, tells you the time: 'at the third stroke it will be eleven thirty-two and twenty seconds.' The Weatherline passes on information supplied by the Meteorological Office about present and future weather conditions in various areas.

The telephone numbers of these and all other telephone information services are listed in your telephone directory and dialling code booklet.

3.9 Telemessages and Telex

There are two further ways in which the telecommunications companies can help in the communication of business information. Both allow a written record to be available.

(a) Telemessages

If you are trying to contact someone urgently and he or she cannot be reached by telephone, you can send a telemessage.

All that is necessary is a telephone call or telex to the telemessage service—

the number is in your directory or dialling code booklet. You give your message to the operator, and it will be delivered on the next working day anywhere in the world.

(b) **Telex**

In many countries, there is a 24-hour telex service. Any form of printed message, including lists of figures, requests for information, instructions and orders, can be sent from one telex machine, a *teleprinter*, to another, which may be in the same country or at the other end of the world, at any hour of the day or night. A copy of what has been transmitted is available for the sender, and the person receiving the telex has a printout of the same information.

The telex machine is a cross between a typewriter and a telephone (Fig. 3.11).

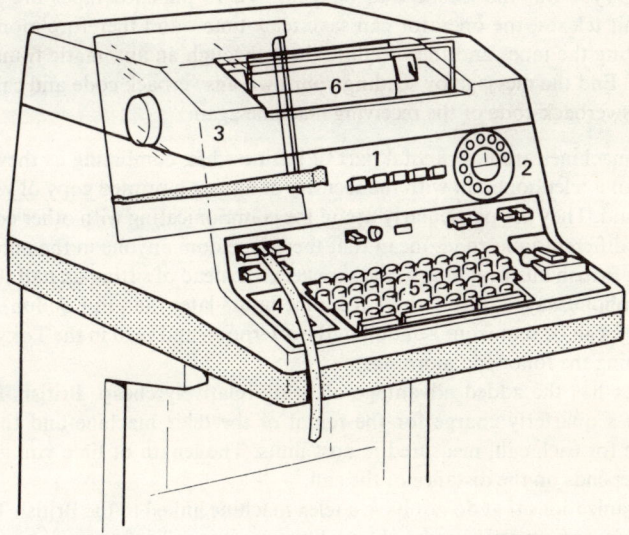

Fig. 3.11 Telex machine. 1. Dial button. 2. Dial. 3. Document support, made of clear plastic: you place the text to be transmitted here, for easy reading. 4. Punched paper tape. 5. Keyboard. 6. Printed telex message

As long as the machine is switched on, it receives, acknowledges and prints out incoming messages automatically. When messages are to be sent, a telex operator is needed. The teleprinter keyboard is similar to that of a typewriter, and the operator should have the skills of a good typist.

The procedure for sending a telex message is as follows:

(i) Look up the telex number of the organization to which the telex is to be sent, either on its letterhead or in the telex directory for the country concerned. (The telex number is not the same as the telephone number.)

(ii) Check the organization's *answerback code*. This is a code name/number, unique to the subscriber to whom it has been allocated. All answerback codes are also listed in alphabetical order in the telex directory.

(iii) Check the message to be sent, making sure that it is clear. Most firms use special telex forms on which the person wishing to send the message writes down what he or she wants to say. The telex operator sends the message exactly as it is written.

(iv) Dial (or type in, according to the machine you are using) the telex number of the organization to which the telex is addressed.

(v) Wait for the answerback code of the receiving teleprinter to appear on the paper in the machine, and check that it is correct. If not, an error in dialling has been made; re-check the telex number and then re-dial.

(vi) Enter your own answerback code.

(vii) Type out the message to be sent. Where punched tapes are used to transmit telexes, the operator can save telex time—and therefore money—by precoding the tapes and then feeding them through an automatic transmitter.

(viii) End the message by sending your own answerback code and calling up the answerback code of the receiving machine again.

Telex machines are now a vital part of business life, combining as they do the speed of a telephone call with the security of having a printed copy of what has been said. They are particularly useful for communicating with other countries where different time zones mean that there is seldom anyone in the office there during British business hours, and vice versa. Instead of sitting up half the night to telephone, say, Tokyo (where it is nine hours later than in London), a telex message can be sent from London in the afternoon and read in the Tokyo office first thing the following morning.

Telex has the added advantage of being relatively cheap. British Telecom makes a quarterly charge for the rental of the telex machine and there is a charge for each call, measured in cost units. The length of time you get for a unit depends on the distance of the call.

Organizations that do not have a telex machine linked to the British Telecom network may nevertheless be able to link company offices on various sites and offices of associated companies by a *private teleprinter circuit*. The teleprinters can be used to communicate with other machines on the same circuit, but not with the telex network.

Although the communication of the spoken word is vital to all modern businesses, communication in writing is also crucial. In the next Unit, we shall look at various forms of written communication.

3.10 Quick Questions

1. What is a telephone extension?

2. What do the letters PABX stand for?

3. Name two stationery items which should be kept close to the telephone.

4. In what circumstances might you have occasion to contact Directory Enquiries? What action would you take before doing so?

5. What do the letters (a) STD and (b) IDD stand for?

6. List three methods by which an incoming telephone call can be paid for by the receiver of the call, rather than by the caller.

3.11 Short Exercises

1. 'A good telephone manner is an asset in business.' Consider this statement, and write down (a) some ways in which the bad telephone manner of a member of staff might affect a company, and (b) the things that someone who had a 'good telephone manner' would do.

2. Identify the types of telephone equipment and telecommunications services with which you have come into contact. For each, describe its main purpose, the circumstances in which it is useful and any particular advantages and disadvantages you feel it has.

Unit Four
Written Communication

4.1 Introduction

On many occasions in business spoken communication is not enough. The written word has several advantages.

(*a*) Complex information can become muddled when it is passed on by word of mouth; in written form, it is clearer and easier to understand. It can be read and absorbed at the reader's own speed.

(*b*) Having things written down in black and white helps to avoid the disputes that can arise when people rely only on their memories.

(*c*) A written document can be produced as proof, in a court of law if necessary, of statements made or agreements reached.

(*d*) The sender and the recipient can each have the same information written down in front of them as a basis for future discussions, provided that the sender keeps a copy.

4.2 Business Forms

Preprinted forms are used in many offices as a simple and efficient means of recording and passing on standard information. Filling in a form is usually much quicker than writing a letter, and does not require the same literary skill.

When customers are ordering goods, for example, it is important that the supplier has all the necessary information about numbers, types, prices, delivery dates, addresses and so on. With the headings of a preprinted form as a guide, the person placing the order can see at once what information is needed, and can write in the details in the spaces on the form. The sales clerk who handles the order, and who deals with such forms every day, becomes very quick at extracting the information needed at each stage of the process and can tell at a glance if any information is missing.

Forms can be completed in three ways: by hand, with a typewriter or using a computer. One of these will be the method in general use in your organization. So find out what this is, straight away.

(*a*) Handwritten Forms

You can write in ink or in ballpoint pen in the spaces on the form. (If carbon paper or carbonless copy paper is used, ballpoint pen works best.) Write clearly, lining up each item under the proper heading, particularly where money is concerned: putting pounds in the pence column produces a muddle.

Handwritten forms are usually acceptable where (i) the form is for internal use only, and (ii) the handwriting is clear and readable. Company forms for external use should not be handwritten unless (i) they are to be completed by a private individual (job application forms, for instance) or (ii) they are to be routinely exchanged between one organization and another, where speed rather than appearance is important or where forms are provided in booklets and typing is therefore difficult. The bank giro credit (see Unit 14.3) is an example.

(b) Typewritten Forms
Typewritten forms are easier to read than handwritten ones, and convey a more professional impression. But if the person supplying the required information cannot type and must ask a typist to fill it in, producing the completed form is slower and more expensive. The typing of documents like invoices requires particular care, to ensure that words and figures are correctly lined up.

(c) Computerized Formfilling
Basic information about the sale of goods or services by one organization to another is normally produced in several stages, which we shall deal with in Unit 17. If, as soon as an order is received, the details are fed into a computer (these are discussed in Unit 15), invoices, dispatch notes, statements and a variety of other documents can be printed out on specially designed business stationery, when they are needed.

This computerized 'formfilling' saves a typist's time and effort, and also reduces errors by making sure that all the information about a particular transaction is consistent.

Although preprinted forms speed up the exchange of routine information between departments and organizations, their use is limited. Other methods must be used where, for instance,

(i) non-standard information is to be passed on—no organization can have preprinted forms to cover every circumstance;

(ii) a point of view, or an opinion, rather than straight facts, is needed;

(iii) a form on its own would convey too impersonal an impression.

In such cases, a letter or memorandum must be composed.

4.3 Business Letters and Memoranda

Letters are sent to people outside the organization. A *memorandum* or *memo* (*memoranda* if there is more than one) is for internal use. Both letters and memoranda contain a small amount of standard information in their headings, but in both the remainder of the message may be quite short, very lengthy or anything in between.

You are not likely to have to compose completely original business letters until later in your office career. But you may be asked to send out routine letters and memos following a standard format.

(a) Letters

(i) Letter heading. Most organizations use headed paper for correspondence. The style and colour used for the printed heading is always carefully chosen, and the firm's *logo* or house symbol can be incorporated if this is felt appropriate. The heading usually includes the following:

> name of the organization
> address
> names of directors, company secretary and chairman
> nature of business
> telephone number
> telex number
> address of company's registered office
> company registration number and place of registration.

Not all of this information needs to be given at the top of the page. Fig. 4.1 shows how it can be broken up to improve the layout.

(ii) References. Some organizations have the words 'Your ref' and 'Our ref' preprinted on their headed stationery. Others leave the typist to insert them. The reference number is often the number of the file relating to the individual or company concerned (see Units 7.4 and 7.5).

(iii) Date. All documents should bear the date on which they were issued.

(iv) Inside name and address. The person to whom the letter is to be sent, the *addressee*, should be identified in the top left-hand corner. The addressee's full name, qualifications and position in the firm should be shown. In the United Kingdom, 'Esq' is sometimes used instead of (never as well as) 'Mr', though some people regard it as old-fashioned. In the USA the word is used in full— Esquire—but only for professional people, like lawyers. The members of a business partnership should be addressed as, for example, Messrs Watson and Holmes. But if the company is a limited liability company (see Unit 1.6(a)(iii)), the name of the firm should be followed by 'Ltd' or 'p.l.c.', as appropriate. Always give the full address, with the postcode on the last line.

(v) Additional addressees. If carbon copies are to be sent to other addressees the inside name and address of the first addressee appears in the usual place, but in the bottom left-hand corner of the page the words 'copies to' or 'cc' (carbon copies), are added, with a list of the names of the additional addressees.

Occasionally a 'blind' copy is sent. In this case the names of additional addressees appear on the carbon copies, but not on the top or *original* copy. The letters 'NOO' (not on original) may precede 'cc' to indicate this.

Each carbon copy must be marked to show to which of the additional addressees it is to be sent. The name may be ticked or underlined, or a cross placed beside it.

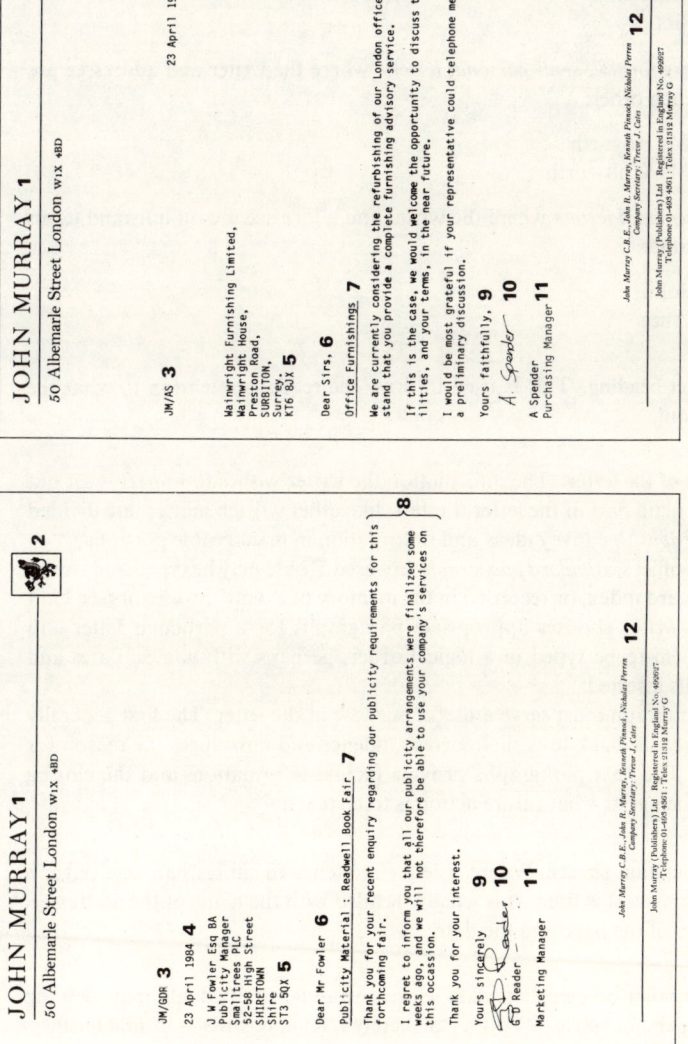

Fig. 4.1 Business letters: (a) a semi-formal letter to an individual, (b) a formal letter to a company. 1. Preprinted letter heading. 2. Company logo. 3. Reference. 4. Date. 5. Inside name and address. 6. Salutation. 7. Heading. 8. Body of the letter, divided into paragraphs. 9. Complimentary close. 10. Signature. 11. Name and position of the writer. 12. Company information

(vi) **The opening of the letter.** This *salutation* sets the tone for what follows. Forms in common use include:

1. *For formal letters* or where the addressee's name is not known to the writer:

Dear Sir
Dear Madam
Dear Sirs

2. *For less formal, semi-personal letters*, where the writer and addressee are known to each other:

Dear Mr Hogarth
Dear Ms Whitworth

3. *For personal letters* where the writer and addressee are on informal terms with each other:

Dear John
Dear Alice

(vii) **Subject heading.** This is used to draw the reader's attention to what the letter is about.

(viii) **Body of the letter.** The information the writer wishes to impart is set out in this, the main part of the letter. Letters, like other written matter, are divided into *paragraphs* to convey ideas and information in manageable portions.

In many offices, *standard paragraphs* are used. These may be typed and stored in a file or card index, or recorded in the memory of a word-processor (see Unit 15.6). The writer chooses appropriate paragraphs for a particular letter and asks for them to be typed in a logical order, perhaps with names, dates and other details inserted.

Each paragraph must serve a useful purpose in the letter. The first generally refers the reader back to earlier correspondence and introduces the reason for this letter. The next paragraphs provide factual information, and the closing paragraph suggests what future action is to be taken.

(ix) **Continuation sheets.** Where a letter stretches to more than one page, a continuation sheet is used. It is usually headed with the name of the addressee, the number of the page and the date.

(x) **Subscription or complimentary close.** Although individuals may develop their own personal style—'Yours', 'Sincerely', 'Kind regards'—formal business procedure requires the use of a subscription or closing remark in keeping with the salutation. A letter starting with a formal 'Dear Sir', should end with an equally formal 'Yours faithfully' or 'Yours truly'. A letter starting with 'Dear Mr Hogarth' should end 'Yours sincerely', while a letter starting 'Dear John' can end in the writer's own personal style.

(xi) **Signature.** The writer of the letter signs it below the subscription. His or her name and position in the organization are typed below the signature.

(xii) **Enclosures.** If other documents are to be sent with the letter, the word 'Enclosure', often shortened to 'Enc', appears in the bottom left-hand corner of the letter. Where there is more than one enclosure, the number should be shown—'Enc 4', for example.

(xiii) **Special instructions.** If a letter is confidential, in the sense that it is to be opened and read only by the addressee or his or her authorized deputy, the word 'Confidential' should be typed immediately above the inside name and address. For letters to be read by the addressee only, the word 'Personal' should be typed there instead. Other special instructions—'For the attention of Mrs A. B. Cedar', for example, or 'Registered', 'Recorded' or other mailing directions— are also inserted above the inside name and address.

Many organizations have developed their own *house style* for business correspondence. This means that particular rules or *conventions* are adopted for layout and punctuation. For instance, find out whether the house style in your organization is for paragraphs to be *indented*, with the first letter of the first word of each paragraph five spaces or so in from the margin, or *blocked*, with all lines starting at the left-hand margin. Also ask whether the preference is for *close* punctuation, with commas and full stops punctuating the name and address, salutation and subscription, or for an *open* style, without these marks.

(b) Memoranda

The heading and framework of an internal memo is usually much simpler than that for external correspondence. Fig. 4.2 illustrates the main features.

Addresses are not usually needed on memos—the name and the department or position are enough to identify the sender and the addressee. Nor is it necessary to waste time and space inserting formal salutations and subscriptions. As the sender's name appears on the memo, it need not be repeated after the signature. Often memos are just initialled, rather than signed in full.

The body of a memo, like that of a letter, may vary in length from a few lines to several pages. It can be divided into paragraphs if necessary.

(c) Envelopes

For external mail, the way the envelope is addressed is very important. The inside name and full address, including the postcode, should be typed neatly on to the envelope, or on to a sticky address label if the envelope is too large to fit in the carriage of the typewriter. Either way, make sure that the position of the address allows sufficient room for stamps or franking (see Unit 11.5). Lay out the address in the same way as the inside name and address, with the name of the town or city in capital letters.

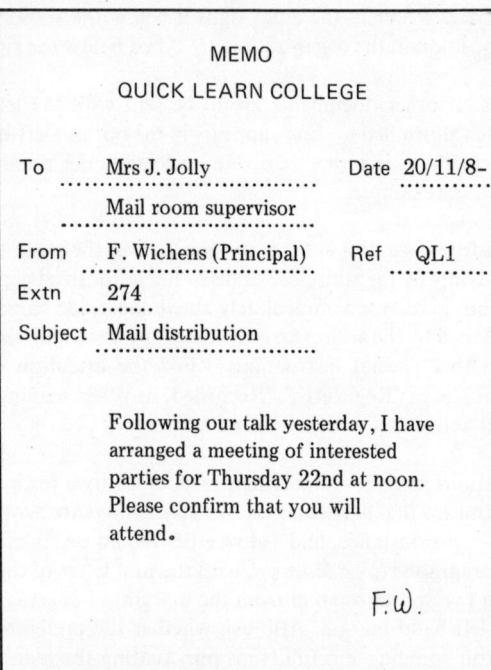

Fig. 4.2   An internal memorandum

4.4 Business English

Mis-spelt or badly written letters give a bad impression of an organization. If you are asked to add a few words or a paragraph to a standard letter, be careful to use the right words, to spell them properly and to draw up logical and grammatical sentences. This takes both practice and patience. Here are a few guidelines.

(i) Plan your letter before you start. Type out a draft if necessary, and check its grammar and spelling.

(ii) Unless you have been told otherwise, write your business correspondence in the *first person plural*—'we', 'us' and 'our', rather than 'I', 'me', 'my'. This is because you are writing on behalf of the organization.

(iii) Don't decorate your correspondence with unnecessary or outdated phrases. 'We are in receipt of your highly esteemed favour of 10th ult' and 'we anxiously await the honour of your esteemed reply' sound far too servile for today's communications. 'Thank you for your letter of 10 April' and 'we look forward to hearing from you further' sound much more positive.

(iv) Don't use slang. Use 'he was absent that day' rather than 'he'd skived off', 'she was dismissed instantly' rather than 'she was given the boot right then and there'.

(v) Avoid phrases of the 'I would' variety. 'We should be grateful if you would' is a useful form of words.

(vi) Keep your wording simple, but without overdoing it. Too much use of words like 'got' and 'a lot of' makes your letters sound rather childish. Try the occasional 'obtained' and 'many' or 'numerous', where the context is right.

(vii) Don't waffle, and don't repeat yourself. Make each point clearly, but make it once only. If the addressee wants to check anything, he or she can re-read the letter.

(viii) Keep your sentences fairly short. A full stop every four or five words makes a letter sound too staccato. But if you write line after line without allowing the reader to pause for breath, you will probably lose him—and yourself.

(ix) Use commas to separate one point from another, as in 'our new machine operates quickly, silently and most efficiently' and 'letters should be clearly written, correctly spelt and to the point'.

(x) Invest in a good dictionary and use it to check your spelling and the meaning of words. Using a dictionary, you can also find out what part of speech a word is (noun, verb and so on); some dictionaries give examples of how the word may be used. A little pocket guide to the use of English can be helpful too: one is *Get it Right* by Michael Temple (published by John Murray).

(xi) When you are composing each sentence, make sure you know what message you want it to get across to the reader. Read through what you have written, to make sure the message comes over as you intended.

4.5 Visual Aids

Written information, especially figures, is sometimes easier to understand if it is presented in an alternative form. There are several ways in which you can bring your written communication to life by the use of visual aids.

(a) Tables

Table 4.1 shows some sales figures in tabular form. This allows us to compare the figures for each month with both the planned and previous year's figures, in

Table 4.1 Travel sales from January to June

Month	Last year's sales (£)	This year's sales: planned (£)	This year's sales: actual (£)	Variance on last year (+/-%)	Variance on plan (+/-%)
January	320 000	340 000	300 000	−6.25	−11.76
February	330 000	350 000	290 000	−12.12	−17.14
March	340 000	360 000	280 000	−17.64	−22.22
April	310 000	330 000	300 000	−3.20	−9.09
May	300 000	320 000	310 000	+3.33	−3.13
June	250 000	270 000	260 000	+4.00	−3.70

a way that is much easier to follow than any description of the position in words. In addition, the point of making the presentation can be clearly made. By including the two variance (difference) columns, and presenting the information in them in the form of the percentage difference between the figures, the shortfall on the planned sales becomes obvious. (The figure in the 'variance on plan' column is the difference between the planned and actual sales figures, expressed as a percentage of the planned figure. The figure in the 'variance on last year' column is the difference between this year's actual figure and last year's, expressed as a percentage of last year's figure.)

(b) Line Graphs

Although clearer than a written narrative, the table has little immediate visual impact. Nor are the trends in the figures instantly seen. Are the sales tending to get better or worse each month? Is the 'variance on plan' greater in some months than others? Can we draw any conclusions about the trading pattern this year— have sales risen in months when we expected them to fall off, or dropped when we expected them to rise? *Line graphs* can help on all these points, enabling us

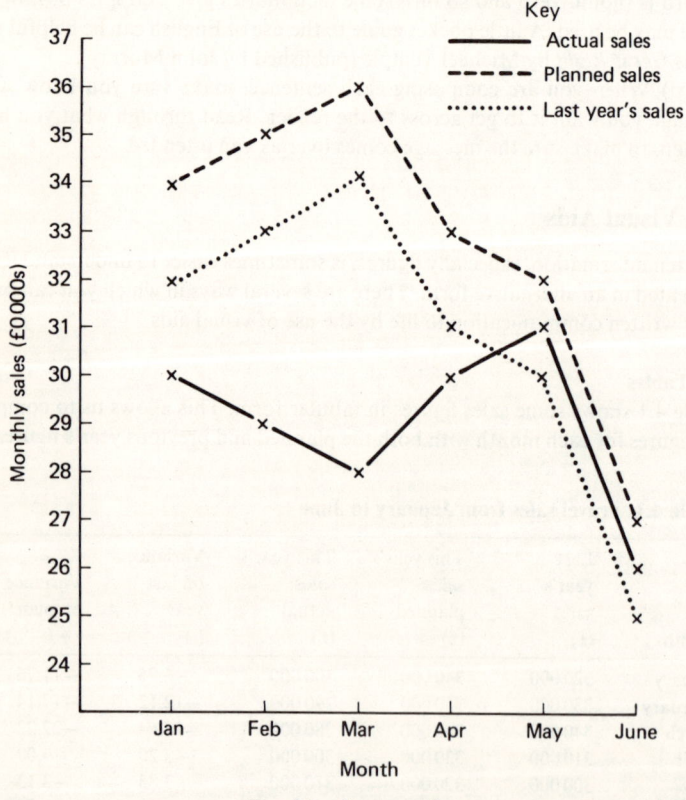

Fig. 4.3   Line graph

to see clearly what the figures are really telling us about the sales position (Fig. 4.3).

The horizontal line or *axis* at the bottom of the graph shows the months of the year to date. In Fig. 4.3 the vertical axis is marked off in steps of £10 000, starting at £230 000 and rising to £370 000, to indicate the value of sales. To plot the graph we need to know how much was sold, and when. Table 4.1 shows that sales in January were £300 000. Move up the vertical axis until you reach the figure 30. (The £0 000s on the vertical axis shows that the numbers there represent tens of thousands of pounds and that four zeros must be added to obtain the actual values.) Move sideways until you are above the point marked 'Jan' on the horizontal axis. Draw a cross at the point you have now reached. For February you need to move down the vertical axis, because sales have dropped to £290 000, and across the horizontal axis until you are above the point marked 'Feb'. Make another cross here. When you have plotted all the points, join them together. Then use the same procedure for the planned figures and for last year's figures.

The unbroken line in Fig. 4.3 shows the pattern of this year's sales, while the broken and the dotted lines indicate the information with which the actual sales figures are being compared. Using a different colour or style for each line adds impact and clarity, but a key (as in the top right-hand corner) is necessary to explain what each line represents.

(c) Bar Charts

A third way of presenting the same sales figures is on a bar chart or *histogram*. This form of presentation (see Fig. 4.4) is particularly useful where information about one item or subject is to be compared and contrasted with information about another. Fig. 4.4 again shows the actual, planned and last year's sales figures plotted separately, and again the months appear on the horizontal axis and the value of sales on the vertical axis. This time, however, there is a separate block or bar on the chart for each of the items to be compared. The solid blocks are easier to see than a single line, and the varying heights of the bars give a clear picture of the relative sales levels. Different colours or shadings can be used for the different items represented.

(d) Pie Charts

Tables and graphs help to highlight trends, changes in sales, costs and so on. But they don't show us what *proportion* of, say, the package holiday market figures represent. If we know the total size of this particular 'pie'—that is, the amount spent on certain types of package holiday during the first three months of the year—and the company's own sales figures for the period, we can draw a *pie chart* (Fig. 4.5). The whole pie or circle represents 100 per cent of the market for this particular product. Costalot's share last year was 35 per cent. This year it has dropped to 25 per cent, while Bumpytours have increased from 25 to 40 per cent over the same period.

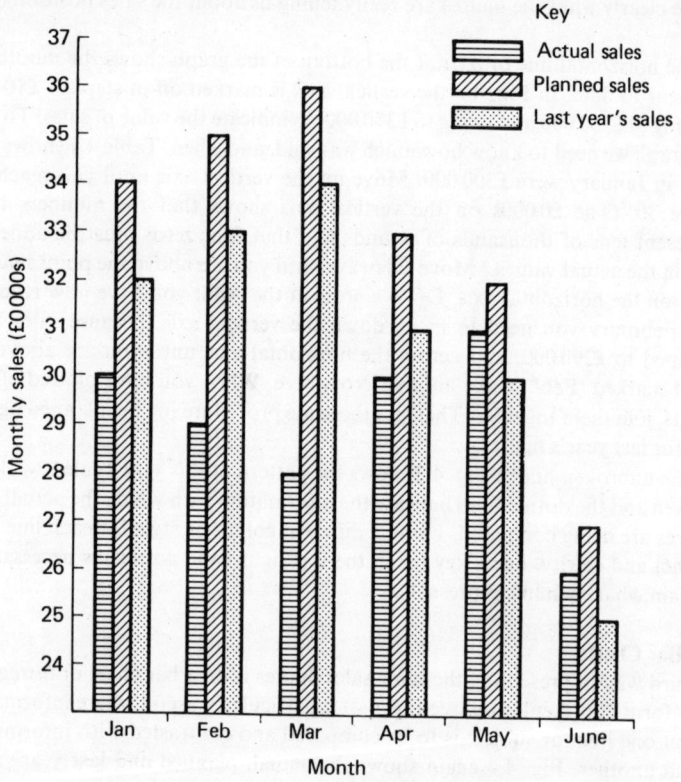

Fig. 4.4   A bar chart or histogram

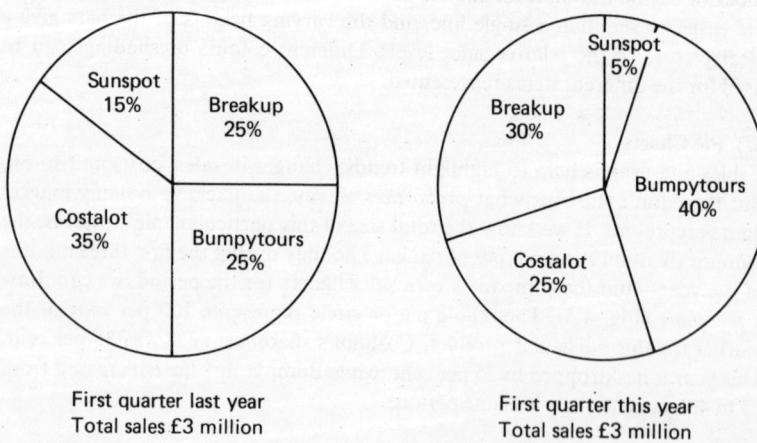

Fig. 4.5   Pie charts

4.6 Sources of Information

Knowing how to write and present information is only half the battle. You must also know *what* to write. Much of the information communicated by office workers is internal to the organization, and is stored in its files and computers. From time to time, however, you will need to consult sources of information produced outside your organization. A checklist of the kinds of problem with which help may be needed is given in Table 4.2, with guidance on reference books and other appropriate sources and how to use them.

When using a reference book, first turn to the section at the beginning of the book which explains how the volume should be used, how the contents are arranged and where to search for what you want. Some books include an alphabetical index, usually at the back, and this can help you to track down information on a particular topic.

Table 4.2 Some sources of information

Information required on:	Reference source	How to use
Spelling	English dictionary, e.g. *Concise Oxford* or *Chambers Twentieth Century*	Words are listed in alphabetical order; scan tops of pages for headlines to see where each page starts and finishes; if unsure of first few letters, check possible alternatives
Part of speech or meaning of word	English dictionary	Locate word as above; a letter after the word tells you the part of speech, *n.* for noun, *v.* for verb, *a.* for adjective, *adv.* for adverb; read through all possible meanings given
Alternative words	Roget's *Thesaurus of English Words and Phrases*	Use alphabetical word index, which comprises second half of thesaurus, to look up word for which alternative is required; this usually refers to several sections of the book, depending on part of speech and context; words with the same meaning will be found in these sections
Grammar and usage	Fowler's *Dictionary of Modern English Usage*	Words arranged alphabetically as in dictionary, but entries explain, with examples, how word is used

Information required on:	Reference source	How to use
Preparation of text for publication, proofreading	British Standards *Copy Preparation and Proof Correction*	The special symbols used are illustrated and explained
Address and/or telephone number where name is known	Relevant UK or overseas telephone directory or, for UK businesses, use *Kompass Dial Industry* which also gives telex numbers (Kompass Publishers Ltd, East Grinstead)	Names listed in alphabetical order; look up as in dictionary
Address and/or telephone number of tradesmen	*Yellow Pages* telephone directory	Look up appropriate classification, e.g. insurance brokers, plumbers; classifications arranged alphabetically and subscribers listed alphabetically within sections; look for an appropriate entry; some cross-referencing between classifications
Address/telephone number/ telegraphic address/telex number of manufacturers, wholesalers, merchants and firms offering services to industry	*Kelly's Directory of Manufacturers and Merchants*, including industrial services (Kelly's Directories Ltd, East Grinstead)	Alphabetical section for use where name is known; classified section to identify firms manufacturing particular products; use this section like classified telephone directory—look up product required in alphabetical sequence, with noun appearing first (e.g. 'hammers, hydraulic'); suppliers are listed alphabetically within each classification

Information required on:	Reference source	How to use
Company details including hours of business, directors' names, bank, number employed, turnover, nature of business	*Kompass UK* (two volumes) for UK companies, or relevant European editions (Kompass Publishers Ltd)	To find suppliers of particular product (vol. 1), use alphabetical product sequence to find six-figure numerical code for product— procedure explained in front of volume. To locate named company, use alphabetical index of companies in vol. 2 to find out where company is situated; turn to appropriate county and town using headlines at top of each page; companies are listed alphabetically under towns
Worldwide information and statistics for revenue, population, industry, national institutions	*Whitaker's Almanack*	Refer to contents and index pages
Weather forecast and travel news	British Telecom Weatherline and Traveline	Find in list of telephone services in telephone directory or dialling code booklet
Biographical details of important people	*International Yearbook and Statesman's Who's Who* (published by Kelly's Directories Ltd)	Names listed alphabetically (first section gives information on international organizations and states of the world): there are other specialized *Who's Whos* for people in particular sectors, e.g. *Who's Who in Education, Business Who's Who of British Chairmen, Chief Executives and Managing Directors*
Train times and fares to and from London	*ABC Rail Guide*	Look up town in alphabetical sequence; also gives local services around London in separate tables

Information required on:	Reference source	How to use
Air travel information	*ABC World Airways Guide*, or individual timetables produced by airlines, or consult a reputable travel agent	Look up departure point in alphabetical sequence; look up destination in alphabetical list of destinations: e.g. for flights from London to Toronto look up London, and then find Toronto in the London section
Hotel information	AA or RAC handbook or reputable hotel guide	Look up town in alphabetical sequence: the best hotels have four stars ****, less highly rated ones are just listed
Restaurants	*Good Food Guide* (Consumers' Association)	Look up town in alphabetical sequence; a rating system is used and an indication of prices is given
Advice on employment matters, help in resolving industrial disputes	Advisory Conciliation and Arbitration Service (ACAS)	Find regional office through list published in *Croner's Reference Book for Employers* (Croner Publications, New Malden)
Postal services	*Post Office Guide*, produced annually (see Unit 12.1)	Find required service in alphabetical index of services at back of guide, or consult summaries of inland and overseas services; check supplements for changes
Postal charges	*Postal Rates Compendium* (inland or overseas)	Check service, weight and, for overseas mail, destination
Telecommunications services	*British Telecom Guide* (produced annually)	Find required service in alphabetical index of services; check supplements for changes

Clearly, the list in Table 4.2 is not comprehensive. If you need help not mentioned here, your local librarian or the staff of the Citizens' Advice Bureau can probably help you. The *Financial Times*, the *Daily Telegraph* and some other national newspapers have libraries which can answer queries by letter or telephone, or suggest suitable sources of help. The British Institute of Management's information service, the Confederation of British Industry and the London and local Chambers of Commerce can also help on most queries relating to British business.

4.7 Quick Questions

1. List eight items of information that should be included in a firm's preprinted letter heading.

2. What is a salutation? Give examples of salutations which are (*a*) informal, (*b*) semi-formal, and (*c*) formal.

3. What is a subscription or complimentary close? Give examples of subscriptions which are (*a*) informal, (*b*) semi-formal, and (*c*) formal.

4. List four ways of presenting numerical information, and indicate briefly the advantages of each.

5. Which reference book(s) would you consult to find out (*a*) the meaning of a word, (*b*) a tradesman's address or telephone number, (*c*) the names of a firm's directors, and (*d*) train times to or from London?

6. Say why you might consult (*a*) the *Post Office Guide*, (*b*) the *British Telecom Guide*, (*c*) the Advisory Conciliation and Arbitration Service (ACAS) (or comparable publications or organizations in your own country).

4.8 Short Exercises

1. Examine any business forms of which you can get copies, either from friends or colleagues or from traders from whom you have bought goods or services. For each form, make notes on (*a*) its purpose, and (*b*) your opinion as to its relevance and suitability for its purpose.

2. You have been asked to draft a letter to the manager of a local hotel confirming that fifteen of your company's representatives will be meeting there for a conference on 15 May. List the points you should include, and then draft the letter.

Unit Five

Stationery and Equipment

5.1 Introduction

Next time you are near an office supplies store, go in and look round. Count how many different kinds of paper, envelopes and business machines are on display. You will probably see hundreds of items, each with its own special use and its own claim to a share in your office manager's stationery budget.

Selecting the right stationery or equipment for a particular task is never easy, even when you are choosing from the more limited range available within your own office. To begin with, you will probably be told which materials to use for each task. Four factors have to be considered:

(i) **Expense.** There is no point in using costly items if a cheaper alternative is available.

(ii) **Efficiency.** Time and effort cost money. So it may sometimes be worth paying a little extra—for a preprinted form or a faster copier, say—in order to save money in the long run.

(iii) **Durability.** Things that will be kept for a long time must be of better quality, and therefore probably be more expensive, than those that have a more limited life.

(iv) **Public relations.** The use of good-quality materials helps an organization to convey a smart and businesslike impression to customers.

Care must be taken not to overdo it, though. If a local authority uses heavyweight embossed stationery when writing to advise the ratepayers of an increase in rates, for instance, there are likely to be harsh comments about the use to which public money is put.

5.2 Paper and Envelopes

Paper comes in various thicknesses or *weights*, which are measured in *grams per square metre* (gsm or g/m^2). It also comes in many different sizes (Fig. 5.1 and Table 5.1). It is important to choose the right kind for each task.

(*a*) Letter Paper

The quality of paper that is used for business correspondence is called *bond* paper, and normally weighs 70 to 90 gsm. It is thick enough not to crease or tear easily, but not so thick that it looks ostentatious. All but the very smallest firms use paper that carries a preprinted letter heading (see Unit 4.3(*a*)(i)).

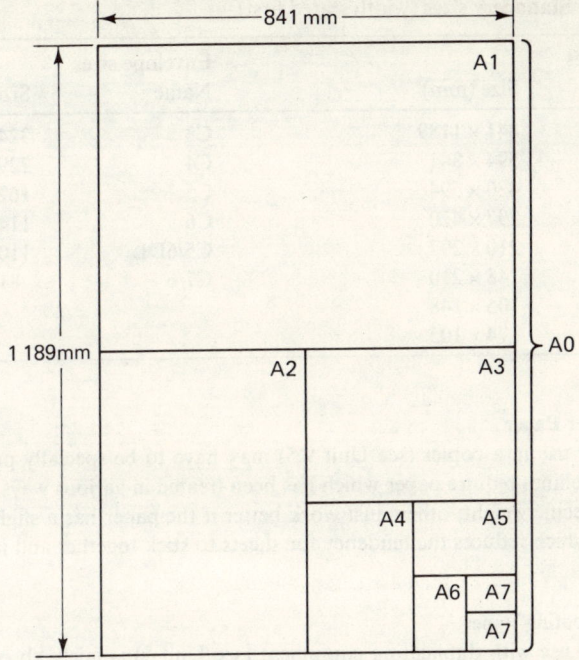

Fig. 5.1 Stationery sizes: each size is exactly half as big as the next larger size— for instance, a sheet of A4 is half the size of a sheet of A3

White paper is usually used for correspondence, with plain white bond continuation sheets. Some organizations, however, try to make their letters stand out by using coloured paper.

For correspondence, the size of paper used is generally either A4 or A5. A size between the two, called 'two-thirds A4', measuring 210 × 198 mm, is also available.

(b) Carbon Copies

Back copies of letters are made by *interleaving* (placing in alternate layers) sheets of carbon paper and sheets of thin (flimsy) paper. This paper is called *bank* paper; it weighs 40 to 45 gsm, and may be either white or coloured.

Carbon paper is also sold by weight. The heavier it is, the more times each sheet can be re-used.

Always make sure that you are using carbon paper the right side up, with the coated (plain) side next to the bank paper.

Bank and carbon paper are sold in the same sizes as bond paper.

(c) Airmail Letters

Letters which are to be sent by air must be as light as possible. Airmail paper weighs only 25 to 30 gsm.

Table 5.1 Stationery sizes (width stated first)

Paper sizes Name	Size (mm)	Envelope sizes Name	Size (mm)
A0	841 × 1189	C3	324 × 458
A1	594 × 841	C4	229 × 324
A2	420 × 594	C5	162 × 229
A3	297 × 420	C6	114 × 162
A4	210 × 297	C5/6DL	110 × 220
A5	148 × 210	C7/6	81 × 162
A6	105 × 148		
A7	74 × 105		

(d) Copier Paper

Paper for use in a copier (see Unit 9.5) may have to be specially purchased. Some machines require paper which has been treated in various ways or which is of a specific weight; others just work better if the paper has a slightly shiny surface, which reduces the tendency for sheets to stick together and jam in the machine.

(e) Duplicating Paper

Paper for use with duplicating equipment (see Unit 9) is fairly absorbent, so that the ink which is applied to it during the duplicating process dries quickly. It weighs about 60 to 70 gsm, and may be white or coloured.

(f) Carbonless Copy Paper

This is sometimes called NCR ('No Carbon Required') paper. The writing surface looks normal, but the paper is treated on the other side with a special substance. This produces an image, like a carbon image, on the sheet below, without the need for carbon paper.

Carbonless copy paper avoids the pitfalls of carbon paper being inserted back to front, left out altogether, or used until its surface is so worn that the back copy is unreadable. It is much quicker to use than interleaved carbon and bank paper, especially where several copies are needed.

On the other hand, it is more expensive, and requires care to be taken to insert a backing card behind the last copy sheet, or the image will go through to the sheets behind. Carbonless copy paper is often used for pads of business forms.

(g) Memo Paper

This is usually of medium, rather than top, quality, as it is for internal use only, and is generally preprinted (Fig. 4.2). A4 and A5 are common sizes.

(h) Compliments Slips

These are small pieces of paper, usually not more than about 10 cm square, which have brief details of the organization and the words 'with compliments' printed on them (Fig. 5.2).

With Compliments

QUICK LEARN COLLEGE

Durham House
51 – 65 Lower Green Kendal Cumbria LA5 4PZ

Fig. 5.2   Compliments slip

They can be sent out with catalogues, price lists or any other documents, to show where they have come from. This saves writing an accompanying (*covering*) letter. A short message and the sender's signature may be written on the slip.

(*i*) Envelopes

Like paper, envelopes come in various weights, from airmail to heavy duty. The normal rule is to use an envelope which matches the quality of the paper used. Fig. 5.3 shows how A4 and A5 paper must be folded to fit into the various sizes.

(i) **Banker envelopes** have the opening and the flap on the longer side. They are usually used for letters.

(ii) **Pocket envelopes** have the opening and the flap on the shorter side, and are used for documents and reports.

(iii) **Gusset** and **padded envelopes** will take more bulky material and are used for sending thick documents, books and so on. Padded envelopes are useful for sending fragile articles, and card-backed envelopes are used for photographs to prevent the risk of bending.

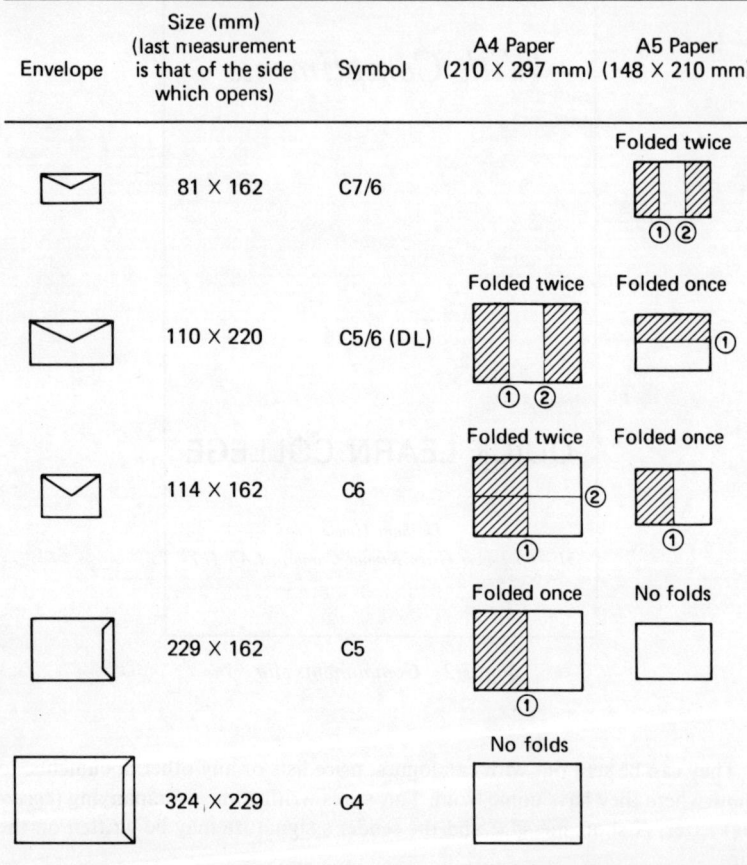

Envelope	Size (mm) (last measurement is that of the side which opens)	Symbol	A4 Paper (210 × 297 mm)	A5 Paper (148 × 210 mm)
	81 × 162	C7/6		Folded twice ① ②
	110 × 220	C5/6 (DL)	Folded twice ① ②	Folded once ①
	114 × 162	C6	Folded twice ① ②	Folded once ①
	229 × 162	C5	Folded once ①	No folds
	324 × 229	C4	No folds	

Fig. 5.3   Envelopes of various sizes, and how to fold A4 and A5 paper to fit them

(iv) **Window envelopes** have an oblong hole in the front, covered with transparent material to form a 'window'. Letters are folded in such a way that the inside name and address can be seen through the 'window' and do not have to be typed again on the envelope.

(v) **Reply-paid envelopes** (see Unit 12.6(*b*)(ii)) don't need postage stamps.

(vi) **Post Office Preferred (POP) sizes.** In the United Kingdom, the Post Office prefers envelopes of a certain size to be used. Envelopes should be oblong in shape, not smaller than 90 × 140 mm and not larger than 120 × 235 mm.

(vii) **Internal envelopes** for use inside the organization are generally of lower quality than those for external use. Sometimes old envelopes are re-used, perhaps with a sticky label to conceal the original address. Sometimes there are special heavy-duty envelopes suitable for repeated re-use, with spaces for re-entry of different addressees' names.

(*j*) **Notebooks and Pads**
These vary in size, quality and type.

(i) **A hardbacked memo book** will last a long time, but is expensive. The pages are not meant to be torn out, so it is more suitable for a permanent record than for day-to-day notes.

(ii) **A spirally bound shorthand notebook** is designed so that the pages can be torn out easily. It is therefore useful for taking notes, especially shorthand dictation, which only have to be kept for a short time.

(iii) **Loose-leaf refill pads** are available in sizes from 330 × 203 mm (foolscap) to 210 × 148 mm (A5). Their pages are lined, with wide or narrow rulings. The paper is of medium quality, suitable for writing in ink, ballpoint or pencil. The pads have holes punched in the margin, so that pages can be torn out and kept in a ring binder (see Unit 6.3(*b*)).

(iv) **Message pads** remind you what information you need to give to enable the addressee to understand your memo. The telephone message pad (Fig. 3.10) is an example.

(v) **Preprinted forms** are often supplied in pads. Sometimes they carry a serial number on each page, especially where money is concerned, to make it easy to check for a missing receipt or invoice that could mean that goods have not been paid for.
    If the forms need to be completed in *duplicate* (two copies) or *triplicate* (three copies), carbonless copy paper is sometimes used. The second and third copies may be distinctively coloured, to avoid confusion.

5.3 Other Items of Stationery

Although paper and envelopes are the first things we think of when we talk about office stationery, many other things are used in the office to aid written communication. Some of these are listed in Table 5.2 (overleaf).

5.4 Using Stationery Economically

All the items we have mentioned have to be bought and paid for by the organization. Here are a few ways in which you can help your firm to save money.

Table 5.2 Office stationery (excluding paper and envelopes)

Adding machine rolls (tally rolls)	Markers (water colour and
Address labels	permanent)
Adhesive (glue)	Paper-clips
Adhesive tape (sticky tape)	Paper drills/punches/perforators
Ballpoint pens	(hole punchers)
Binders (ring, punched)	Paper-fasteners
Blotting paper	Pencils
Box files	Pencil-sharpeners
Bulldog clips	Photocopy correction fluid
Calculator rolls	Pins
Calendars	Plastic folders
Chinagraph pencils	Postal tubes
Clipboards	Postcards
Correction fluid/strips (for typing	Record cards
errors)	Reinforcing washers (for punched
Correction fluid thinner	holes)
Corrugated card	Report covers
Dampers (moistened rollers, for	Ring binders
envelopes, stamps, etc)	Rubber bands
Date stamps	Rubber stamps
Diaries	Rulers
Double-face tape (sticky on both	Scissors
sides)	Sealing wax
Drawing pins	Self-adhesive labels
Dusters	Self-adhesive tape
Erasers	Staple extractor
Fibre-tip pens	Stapler and staples
File laces	Stencil correcting fluid
Filing clips	Stencils
Fingerettes (rubber thimbles)	String
Flat files and folders	Strip index strips
Guide cards	Tags
Gummed labels	Tape dispenser
Gummed tape	Tissue paper
Holiday planners	Transparent tape
Index card boxes	Treasury tags
Index cards	Twine
Ink	Type cleaner
Ink pads	Typewriter ribbons
Labels	Wrapping paper
Letter openers	Year planners
Lever-arch files	

(*a*) **Things to Do**

    (i) Do make sure you have the right paper or equipment for the job—check

      size and quality of paper
      size and strength of envelopes and folders
      size of rubber bands and staples
      length of tape or string required
      size of labels.

    (ii) Do make sure you finish one box before opening another when you are using such items as pins, paper-clips, paper and typewriter correction strips or fluid.

    (iii) Do use items more than once if possible: envelopes can be re-used for internal mail, and discarded typescript and photocopies can be used as scrap paper. Re-use folders, binders and files by changing labels.

    (iv) Do keep items clean and in usable condition. Paper and envelopes should be stored in boxes until required, typewriters should be kept clean, paper punches and pencil-sharpeners should be emptied regularly and staplers should be used with care to avoid jamming.

(*b*) **Things Not to Do**

    (i) Don't throw anything away until it is finished. Bottles of typewriter correction fluid, for instance, can appear empty but may only have dried up and can be rescued by adding thinner.

    (ii) Don't leave pencils, pens, rubbers, staplers, pencil-sharpeners, paper punches or other items lying about where they might be mislaid or misappropriated.

    (iii) Don't use expensive items where cheaper ones could be used without giving a bad impression.

    (iv) Don't carry heavy stocks of items that are not often used. Money invested in paper might be needed for other things. You may also find, particularly where preprinted stationery is concerned, that designs have changed and you are left with obsolete stock.

    (v) Don't allow yourself to run out of an item which is normally ordered in large quantities from a supplier. If you have to rush out to buy single items it will cost your firm more than buying in quantity.

These last two problems could both be prevented by the operation of some simple stock control.

5.5 Stationery Stock Control

If your office is part of a large organization, there is probably a centralized system of buying stationery in large quantities from manufacturers or wholesale distributors. Once delivered, the stationery will be kept in a *stationery store*. An *inventory* or list of available stock may be issued. Each department is usually responsible for ordering its own stationery from the stationery store, using a

Success in Office Practice

68

REQUISITION

Department .... Requisition no. ....

Supplier's name (if known) ....

Date ....

Quantity	Details	Catalogue no.	Unit price

Authorized
signature:

Fig. 5.4   Requisition slip

form called a *requisition* (Fig. 5.4). If the stationery store and the office are some distance apart, it may take several days for a requisition to be dealt with and the required stationery to be delivered to the user department. Each department has to monitor its use of stationery so that the stock kept for daily needs is enough, although not so much that valuable space and money are wasted on storage.

In most departments, one person takes on the task of looking after the stationery stock. If you are given this responsibility, you should:

(i) Find out which items are regularly used in the department. You can ask the supervisor and individual members of staff for this information.

(ii) Count up how much of each item is used each week, over a period of several weeks.

(iii) Ask whether the weeks you have been monitoring are likely to be fairly typical—has it been a particularly busy or a particularly quiet period?

(iv) Ask whether there are any particular activities, such as stocktaking, for which special forms are required that are not normally in use.

(v) Agree with your supervisor an appropriate stock level for each item. If, for example, over a period of three weeks you found that, on average, eight shorthand notebooks were used each week, and if it takes between ten days and two weeks for a requisition from your department to be dealt with by the central stationery store, you might decide to have a basic stock of four weeks' supply—32 notebooks. As soon as your stock falls to 16 you should reorder to bring in another 32 notebooks, using the company's requisition form (see Fig. 5.4) and keeping a copy for your own use.

(vi) When your stocks are delivered, check them carefully against your copy of the requisition. Make sure that you have been sent the type and number of each item that you asked for, and that all are in good condition. Remember that your department will probably be charged, through the firm's accounting system, for the stationery it orders. You shouldn't pay for items that have been damaged elsewhere.

(vii) Keep the stationery neatly on shelves, not on the floor. In a large store, each shelf and section should be labelled so that, for instance, paper of various types is kept in one area, but the different sizes and weights are not muddled together. Resist the temptation to put new stock, particularly paper in any form, in front of the old on the shelf, so that packets of paper cannot remain at the back of a shelf for years, becoming yellow and unusable. Using *stock rotation* (bringing forward the stock at the back) eliminates this risk.

(viii) Make sure that the cupboard or store room is kept clean, dry and tidy. Items should be stored in their wrappers or containers until used. Old wrappers should be thrown away, not left lying about on the shelf or on the floor.

5.6 Office Equipment

Office equipment ranges from simple stationery items, like paper punches and staplers, to copiers, duplicators and computers. Table 5.3 lists some of these; use the Index at the back of this book to find detailed descriptions of major items.

The operating instructions for each machine depend on its make and design. For many you will need special training before you attempt to operate them. There are, though, a few general principles to be borne in mind when handling and using equipment.

(a) Things to Do

(i) Do find out what each item of business equipment is for.

(ii) Do find out who is allowed to use it.

(iii) Do find out how to operate this particular make of machine.

(iv) Always follow the manufacturer's instructions carefully.

(v) If a record is kept of the machine's users, make sure you enter details each time you use it.

(vi) Do operate the machine as economically as possible, and switch off electrical equipment when not in use.

(vii) Keep machines clean and well maintained. Most manufacturers undertake regular servicing and will send you an engineer to correct faults that cannot be dealt with by the operator.

(viii) Pay careful attention to safety (see Unit 5.10).

Table 5.3 Office equipment

Equipment	Equipment
Adding machine	Intercom system
Accounting machine	Letter-opening machine
Addressing machine	Letter rack
Binding machine	Letter sorter
Bin (waste-paper)	Letter tray
Cabinet	Photocopier
Calculator	Printing equipment
Cash box	Scales (postal)
Cash register	Shredder
Computer system	Strip index
Cupboard	Telephone amplifier
Dictation equipment	Telephone answering
Duplicating equipment	machine
Electrostatic copier	Telephone switchboard
Filing cabinet	Typewriter
Filing trolley	Viewdata equipment
Franking machine	Visual display unit
Guillotine	Word-processor

(b) **Things Not to Do**

(i) Never assume that the machine will do all the work. Even the most sophisticated equipment can fall prey to 'operator error'. While some, such as the key-to-disc computer input systems discussed in Unit 15.2(b), will alert you if you attempt to feed in information that does not fit what the computer has been programmed to expect, many more accept your errors, and you may not discover them until you are trying to balance your entries later in the day. It can then be quite hard to pinpoint what it is that is making nonsense of your calculations.

(ii) Never use the machines for private purposes without getting permission first. Some employers allow staff to use copiers and other equipment for a small fee, others prefer these not to be used for anything other than company business. Find out your firm's policy, and abide by it.

(iii) Although respect for powerful and expensive machinery is healthy, don't be so overawed by mechanical gadgetry that you become reluctant to use it to the full. If you find yourself reacting in this way, ask a more experienced operator to watch you operate the machine once or twice so you will not panic if anything goes wrong. The machine is there to help you do your job more efficiently, but it can only do so if you use it correctly.

(iv) Don't be afraid of machines. Some people worry that the more automation there is in the office, the fewer people will need to be employed. Up to a point this is true, but quite often the introduction of new machines creates new, but different, jobs.

Each year, bigger, better and faster office machines are developed. Even that most familiar piece of equipment, the office typewriter, is changing.

5.7 Office Typewriters

The typewriter is essential for the production of all business correspondence and reports: a typed document is both easier to read than a handwritten one and looks more professional.

The central feature of all typewriters is the *keyboard*. This usually consists of four rows of 11 or 12 keys, denoting letters, figures, and symbols. The order of the keys nearly always follows the pattern in Fig. 5.5. This is the Universal keyboard, sometimes referred to as the 'QWERTY' keyboard, from the first six keys on the top row of letters.

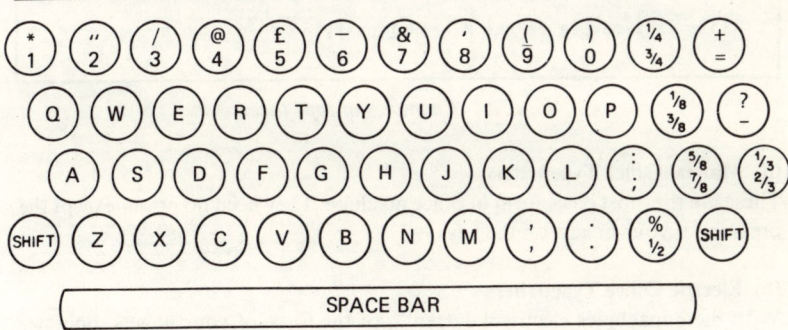

Fig. 5.5   The layout of the Universal or 'QWERTY' keyboard

When you strike one of the keys on the keyboard, the metal *type* which bears the *characters* (letters, numbers and symbols) strikes a *ribbon*. The ribbon may be either carbon or fabric. It is loaded on to two spools, which may be encased in a cassette, and travels automatically from spool to spool as you type. When the type strikes the ribbon against the paper, the impression of the character is left on the page.

The size and shape of the finished type depend on the *pitch* and the *type face* or *fount*. Pitch means the width in millimetres of each character of type. The two most common pitches are pica—each character 2.54 mm wide—and elite—each character 2.12 mm wide. Some different type faces are shown in Fig. 5.6. There are four main kinds of typewriter.

```
This is a sample of the Pica Typestyle

This is a sample of the Victoria Typestyle

This is a sample of the Livius Typestyle

This is a sample of the Eletto Typestyle

This is a sample of the Letter Gothic Typestyle

This is a sample of the Britannia Typestyle

This is a sample of the Italico 1 Typestyle

This is a sample of the Italic Typestyle

This is a sample of the Mikron Typestyle
```

Fig. 5.6   Examples of type faces

(a) Manual Office Typewriters
These are the most basic form of office machine. They need no power except the pressure of your fingers on the keys.

(b) Electric Office Typewriters
With these machines electrical current, not the force of your fingers, operates the type-bar and produces an even, firm impression, regardless of the pressure applied to the keys. This makes them less tiring to use than manual machines. In addition, many automatic features help to increase typing speeds: carriage return, spacing and repeat character keys save the typist's time and effort.

Many electric typewriters now have a *single-element* typing mechanism. Often called 'golf-ball' machines, these have just one spherical typing head, around which all the characters are spaced. With most machines, the typing head itself moves across the page. As the ball can rotate at least twice as fast as most typists can type, there is no danger of the jamming that can occur with sluggish manual type-bars. When a different type face is wanted, a new 'golf-ball' can be inserted.

Some typewriters are fitted with a correcting ribbon, either lift-off (for use with carbon ribbons) or cover-up (for use with fabric ribbons). If a correcting ribbon is not fitted, conventional correcting materials, such as correcting fluid or paper or an eraser, are needed.

(c) Special-purpose Typewriters

Large document typewriters have a longer carriage than that of the standard machine, so that extra wide paper can be inserted. They are used for typing legal and other big documents.

In the accounts department (see Unit 19), you might find a *dual-feed* machine, so called because two documents can be fed into it at the same time. The edge of the back document sticks out beyond the front one, and entries can be made on both at once. This is useful where, for instance, a ledger card is kept to record dealings with each supplier or customer, and a summary sheet, showing all the day's transactions, is also needed. In one line of type, both documents can be brought up to date at once.

Another kind of special-purpose typewriter is the *continuous stationery* machine. This uses paper folded concertina-style, with perforations along the folds so that you can tear off what you have used. The paper is fed through the typewriter automatically, and so the chore of feeding fresh paper into the machine disappears. This typewriter, too, is most likely to be found in the accounts department, where a constant series of invoices is being typed.

(d) Electronic Typewriters

Electronic typewriters do not look very different from electric machines, except that some have a one-line thin window strip or *visual display screen*, usually just above the keys (Fig. 5.7). After you have typed a line you can inspect it. If it's right, the operation of the carriage return causes the line to be printed out on the paper. This delay between the typing of the characters and their appearance on the final copy allows the electronic machine to offer other features which cannot be obtained with an ordinary typewriter.

Many electronic machines can automatically *justify* both right- and left-hand margins; this means that all the completed lines of type are of equal length, as they are in a printed book. They can adjust the layout of typed material, for example, by centring headings or moving them to the side of the page. Errors can often be corrected without the need for special ribbons or correcting fluids.

In addition, some electronic machines are what is known as *intelligent* typewriters. These can take information stored on magnetic cards or floppy discs (see Unit 15.4) and include it in the text of a letter. Standard paragraphs—those which are used repeatedly in letters to suppliers, customers or staff—can be stored and indexed. When you want to produce a letter using the standard format, you insert the appropriate card or disc and instruct the machine to print it out. You can add in new information, such as names, dates, addresses, prices and so on, at various points in the text.

You will find electronic typewriters are:

(i) *Reliable.* They have only about 100 moving parts inside them, compared

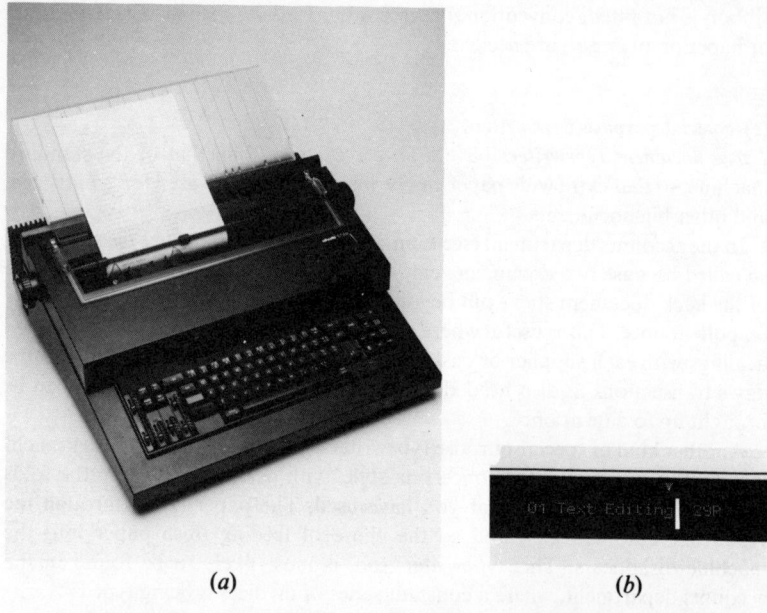

(a)   *(b)*

Fig. 5.7 (a) An electronic typewriter and (b) its visual display, enlarged

with the traditional electric typewriter, which has about 2500, all of which can go wrong and lead to frustrating and timewasting breakdowns.

(ii) *Quiet.*

(iii) *Capable of high-quality output.* Instead of type-bars or a golf-ball, electronic typewriters may use a *daisy wheel* typing element. So called because the characters are arranged around the element like the petals of a daisy, the daisy wheel produces a clean, clear type, with all the characters evenly placed. The daisy wheel can be changed to give a different type face when needed. It is also used in some high-quality computer printers (see Unit 15.3(*b*)) and in word-processors (see Unit 15.6).

(iv) *Quick.* Operating speeds are high, and typists find that they can work much faster, once they are used to the machine.

Most offices possess at least one typewriter. Sometimes the machine is used purely for *copy typing* (transferring information from a handwritten draft). But often the typist works from the spoken word, dictated on to an *audio dictation machine.*

5.8 Audio Dictation Equipment

The dictation machine is an essential piece of equipment in many offices. Letters, reports and other information are dictated into the microphone of a *dictation unit.* The completed recording is passed to a typist who plays it back on a separate *transcription unit* and types it out. Some machines are dual-purpose, and can be used for both dictating and transcribing.

(a) Dictation Units

The dictation unit is made up of a microphone and a recording machine. *Magnetic media*—sheets, belts or tape cassettes—are generally used for recording. These have the advantage of being re-usable, so the dictator can change his or her mind and correct the dictation over the top of what has just been said, provided the errors are noticed quickly enough. The belts can also be re-used when the first recording has been transcribed. *Non-magnetic media* are available too. These are not re-usable, so can be kept as a permanent record, if required. As corrections on these cannot be made by re-recording over the passage, the dictator has to mark them on an index strip, usually by writing a letter C.

The *index strip* is a vital part of the machine whatever medium is used. A *cursor* or metal point moves across the belt as recording proceeds and indicates the length of the dictation on the index strip on the machine. When the end of a document is reached, the dictator makes a pencil mark on the index strip, opposite the cursor. By looking at the distance between pencil marks, the typist can judge the length of a piece of dictation and so plan the layout. In some machines, pencil marks on the index strip can be replaced by re-usable indexes which are marked with dots or other indicators simply by pressing a button on the microphone.

The dictation unit has a playback button and a loudspeaker as well, so that the dictator can play the tape back and check its contents before sending it to the typist.

(b) Transcription Units

The transcription unit consists of a transcription machine and a headset. The typist inserts the medium into the transcription machine and listens to the dictator's voice through the headset or earphones, using a foot pedal to stop and start the tape. The typist looks at the index strip to assess the length of dictation, to pinpoint special messages and, where non-magnetic media are used, for correction. If the sense of the dictation is not immediately clear, the typist can replay the relevant section to make quite sure that he or she has got it right.

Audio units come in many different shapes and sizes. Fig. 5.8 shows a decentralized, office-based system. The dictator records communications sitting at his or her desk. The typist plays back and types in another part of the same department. There are two major variations.

(i) **Pocket recorders.** These mini dictation units are designed for people on the move who may want to compose reports or write letters while events are still fresh in their minds.

(ii) **Centralized dictation systems.** Many organizations believe that it helps

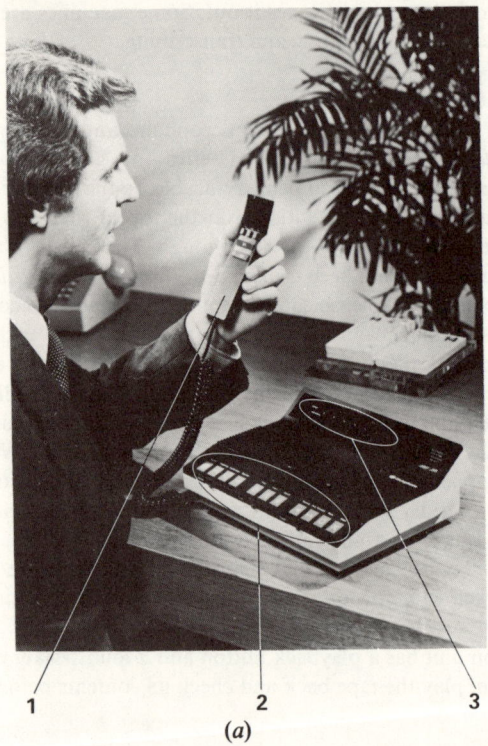

1   2   3
(a)

Fig. 5.8   Office-based dictation/transcription system set up (a) for dictation, (b) for transcription. 1. Microphone control for stop, start, playback, record, review and signals for typist. 2. Keys for fast forward and rewind tape scanning, afterthought insertion, conference recording and erase. 3. Light signals showing letter

efficiency to bring all audio typists together in one place, since some departments produce more work than others. In a central *audio pool*, *dictation centre* or *secretariat* (see Unit 22.5) the work can be shared so that all the typists are kept fully occupied.

The central unit can use the same equipment as a decentralized, office-based system, with a personal dictation machine for the dictator and a transcription machine for the typist. The use of *remote control* systems means, however, that both units of the dictating system are housed together in the central unit, away from both the dictator and the typist. The dictator has a microphone with the usual controls, and this microphone can be wired into the internal telephone system. When he or she wishes to dictate, the dictator lifts the telephone receiver, dials a code to obtain a connection to the audio pool and waits for a signal which indicates that there is a dictating machine free. The dictator then dictates into the receiver. When dictation is complete the audio supervisor passes the recording to a typist for transcription.

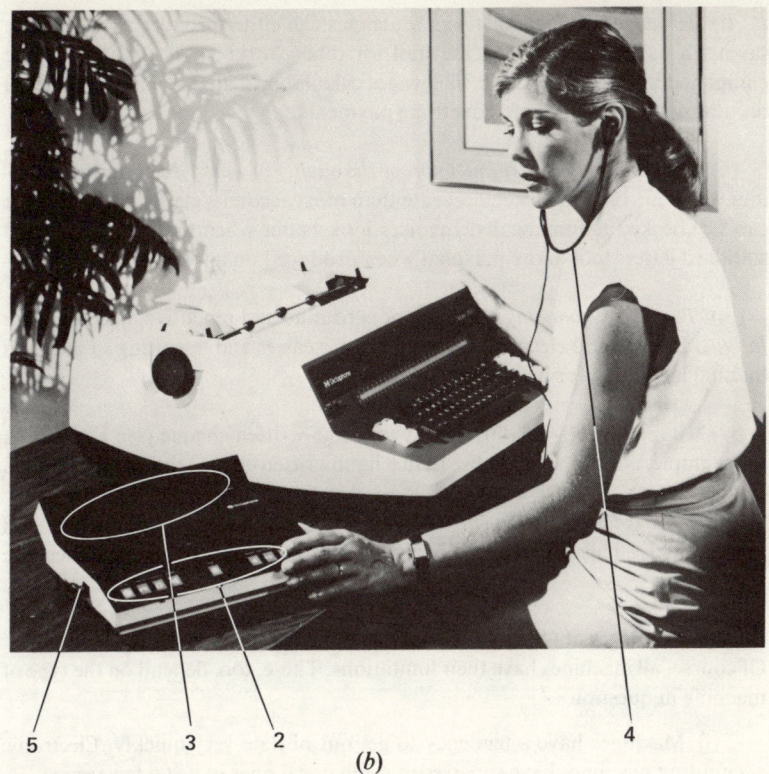

(b)

lengths, tape capacity used, instructions and afterthought insertions. 4. Headset.
5. Headset plug. Slider controls for volume, speed and tone are at the front of the
unit. The typist uses a foot control, which is not shown

While centralized dictation services can increase the speed with which dictation can be processed, they are highly impersonal. The typist may never meet the dictator and has little opportunity of getting to know the work of any particular department.

5.9 People versus Machines

Increasingly often today, management has to decide whether to invest in certain types of office machines or to rely on traditional 'human' methods. Machinery has both advantages and disadvantages.

(a) Advantages of Office Machines

There are several benefits to be gained from the use of most office equipment, although the degree of benefit clearly depends on the nature of the machine concerned.

(i) *To save labour and/or time.* Machines can either produce a measurable saving in payroll costs or release staff for other work. Tasks that have to be completed by a fixed deadline, like wages calculations, are normally completed on time without the need for overtime payments.

(ii) *To promote accuracy and improve the quality of work.* Accounting machines (see Unit 19.6) are more accurate than most accounts clerks are, and work can be checked automatically. Invoices look better when they are typed, and standard letters look more personal when produced on a word-processor.

(iii) *To relieve monotony* where work is routine and repetitive, and *to reduce fatigue.* Electric and electronic typewriters are easier and less tiring to use than manual machines, for instance.

(iv) *To reduce the risk of fraud.* A machine-written cheque (see Unit 14.2), for example, is less open to abuse than a handwritten cheque that can be altered.

(v) *To provide management with more information,* more accurately and more quickly. This is one of the useful aspects of computers, for instance (see Unit 15).

(*b*) **Disadvantages of Office Machines**
Of course, all machines have their limitations. These, too, depend on the type of machine in question.

(i) Machines have a tendency to get out of date very quickly. Electronic accounting machines have superseded mechanical ones in just a few years.

(ii) Trained machine operators may be difficult to recruit, and training unskilled staff can be expensive.

(iii) Special stationery and printing may be necessary. These too are often more expensive than the materials needed for the equivalent manual method.

(iv) The introduction of a new machine, such as a computer, may mean that the whole office system has to be changed to accommodate it: paperwork may have to be redesigned and staff retrained.

(v) Some machines are not very flexible—they can only do what they have been programmed to do. People, on the other hand, can be retrained and moved between departments if necessary.

(vi) Although machines handle routine work well, they cannot do work that requires intelligence and initiative. An accountant is still needed, even where accounting machines are used.

(vii) Some machines are rather noisy and can make working conditions difficult unless they are kept separate or properly screened.

(viii) Machines are often expensive, and tie up a large amount of capital. Many machines can be leased (rented) instead, however, which cuts the initial cost while allowing the machine to be exchanged when it becomes obsolete.

5.10 Health and Safety in the Office

Whether you are operating business equipment or working quietly at your desk, you and your colleagues, as well as your employer, must do everything possible to ensure that you are working safely as well as efficiently. In various parts of this book you will find suggestions concerning health and safety in carrying out particular tasks. Here are some more general points.

(a) Things to Do

(i) Read carefully the instructions provided by your employer about what to do in the event of fire. Locate the nearest exit and remember where you are to meet for roll call outside the building.

(ii) When your employer has a fire practice, treat it seriously. In a real emergency, panic is often a killer. People who have practised the procedure and know what to do are much less likely to panic.

(iii) Read carefully through the manufacturer's operating instructions before operating a new machine for the first time. Before you start up any machine, make sure you know how to stop it.

(iv) Switch off electricity at the mains and disconnect the plug before opening up enclosed electrical machinery (copiers, shredders, typewriters or any other equipment which is plugged in to the electricity supply). Always switch off and unplug them at the end of the day.

(v) Check that your wiring, fuses, switches and so on will be able to cope before you plug in a new typewriter, copier or kettle.

(vi) Keep your own work area clean and tidy. Trailing wires, spikes, sharp implements like letter-openers, should all be kept out of other people's way.

(vii) Do not cover heaters by piling files or books on top.

(viii) Pay attention to storage on high-level shelving. Even quite small things can hurt when they fall from a height, and a loaded box file dropping on someone's head can inflict serious injury.

(ix) Take care when lifting heavy items, and always make sure you can see over any load you are carrying.

(x) Always think through the consequences of your actions. Pulling out a file from the bottom of the pile may be quicker than removing all the other files to get at it. But if the pile collapses on top of you or someone else, you might wish you had taken the extra trouble.

(xi) If and when an accident occurs, report it *immediately*. Your firm should keep an accident book and may have a doctor or nurse on the premises. Prompt action can prevent accidents: the loose piece of carpet which caused you to trip and bruise your knee should be fixed before it causes someone else to fall and break a leg. Besides, even minor cuts and bruises can give trouble later. Should this happen, perhaps because a cut has turned septic, you may wish to claim compensation from the firm, or to prove that you are eligible for disablement benefit under the industrial injuries scheme. If you did not report the accident at the time, it might not be accepted that you were injured while you were at work.

(xii) Always be on the watch for possible hazards: exposed wiring, power points not switched off, wet or highly polished floors, trailing wires, unprotected blades, loose carpet, wobbly window frames, rickety cupboards or doors, unstable filing cabinets—the list is endless. If you come across these or other dangers, don't just grumble about them. Point them out to someone in authority or raise them with your safety representative for discussion at the next meeting of the safety committee (if there is one). Your firm's safety policy statement should be displayed on notice boards, and will tell you who has overall responsibility for the safety of your systems and conditions of work.

(xiii) The law in Britain lays on you a duty to take reasonable care for your own health and safety and for that of other people who may be affected by what you do and do not do. You also have a duty to co-operate with your employer and other people where safety is concerned, and not to misuse or damage things that are provided for your safety.

(b) Things Not to Do

(i) Never smoke in the office, or any other part of the building, unless you are specifically authorized to do so. If you do smoke, never put your cigarette ends into a waste-paper basket; always use an ash-tray.

(ii) Don't tamper with or remove fire extinguishers or instructions for their use.

(iii) Don't prop open fireproof doors.

(iv) Don't leave things lying about in corridors or on the stairs where they can catch fire or cause someone to fall.

(v) Don't remove protective guards from equipment. Guillotines and paper-trimmers are designed to avoid slicing your fingers; removing the guard to expose the blade is extremely dangerous. Lifts and conveyor belts—indeed, all machines with moving parts—should be fenced or protected so that fingers, feet and so on cannot become trapped.

(vi) Avoid sniffing the fumes of correcting fluid or glue.

(vii) Never attempt to mend or maintain electrical equipment unless you have been trained to do so. Call in an expert.

(viii) Never remove the casing of any machine while the machine is in use.

(ix) Don't make do and mend by using anything other than the materials and components specified by the manufacturer for use with his machine. Substitutes are usually less efficient, and sometimes dangerous.

(x) Never forget that it is better to be overcautious and safe than reckless—and injured or dead.

5.11 Quick Questions

1. What do the following letters stand for: (a) gsm, (b) NCR, (c) POP?

2. List four things that you should do, and four things that you should not do, when using business stationery supplies.

3. What is an inventory?

4. Give the names by which the following are often known: (*a*) the Universal keyboard, (*b*) single-element typewriters.

5. List four advantages of (*a*) electronic typewriters, and (*b*) office machines in general.

6. List ten things you should bear in mind to safeguard your own and other people's health and safety in the office.

5.12 Short Exercises

1. 'A typist is only as good as his or her machine.' 'A typewriter is only as good as its typist.' Which of these two statements do you think comes nearer to the truth? Prepare brief notes to support your argument.

2. One of your colleagues is reluctant to use a new business machine. Consider some ways in which you might be able to persuade him or her that the equipment 'won't bite'. Make notes to support your argument.

Unit Six

Filing: Equipment

6.1 Introduction

The written communication we discussed in Unit 5 can lead to mountains of paper. If the information they contain may be needed again in the future, these papers must be kept in a systematic way, that is, they must be *filed*.

Many different kinds of filing equipment are available. They are all designed to ensure that forms, documents and correspondence can be kept where they will be safe, easily found, tidy and clean, in a way that heaps of papers scattered around the office can never be.

Your office manager will choose the most appropriate system for your office. But you need to know what each can do, and understand its limitations.

6.2 Short-term Storage

For documents which need to be kept close at hand for a few days while action is being taken, there are several possibilities.

(*a*) Clips and Clipboards
These are used for papers which have to be (or have been) dealt with in a particular sequence. Worksheets for mechanics in a car service garage are sometimes handled in this way. Such methods are best kept for dealing with single sheets of paper, and the documents should be removed after each day's work.

(*b*) Spikes
Single sheets of paper, such as orders taken in a restaurant, can be kept transfixed on a spike in the order in which they are taken. These, too, should be cleared each day.

(*c*) Rising Trays or Baskets
The type of tray shown in Fig. 6.1 allows papers to be stored neatly during the working day. The trays can be bought separately and then stacked on top of each other or hung on the wall. Each tray is labelled with an appropriate title—filing, post, typing and so on. Some people have just two—an *in-tray* and an *out-tray*. The in-tray is used for all incoming files, correspondence and documents while they are waiting to be dealt with. Once the required action has been taken, they are transferred to the out-tray for mailing or filing.

6.3 Sets of Similar Documents

Where a more permanent home is needed for a collection of, say, invoices, price lists, orders or catalogues, a box file or binder of some sort may be the answer.

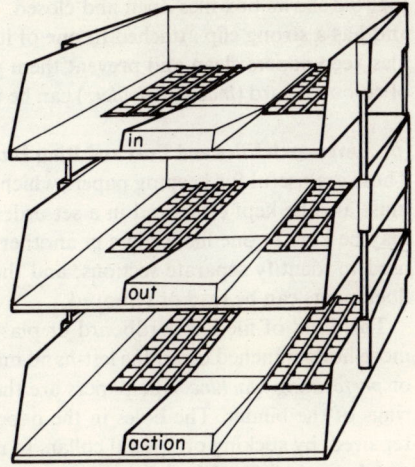

Fig. 6.1   Filing trays

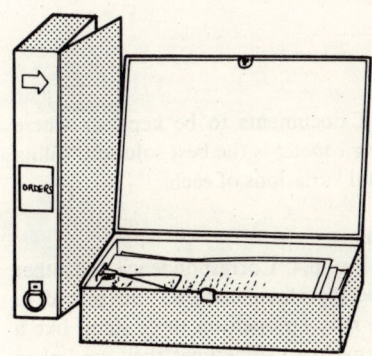

Fig. 6.2   Box files

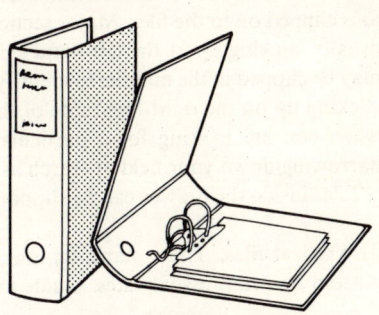

Fig. 6.3   Lever-arch files

(a) Box Files

Fig. 6.2 shows box files open and closed. The box is usually about $7\frac{1}{2}$ cm deep and has a strong clip attached to one of its walls, to keep papers in place. Box files keep papers clean and prevent them getting crumpled at the edges. Pieces of coloured card (*indexed dividers*) can be used to separate papers into sections.

(b) Lever-arch Files and Post and Ring Binders

These are useful for keeping papers which are referred to frequently but which must also be kept clean and in a set order—date order, for instance. Invoices may be kept in one file, orders in another, and so on. Indexed dividers can be used to identify separate sections, and the file can be opened at any point so documents can be read or removed.

This kind of file has cardboard or plastic covers. Papers must have two or more holes punched down the left-hand margin. This can be done using a *punch* or *perforating machine*. The papers are then placed over the spindles, posts or rings of the binder. The holes in the paper can be prevented from tearing, or repaired, by sticking on special collars to reinforce their edges.

A lever-arch file (Fig. 6.3) holds more papers than a ring binder can. But care must be taken not to overfill either, as the pages become difficult to turn and extra strain is put on the punched holes.

6.4 Large-scale Filing

Where there are many different kinds of documents to be kept, or where documents need to be locked away, a *filing cabinet* is the best solution. Filing cabinets are of two main forms, with several variations of each.

(a) Three/Four/Five-drawer Filing Cabinets

A four-drawer filing cabinet is shown in Fig. 6.4. Correspondence and other documents are grouped according to specific classifications, and placed in pocket files made of strong paper. These may be open on three sides, like a folder, or closed on three sides, like an envelope; sometimes they are linked together, concertina-style.

The filing drawer is divided into sections by the use of *guide cards* or plastic *tabs* clipped on to the files. Major sections are indicated by *primary guide cards*, usually sticking up at the left-hand side of the drawer. *Secondary guide cards* may be clipped in the middle, to identify subsections. Each file has its own *label*, sticking up on the right-hand side of the drawer (see Fig. 7.2 on page 100). So when you are looking for a particular file you can read from left to right, narrowing down your field of search as you go.

Files inside the drawer can be supported in either of two ways:

(i) **Vertical files.** These stand upright, one behind the other, gripped at the bottom by compressor plates. Guide tabs can be cut from the top of each file.

(ii) **Suspension files.** Each file carries a hooked metal strip on each side of the

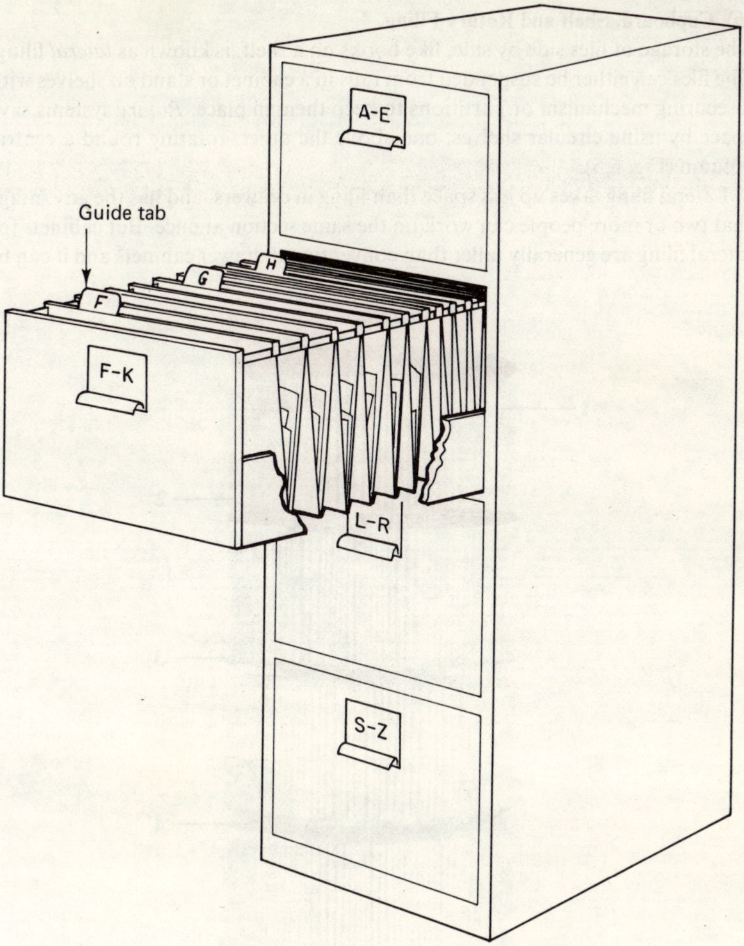

Guide tab

A-E

F-K

F

G

H

L-R

S-Z

Fig. 6.4   A four-drawer filing cabinet, showing suspension filing

top opening. Inside each filing drawer are metal runners, attached at the front and back (Fig. 6.4), on to which the files can be hooked. The files then hang one behind the other, and are always kept in an upright position. The metal strip carries a transparent sleeve into which labels, colour-coded for easy reference, can be slipped.

Many people find the suspension system is the easier of the two to work with, because the files can readily be moved backwards and forwards, the contents can be consulted without taking out the whole file and new labels can easily be typed and inserted.

(b) Cupboard, Shelf and Rotary Filing

The storage of files side by side, like books on a shelf, is known as *lateral* filing. The files can either be suspended from rails in a cabinet or stand on shelves with a securing mechanism or partitions to keep them in place. *Rotary* systems save space by using circular shelves, one above the other, rotating round a central column (Fig. 6.5).

Lateral filing takes up less space than filing in drawers, and has the advantage that two or more people can work on the same section at once. But cabinets for lateral filing are generally taller than conventional drawer cabinets and it can be

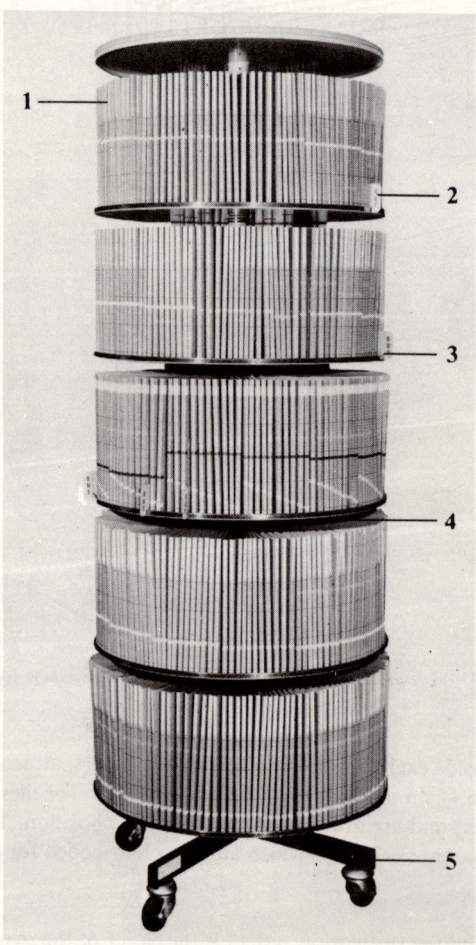

Fig. 6.5 Rotary filing system. 1. File name. 2. Absent card. 3. Shelf. 4. The shelves of files rotate about a central column. 5. The roundabout carriage allows the whole system to be mobile

difficult to read the labels of files on the top shelf without the help of a filing stool.

Filing cabinets generally provide a tidy and efficient way of storing large quantities of paper, but there are several points to watch.

(i) Don't try to put too much paper into the files. This increases wear and tear on the pocket or folder and will warp the metal runners in a suspended system.

(ii) Don't leave the drawers of the filing cabinet open-for other people to trip over or walk into.

(iii) Don't put too much weight in the top drawer of the cabinet or open the top two drawers together; the cabinet could tip over.

(iv) Don't forget that some cabinets are self-locking. It is therefore not a good idea to keep the key in your handbag and your handbag in the cabinet.

(v) Do ensure that papers intended for filing actually go into the file. Unless a concertina system is used, papers can slip down between the folders.

(vi) Do make sure that files which have been removed are returned to the correct place. (We shall discuss the procedure in Unit 8.)

(c) Electronic Filing

Most of these 'points to watch' can be rendered obsolete by the introduction of an electronic filing system (Fig. 6.6). This is a way of storing and retrieving paper information by means of an electronically controlled conveyor, located between two banks of storage containers. The required file can be identified and brought to you in a matter of seconds. When you have finished with the file, it can be replaced in the same way.

6.5 Long-term/Micro Storage

Where documents must be kept for a long time, or where space is limited, files of paper may be too bulky to keep. Almost any document can be reduced, by photography or other means, to a small fraction of its original size and kept in this *microform* until someone wishes to consult it. Then it is inserted into a special viewer which magnifies it and projects the information on a screen. Several different microforms can be used.

(i) **Spools of film.** The film is threaded on to the spool of a scanning machine (Fig. 6.7) and wound through by hand until the required document is reached. In most modern machines the film is stored in a cartridge or cassette, which greatly simplifies the film-handling.

(ii) **Jackets.** Each of these 'mini-files' contains microcopies of up to 60 letters or documents. When a file is needed, an enlarged printed copy can be made, or the jacket can be viewed on a reader.

(iii) **Aperture cards.** Pieces of 35 mm microfilm are stuck on to cards measuring 102 mm × 75 mm. The microfilm takes up only a small area of the card, the rest

Fig. 6.6   Electronic filing system: the clerk enters a three-digit reference number on the keyboard and presses the 'retrieve' button, the appropriate file container is delivered automatically and the clerk selects the file required

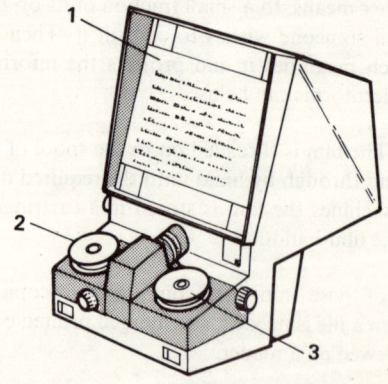

Fig. 6.7   Microfilm reader. 1. Screen. 2. Loaded spool of microfilm.
3. Empty spool

of which is used for identifying the drawing or other document on the film. Aperture cards are mainly used for storing design drawings and similar work.

(iv) **Microfiches.** These are small transparent cards about the size of a postcard (Fig. 6.8). A camera is used to put the image of each document photographed

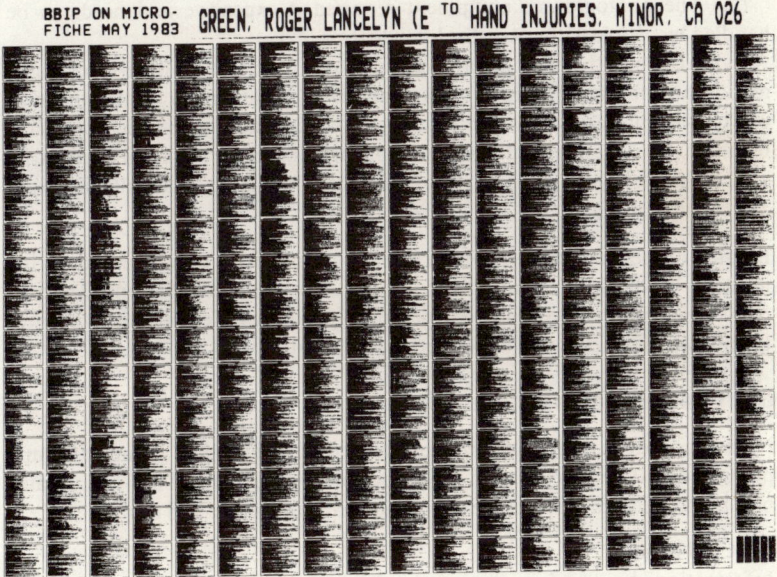

Fig. 6.8   A microfiche (part of the British Books in Print catalogue) giving details of 269 different publications

into a selected position on the fiche. A viewer is used to find and read any part of a document.

Microfiches are often used for cataloguing library information. Each month, as new books are added to the library stock, new fiches can be issued and distributed to the libraries using the system. With the most recent equipment it is possible to alter part of a fiche, leaving the rest unchanged. With a reader-printer, an enlarged printed copy of microfiche information can be made.

(v) **Computer output microfilm.** Instead of photographing words and figures written on paper, information can be recorded on microfilm direct from a computer. The computer can also be used to find and retrieve microforms which can then be viewed using computer visual display units (see Unit 15.3(*a*)).

(*a*) Advantage of Microform Storage
The major advantage of microform storage of information is compactness. It enables a company to have all the advantages of a complete paper filing system, without taking up nearly so much space.

(b) Disadvantages of Microform Storage

(i) Many people find that the display screens of microform scanners are hard to read or give them a headache.

(ii) It is difficult to 'get the feel' of long microcopied documents. You cannot flip backwards and forwards through the 'pages' quite as readily as you would with sheets of paper.

(iii) The photographic equipment required is expensive and needs to be handled by people with specialist knowledge.

(iv) Although the most advanced microform readers have high-speed automatic search facilities, so that you can find the information you want at the push of a button, many older systems require you to scan through the microfilm page by page. Careful and detailed *indexing* of each document recorded is therefore vital and, unless your recording equipment can do this automatically, indexing can be a tedious task.

Because of these difficulties, your organization is unlikely to use microform for most day-to-day information. But for bulky information that is consulted only occasionally it can be invaluable, especially if you have the equipment to convert the microform back into a paper copy when detailed work is needed.

6.6 Quick Reference/Index Systems

Names, addresses, telephone numbers and other basic details about staff, suppliers and customers may need to be looked up frequently. They can usually best be stored in card systems, which are readily accessible and easy to use.

(a) Card Index

Information about each customer or each member of staff is written on a card, usually a little smaller than a postcard, and the cards kept in alphabetical order

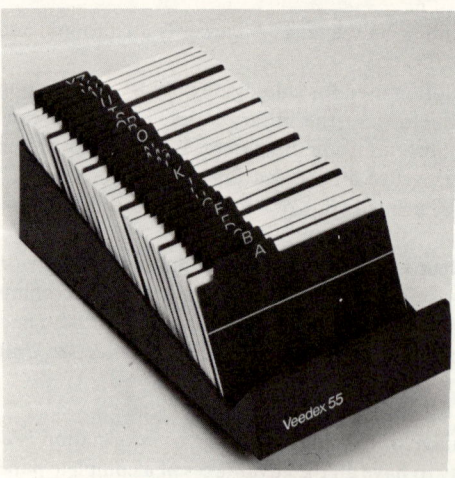

Fig. 6.9   Box card index

in a box (Fig. 6.9). If a customer stops placing orders, or a staff member leaves, that card can be removed without affecting the others. Apart from the information actually on the card, which will be consulted whenever anyone asks for, say, 'the address of Bloggs & Co', you can also extract other information from the system. You can count the total number of cards to find out how many customers (or staff) you have. If you use the alphabetical dividers or guide cards provided with most card index boxes, you can also tell quite easily how many customers have names beginning with a particular letter of the alphabet.

(b) Visible-edge Index Systems
In a simple card index the edges of the cards are all lined up with each other, but in a visible-edge index system a strip at the edge of each card remains visible. The cards are kept in trays (Fig. 6.10) or in cabinets, in alphabetical or any other

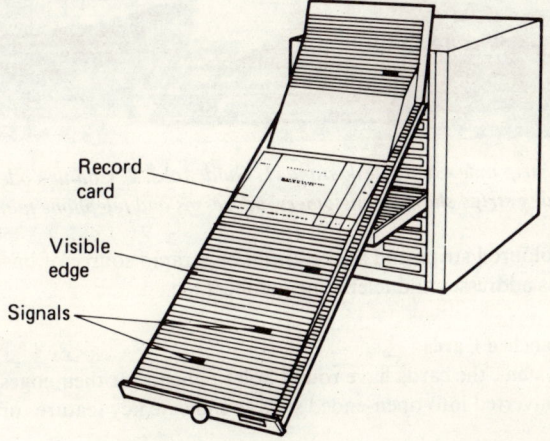

Record card

Visible edge

Signals

Fig. 6.10   Visible-edge card index system

chosen order, and the index strips can be scanned at a glance. Boxed sections with coloured stickers or flags can be used to denote particular characteristics so that you can pick out quickly those cards which have the features you are looking for.

(c) Strip Index Systems
If all the information you really need about a customer or staff member can be contained on the visible index edge of a card, it could be that the rest of the card is unnecessary and that a simple *strip index* could be used. In this system, strips of card are inserted into plastic sleeves, to form the lines of a page in a book (Fig. 6.11). Strips can be removed and replaced as the information they contain goes out of date. Occasionally a page may have to be reorganized entirely, but the existing strips can then be rearranged rather than retyped. Strip indexes therefore have the flexibility of a card index, and with the use of *colour codes*

Fig. 6.11   Strip index, with desk stand. 1. Guide tabs. 2. Colour-coded headings.
3. Index strips showing customers' addresses and telephone numbers

(different coloured strips and stickers) can be a rapid source of basic information, such as addresses and telephone numbers.

(d) Edge-punched Cards

With this system, the cards have round holes punched at their edges, and these holes are converted into open-ended slots to indicate key features or character-

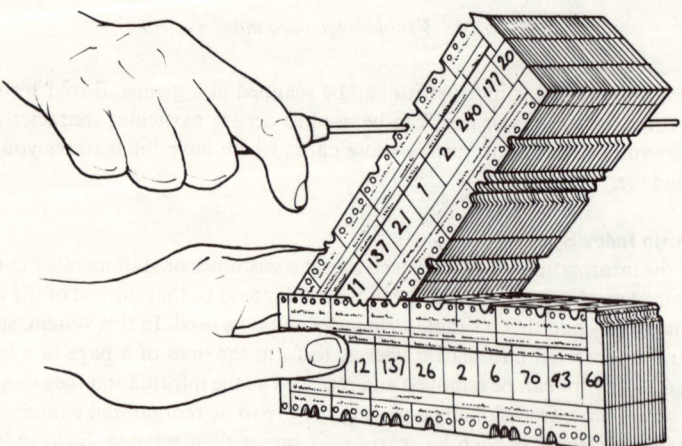

Fig. 6.12   Sorting a pack of edge-punched cards

Table 6.1 Methods of storing and retrieving information

Requirement	Clips, spikes, trays	Box files	Lever-arch files	Vertical/suspension filing	Lateral filing	Electronic filing	Card index systems	Microform	Edge-punched cards
Can be stored on a desk	✓	✓							
Can be stored next to individual workstation		✓	✓				✓		
Can be used to keep documents in a set order			✓	✓	✓	✓			
One item can be removed or amended without disturbing others			✓	✓	✓	✓	✓		
Can be used by more than one person at once				✓	✓	✓			
Can be used for filing large amounts of data on wide range of subjects		✓		✓	✓	✓		✓	
Does not require specialist input/output skills	✓		✓	✓	✓		✓	Depends on availability of readers	
Does not take up much space	✓					✓	✓	✓	✓
Key facts can be established quickly							✓		✓
Basic statistical information can be compiled quickly						✓	✓		✓

istics of the person or company to whom the card relates (staff members over 55 years old, perhaps, or customers in Kent). Cards for the people having the characteristics you are looking for can be separated from the pack using metal rods (Fig. 6.12). You insert a rod through each of the holes that relate to the chosen characteristics, and lift the cards off their rack or container. The cards where all the relevant holes have been converted into slots fall off the metal rods and are left behind, thus providing a quick method of sorting information.

Table 6.1 summarizes the features of the various storage methods we have discussed in this Unit.

6.7 Quick Questions

1. List four reasons why it is important for a business to have an efficient filing system.

2. Name three methods of storing business documents.

3. Say what you understand by the following terms: (a) suspension filing, (b) lateral filing, (c) rotary filing.

4. List five ways of storing information in 'micro' form.

5. List three disadvantages of microfilm as a method of storing information.

6. List four ways of recording information that is likely to be required for quick reference.

6.8 Short Exercises

1. Compare and contrast microfilming and conventional filing cabinets as methods of storing information in the office.

2. If a new office junior showed a tendency to leave papers lying about in a muddle, what arguments would you use to convince him or her that correct filing is necessary?

Unit Seven
Filing: Classification Systems

7.1 Introduction

Efficient filing is not just a matter of having the right size of filing cabinet. It also means having a method of organizing and classifying the information which will enable you to find it again quickly and easily when it is needed. In this Unit we will discuss the classification systems you may come across.

7.2 General Alphabetical Filing

Where the files contain mainly correspondence with individuals and with other organizations, this is the simplest and most logical classification method to adopt.

Each file is given a name, usually the name of the person or organization to which it relates. The files are kept in alphabetical order; those with names beginning with 'A' come first, those with names beginning with 'Z' come last.

Each drawer or shelf of the filing cabinet is labelled: A–E, F–H and so on. Primary guide cards divide it into major sections, one for each letter of the alphabet—A, B, C and so on. If there are many files with names beginning with 'A', the section may be divided using secondary guide cards into Aa–Ad, Ae–Ah, Ai–Al, Am–Ap, Aq–Az. So a file marked ABBOTT is filed in the first of these subsections; AHMED goes in the second, AJAX in the third and ANNETTS in the fourth.

Certain rules or conventions are followed for alphabetical filing. You must abide by these if the items you have filed are to be retrieved without trouble.

(a) Indexing Units

In an alphabetical system, the names of people and organizations are treated as *indexing units*, and the *principal indexing unit*—that which usually determines the file's position in the system—must be identified. Where people's names are used, the surname is generally the principal indexing unit: 'Thomas Ackroyd' is filed before 'Terence Arbuthnot'. The files are called

ACKROYD Thomas
ARBUTHNOT Terence

If two individuals have the same surname, their forenames must also be considered. Thus 'ARBUTHNOT Terence' is filed before 'ARBUTHNOT William'. If initials rather than full forenames are used, then 'ARBUTHNOT T' still comes before 'ARBUTHNOT W', and 'ARBUTHNOT T A' precedes 'ARBUTHNOT T W'. If some files bear initials and others have the names in full, then those with initials come first; for instance, 'ARBUTHNOT T' precedes 'ARBUTHNOT Terence'.

The principal indexing unit for companies or other organizations is normally the first word in its name which distinguishes it from others. The Allbright Steelworks Ltd is filed under 'A' for 'Allbright', not 'T' for 'The'. For local authorities, the name of the town or county is normally used as the principal indexing unit. So 'the Borough of Reigate and Banstead' becomes 'REIGATE AND BANSTEAD, Borough of'.

(b) General Rules

(i) 'St' is read as 'Saint' and filed under SAI. If there are two such names, such as St John and St Michael, the second word determines the order. ST JOHN will therefore come first of these two: both come after SADLER and before SALINGER.

(ii) The prefixes 'Mc' and 'Mac' are both treated as 'Mac', and such names are often filed under a separate subsection (Fig. 7.1). The letter that follows the

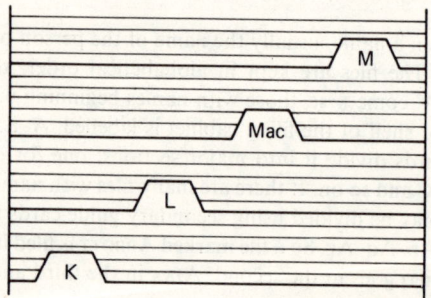

Fig. 7.1   Part of an alphabetical filing system

'c' determines the order of filing within the section, regardless of whether the second part of the name begins with a capital letter, so MCDONALD always comes before MACKAY.

(iii) Hyphenated names are treated as one word, so SIMMINGTON-SMYTHE comes after SHERWIN but before SMITH.

(iv) Titles are not used as indexing units but are shown in brackets after the name and initials: ORMOND F (Dr), for example, or PHILLIPS M (Major).

7.3 Subject Filing

Sometimes documents relate to topics, activities or projects rather than to individual people or firms. An office manager might, for instance, require files on subjects like HEALTH AND SAFETY; OFFICE, SHOPS AND RAILWAY PREMISES ACT; CONTRACT CLEANERS; CONTRACTS OF EMPLOYMENT; SALARY SCALES; RELOCATION (proposals), with a MISCELLANEOUS file for items that do not fit in elsewhere. The subject files are usually kept in alphabetical order, but should be stored in a separate drawer or section of the system, not mixed up with the main alphabetical system.

Since these files may contain documents relating to a number of different people and organizations, it is important to have some means of identifying where, for instance, letters from a particular firm may be found. A card index can help in this: a card is made out for each correspondent, and these are kept in alphabetical order in the index (see Unit 6.6(a)). The name of the subject file where correspondence is kept is written on the card, together with other relevant information, for quick reference. So when the office manager asks for the file on 'SWEEP-IT-UP LTD', you can find the card under 'S' in the index and establish that correspondence relating to the company is filed under CONTRACT CLEANERS in the main filing system.

7.4 Numerical Filing

Sometimes it may be helpful to give a number to each file and to keep the files in numerical, rather than in alphabetical, order:

(a) where many of the files have similar names, which could lead to errors in alphabetical filing;

(b) where names and subjects are to be mixed together;

(c) where the system may need to be expanded to take many more files and reorganizing all the alphabetical sections would be a major task (in a numerical system, new files can be added at the back: in an alphabetical system, they must be inserted under the correct letter of the alphabet);

(d) where some form of numerical code is already available and can be used as a means of identification. Customers' account numbers and staff payroll numbers can be used this way. Numbers allocated for these purposes are unique to the person concerned—even if they share their name with six other George Browns;

(e) where the system is a large one.

Guide cards are used to separate major sections. Thus, in a drawer marked 100–199, guide cards would indicate sections 100–109, 110–119, 120–129 and so on. An alphabetical index is needed, as the key to finding the files you want. The index might tell you that papers relating to 'Sweep-it-Up Ltd' can be found in file number 378. All three of the numbers (*digits*) tell you something about where to find the file:

1. File number 378 would be in the drawer marked 300–399.
2. You should find it in section 370–379.
3. It will be the last file but one in the section.

This basic method of numerical filing is called *consecutive digit filing*. There are two variations.

(i) **Terminal digit filing.** Instead of reading the numbers from left to right, this method starts with the last part of the number. The last two digits are used to show in which section the file belongs; so all the file numbers ending in 30 will be found in section 30. Each section can be divided into subsections, which are themselves numbered from 01 to 99. The second pair of digits in the file number indicates in which of these subsections the file will be found. The first pair of digits indicates whereabouts within the subsection the file should be. So file number 11 12 30 will be found in section number 30, in subsection 12, between file number 10 12 30 and file number 12 12 30.

This section can readily be expanded for the addition of new files or whole new sections, without disturbing the original system.

(ii) **Decimal filing.** This system allows for new files on a particular topic to be kept in the same section as existing files on related topics, and the numbers used, unlike those in the other two numerical systems, themselves indicate the subject to which the files relate.

The principle is the same as that used by libraries when classifying books on what is known as the *Dewey decimal method*. The first group of digits indicates the overall subject classification, the next indicates the particular topic and the final digits identify the specific contents of the file. Your office manager might decide to classify the subjects with which your department is concerned, thus:

> 50—Legislation
> 100—Maintenance
> 150—Staff
> 200—Company projects

and so on.

The maintenance classification (100) could be subdivided into up to nine sections as follows:

> 100.1 Plumbing
> 100.2 Electrical
> 100.3 Cleaning
> 100.4 Decorating
> ⋮

The 100.3 (Cleaning) classification might, in turn, be broken down into a maximum of nine subsections:

> 100.31 Materials
> 100.32 Equipment
> 100.33 Contractors
> ⋮

So correspondence from Sweep-it-Up Ltd should be in file number 100.33.

Once you have learnt the basic classifications, you will recognize what a file is about, just by looking at its number.

7.5 Alpha-numeric Filing

This, as the name implies, is a combination of alphabetical and numerical filing. There are two forms.

(a) Each alphabetical subsection of the system is given a number. Aa–Ad would therefore be A.1, Ae–Ah would be A.2, and so on. The files within the subsections are also numbered, although they are filed in *alphabetical* order. So 'ACKROYD Terence' still comes before 'ACKROYD Thomas', but if Thomas's file is opened first, that is numbered A.1/1 while Terence's file is A.1/2. 'A.1/1 and A.1/2' are *alpha-numeric codes*. Because the files are still arranged alphabetically the code is useful only as a reference to put on correspondence.

(b) Sections are numbered A.1, A.2 and so forth, as in (a), and within these sections files are placed in *numerical* order. If Thomas Ackroyd's was the first to be put in section A.1, it would be numbered A.1/1 and stored in front of Terence's file, A.1/2. When files are subsequently opened for ABIGAIL and Co Ltd and AARON Bros, they will be numbered A.1/3 and A.1/4 and placed behind A.1/1 and A.1/2 (even though, in a purely alphabetical system, both these names would come before ACKROYD).

Because files are stored in numerical order, an alphabetical index is necessary as a key to the position of any given file.

7.6 Chronological Filing

Within each file, documents are normally placed in chronological order, that is, in date sequence. Files themselves are often placed in order on this principle, especially where the most important feature of a subject relates to a date.

Some travel agents, for instance, file their clients' booking documentation according to holiday departure dates. If your holiday starts on 18 August, the sales clerk may use this to track down your papers, rather than your name or the name of the tour operator with whom you have booked. The filing system is divided into twelve sections, one for each month of the year. These sections are divided into subsections—for instance, week beginning 5 August, week beginning 12 August, week beginning 19 August and so on. The travel sales clerk stores the file for 18 August at the back of the second of these subsections.

Dispatch departments (see Unit 16.2), where life is ruled by delivery dates, can also find this a useful way to organize their documentation.

7.7 Geographical Filing

Where places are more relevant than either people, subjects, numbers or dates, the files may be organized by *geographical location*. An export department might therefore have primary guide cards denoting the names of countries in which the firm's products are sold: AFGHANISTAN, BARBADOS, BELGIUM, BOLIVIA,

BRAZIL and so on. Within each section files relating to particular subjects (agents, export credit arrangements, import procedures) and/or people (Kabul Shipping Company, the Herat Distributors Ltd) can be arranged alphabetically, following the normal procedures for subject filing or alphabetical filing (Fig. 7.2).

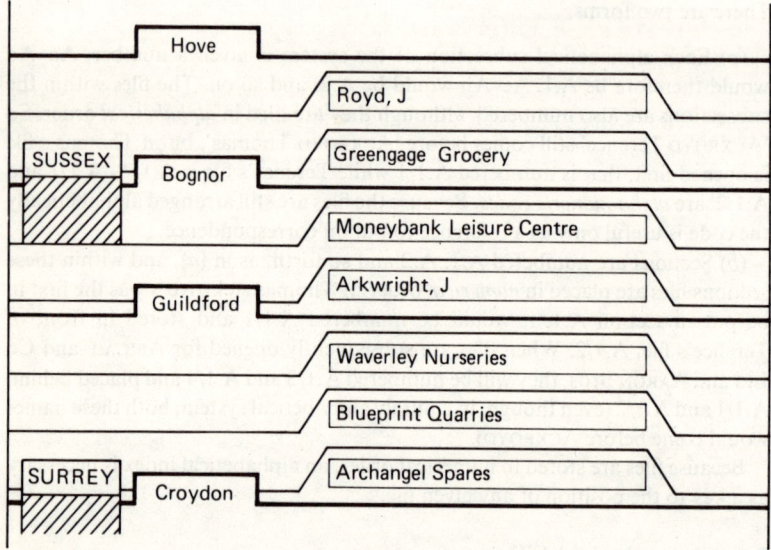

Fig. 7.2   Geographical filing

When you start work in an office, study the filing system carefully. Make sure that you understand the classification used, and that you know what each guide card and number means.

7.8 Quick Questions

1. What is the difference between a classification system and a storage system?

2. List six classification systems.

3. What is a primary guide card, and where would you find one?

4. What is an indexing unit?

5. What do you understand by 'alpha-numeric classification'?

6. What is chronological filing? Name two departments in which it might be used.

7.9 Short Exercises

1. List the surnames and initials of all the members of your study group or office. Place the names in alphabetical filing sequence, using the conventions discussed in Unit 7.2.

2. Work in Totem Toys sales office has been increasing for some time, and a simple alphabetical filing system is no longer adequate. Decide what classification you would recommend for each of the following types of filing, and the kind of storage equipment you would choose:

(a) information and correspondence to sales representatives throughout the country;

(b) information about the different products sold;

(c) confidential information.

Unit Eight

Filing: Operating the System

8.1 Introduction

Whether you are concerned with the files of just one department or are part of a centralized service for the whole organization (see Unit 22.4), keeping the system operating efficiently requires care.

8.2 Opening New Files

Before you open a new file, make sure that you fully understand the classification system used, and that you have been authorized to start new files for documents that do not fit anywhere else. Usually the office manager or supervisor keeps a close eye on file-opening, and will let you know what number or title to give the new file. If a subject or numerical classification is being used, a card or index strip must be made out for the new file and inserted in the alphabetical index. Nearly always there is more than one copy of this index to be updated, because

(*a*) if the index is lost the whole system will grind to a halt;

(*b*) the staff dealing with the information kept in the files need to know what files there are, so that they can decide which one to ask for or where particular new information should be filed.

8.3 Removing a File

There are three main ways in which you may be told that someone needs to consult a particular file.

(*a*) Oral Requests

Other members of staff may ask you, as filing clerk, for a file directly: 'Let me have the file on Sweep-it-Up Ltd, please'. If you have several such requests at the same time, make a note of each and deal with the most urgent first.

(*b*) Written Requests and Requisitions

Occasionally a file will be requested in a polite little note addressed to you, perhaps by a newcomer to the department. Sometimes an official *requisition form* (Fig. 8.1) will be used. But frequently you will have to decipher some form of coded message. Fig. 8.2, for instance, tells you that Mr Winters (the Personnel Manager), having received a memo from Mr Green, wants Margaret Miles-Brown's personal file so that he can check back on the previous correspondence it contains. Your clue to the fact that it is Miss Miles-Brown's file he wants, not his own, Mr Green's or any other, lies in the reference quoted at the top of the memo. Usually letters and memoranda quote

My ref: Your ref:

FILE REQUISITION	
User department:	Date required:
Name:	Expected date of return:
File reference:	Signature:
title: -	Date requested:

Fig. 8.1   File requisition form

> MEMORANDUM
>
> From: J. Green, Accounts Department
>
> To: H. Winters, Personnel Manager
>
> My Ref: JG/M/3   *File pl.*
>
> Your Ref: M/PM/PER/M
>
>   Re Margaret Miles-Brown
>
>   Thank you for your note re the above named. I can confirm
>
> that she has settled into the department very well and that she
>
> is now a satisfactory and competent member of my staff. I
>
> recommend we continue her employment when her probationary
>
> period ends.
>
>   *John Green*

Fig. 8.2   Coded file request memorandum. In the reference, the first code denotes the area of the organization (M = Management), the second the particular department (PM = Personnel Management), the third (PER) means that the file will be found in the alphabetical filing system, where a personal file is kept for each staff member, rather than in the subject classification, and the final code indicates the identity of the correspondent (M = Manager)

'My ref' refers to the filing system used by the person sending the letter or memo. 'Your ref' refers to the filing system used by the person to whom the correspondence is addressed. In this particular filing system the reference can be deciphered as shown in the caption. If there has been no previous correspondence, or if the person sending the letter omits to quote 'Your ref', the filing clerk will have to depend on the heading—in this case 'Margaret Miles-Brown'.

(c) Follow-up/Tickler Systems

Some files are consulted regularly by particular members of staff—on the last day of every month, say; others may be given to you with a request to 'let me have it back on the twenty-fifth, please'. The way to make sure that you produce the files on the dates when they are next required is to operate some form of diary or follow-up filing system.

In a diary you can list the files that are to be sent out on each date and to whom they are to go. Each morning you can then inspect the day's list and distribute the files accordingly. Alternatively, you can start a separate chronological follow-up filing system to 'tickle' your memory of which files are needed, and on what date. A separate drawer or trolley can be used, with a guide card for each month of the year. The current month is subdivided into sections, one for each day of the month (Fig. 8.3), and each section holds the appropriate notes, requisition slips and reminders to be sent to staff who have held files for a while. Each day you remove the papers filed under that day's date, and take the necessary action.

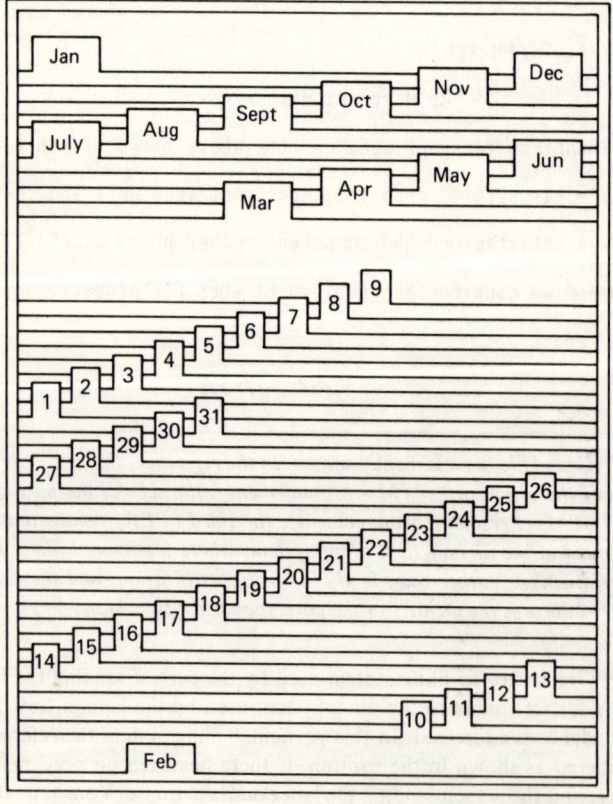

Fig. 8.3   Tickler system

(d) Keeping Track of Files

When you remove a file from the system, the remaining files close their ranks and, particularly in an alphabetical system, no indication remains that the file was ever in the cabinet. It is therefore very important that you know what has happened to files that you (or other people) remove. This can be done in two ways.

(i) **Day-books.** Where files normally go out for only an hour or two, do not leave the department and are returned on the same day, a simple listing works well. Whenever a file is issued, the file name or number, together with the name of the person to whom it has been given and the expected time of return, can be noted on a daily record sheet or in a book with one page for each day. When the file is returned, the entry can be crossed out or the time of return entered.

(ii) **Absent cards.** If files are likely to be removed for longer periods or taken out of the department, an *absent card* or folder, the same size as the file itself, should be used (Fig. 8.4). The name or number on the file and other particulars should be entered carefully, and the absent card or folder can then be placed in the borrowed file's own position in the filing cabinet. If a folder is used, it can provide a temporary substitute for the file, and any additional documents to be placed on the file can be stored in the folder until the file itself is returned.

It may be departmental practice to ask the borrower to 'sign for the file'. If so, always double-check the signature to make sure you can read it; otherwise you will have no way of tracing the borrower should another member of staff ask for the the file before it is returned.

Once you have taken the file from its place in the system and made the appropriate entries on the absent folder or daybook, you are ready to release the file. Attach to the front of the file, using a paper-clip, whatever note, memo,

ABSENT				
Date taken	File no / title	Taken by Name	Department	Date returned
12 Nov 8–	Miles – Brown M.	H. Winters	Personnel	13 Nov 8–
13 Nov 8–	Higgins J.	B. Rogers	Sales ledger	
13 Nov 8–	Graves P.	B. Rogers	Sales ledger	

Fig. 8.4   Absent card

letter or requisition caused you to get the file out. Then the file can be placed in the in-tray of the person who requested it.

8.4 Adding to a File

(a) Insertions
Documents that are to be filed are usually marked with some sort of *release symbol*. The word 'FILE' may be stamped on the document, or a large 'F' (for file) written in the corner. In addition to these self-explanatory release symbols,

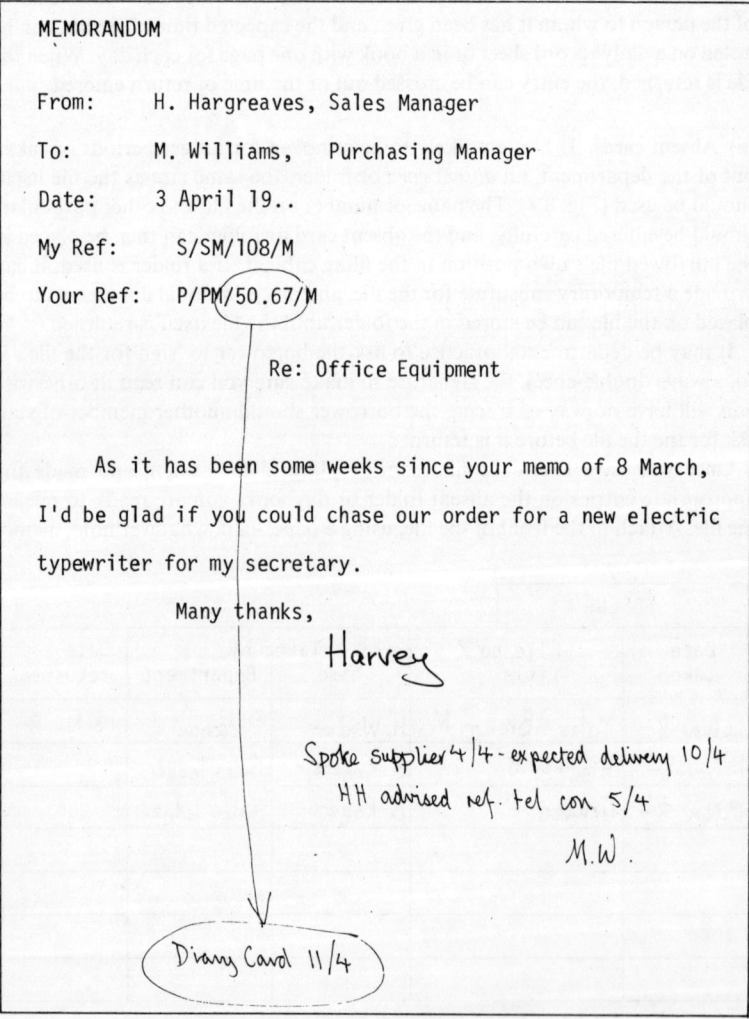

MEMORANDUM

From: H. Hargreaves, Sales Manager

To: M. Williams,   Purchasing Manager

Date: 3 April 19..

My Ref: S/SM/108/M

Your Ref: P/PM/50.67/M

                    Re: Office Equipment

    As it has been some weeks since your memo of 8 March,

I'd be glad if you could chase our order for a new electric

typewriter for my secretary.

        Many thanks,

                    Harvey

        Spoke supplier 4/4 - expected delivery 10/4
        HH advised ref. tel con 5/4
                    M.W.

        Diary Card 11/4

Fig. 8.5   Memorandum to be filed

it is also common to find a large tick or line on the first page, often ending in a circle round the appropriate reference or *filing point*. In Fig. 8.5, for example, Mr Williams, the Purchasing Manager, has taken action by telephone and recorded this on the memo, so the note can go on to the file whose number he has used as a reference in his previous correspondence. He has, however, indicated that he would like to have the file again the day after the typewriter is due to be delivered, probably to check it has arrived.

When you receive this memo:

(i) Record the request for the file to be given back to Mr Williams on 11 April in your follow-up system.

(ii) Find file 50.67 in section 50, subsection 6 in your decimal filing system. (In the system, 50 probably indicates OFFICE EQUIPMENT, 6 could be TYPE-WRITERS, 7 the manufacturer's file.)

(iii) If the contents are filed in chronological (date) order, put this new piece of paper in on top of the documents that are already there. Line up the edges of the papers and secure the clip if the system is a vertical or lateral one, to ensure the paper does not slip out.

In some departments you may find variations on this strictly chronological system—where, for instance, some documents are to be kept indefinitely while others will be removed after a period (see Unit 8.5). You will need to learn the particular conventions which your department is using before you risk adding papers to the wrong end of the file.

(iv) Once the papers have been correctly inserted, replace the file and remove the absent card.

(v) Papers that have been added to a file should not be taken out again without explicit instruction from the office manager. Although you know which memo Mr Williams wants to look at on 11 April, you must give him the whole file.

(*b*) Cross-referencing

Sometimes cross-referencing documents can help people to track down a particular item. In the example in Fig. 8.5, Mr Williams might have asked for the memo to be placed on the Sales Department file, because this is the department with which he has been corresponding. There are two possible courses of action.

(i) Photocopy all relevant correspondence and place a copy on both files. Although this should be foolproof, it is expensive and adds to the volume of paper in the system.

(ii) Cross-reference the files, using a cross-reference sheet stuck to the front of the file, indicating the titles or numbers of other files that contain information relating to that subject.

8.5 Thinning/Removing Dead Files

(*a*) Thinning
Nothing accumulates in the office as fast as paper. Once the items on a file

become too old to be of any use, they should be removed from the file. The filing clerk is not normally the judge of what is or is not useful. But he or she may need to set up a system to pass out a section of files to the office manager at intervals, so that obsolete items can be removed and shredded (see Unit 10.6). Alternatively the filing clerk may be given a fixed time period and told to remove papers older than this. Seven years is a common deadline, because no correspondence older than this can normally be used in a court of law.

Papers removed from a file in this way should be checked to make sure that no recent papers have been misfiled and removed by mistake. A note or cross-reference slip may be placed on the file to indicate that papers have been removed and either destroyed or stored elsewhere.

(b) Dead Files

Occasionally files may become completely obsolete: those for customers who no longer buy from your organization and have not done so for years, staff who no longer work for you, suppliers who have gone out of business, and so on. Once the office manager is satisfied that such files will no longer be referred to on a regular basis, they may be thinned down to the bare essentials and moved to the *archives* where all the company's old records are kept. They may be microfilmed and stored in microform, to save space; after a further period they may finally be destroyed.

8.6 Quick Questions

1. What is a filing index? Why is it important?
2. What is a requisition form?
3. What is a tickler system?
4. What is an absent card used for?
5. Name two common release symbols for filing.
6. Describe two methods of cross-referencing documents.

8.7 Short Exercises

1. Compare and contrast the effectiveness of any two follow-up systems with which you are familiar.
2. Consider the range of requisition procedures and release symbols mentioned in this Unit. Which do you think are the clearest and most easily understood, and why?

Unit Nine

Making Copies

9.1 Introduction

Much of the information produced in the office will be read by more than one person. There are many ways in which extra copies of letters, forms and other documents can be made. These *reprographic systems* range from a simple sheet of carbon or carbonless copy paper (Units 5.2(*b*) and 5.2(*f*)) to complex microprocessor-controlled printers and copiers.

Large offices may boast several different kinds of reprographic equipment. In a small office the choice may be between carbon paper and a trip to the local copy-shop. In the early stages of your career, your office manager will tell you which machine to use for a particular job. The factors which must be considered are:

the number of copies needed;
the cost per copy;
the quality of appearance required;
the kind of *original* (the document to be copied);
the need for a specially prepared master copy;
speed.

Table 9.1, at the end of this Unit, compares various reprographic methods.

9.2 Ink Duplication

Fig. 9.1 shows an electrically operated ink duplicator. Copies are made from specially prepared masters called *stencils* (Fig. 9.2). Stencils have a *headpiece*, with holes or slots in it, by which the stencil is attached to the drum of the duplicator. They also have a backing sheet, which helps to reduce creasing and can be used, with a carbon, to produce a carbon copy. The words, pictures or diagrams to be copied are cut into the surface of the stencil.

The duplicator has a *drum* or cylinder inside it. The surface of the drum allows ink to pass through it. As the cylinder is turned, ink is squeezed through and, through the cuts in the stencil, on to sheets of duplicating paper passing under the cylinder. The paper thus ends up bearing the same image as the original stencil.

Duplicating machines are sometimes referred to as 'Gestetners' or 'Roneos', from the names of two leading manufacturers of ink duplicating equipment. Machines can be either electrically or manually operated.

(*a*) Preparing Stencils
Words and pictures can be cut in the surface of the stencil in four main ways.

(i) **By typing.** The types of the typewriter must be clean and the ribbon set to

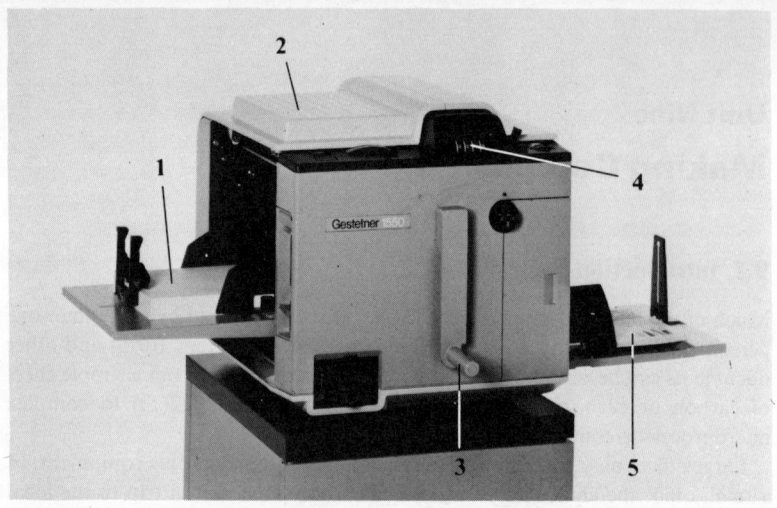

Fig. 9.1 An ink duplicator. 1. Copy paper in feed tray. 2. Cylinder cover (the stencil is fixed to the drum inside). 3. Handle. 4. Copy counter. 5. Duplicated copies

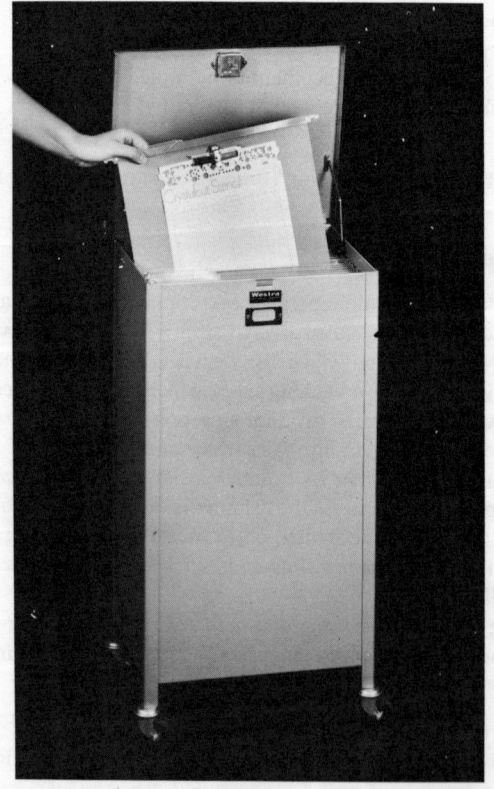

Fig. 9.2 Stencil-storage cabinet showing a stencil, with perforated heading, clipped to a file

the stencil position, usually marked on the machine by a letter 's' or a white dot: the type then bypasses the ribbon and strikes the stencil direct. Errors can be corrected using special correction fluid.

(ii) **By writing or drawing.** When a stencil is to be cut by hand a special stencil pen, with a sharp stylus or rotating wheel, is used. Where an entire document is to be handwritten or drawn, a special drawing or 'brush' stencil is needed.

(iii) **Precut stencils.** Some organizations have stencils with their letter heading already professionally cut. This means that you can type or write on the remaining portion of the stencil, duplicate on to ordinary duplicating paper, and produce a page with the company's letter heading apparently printed at the top.

(iv) **Machine-cut stencils.** Almost any original, from a page of type to magazine clippings and photographs, can be inserted in an *electronic scanner*. The machine cuts the outline on vinyl stencils, which can then be processed in the same way as typed or handwritten ones.

An alternative to the electronic scanner which is still used in some offices is the *thermal stencil processor*, also known as the thermal or heat-transfer copier. These use a heat process to cut the stencils, and can produce them in seconds. The original must be in black and white; colours are not reproduced.

(b) **Advantages of Stencils**

(i) Copies are produced very quickly—150 per minute or more.

(ii) Once a stencil has been cut it can generally be stored (Fig. 9.2) until needed again. The stencil can then be re-fixed to the duplicator and more copies made—up to 10 000 from one 'long-run' stencil.

(iii) Duplicating paper is no more expensive than ordinary bond and the ink for 500 copies costs about the same as 500 sheets of paper. The cost is therefore lower than for most other methods of reproduction.

(iv) If the stencil is machine-cut, it will take less than two minutes to prepare (although the original may have to be typed on ordinary bond paper).

(v) Different coloured inks and different coloured paper can be used to make an attractive effect.

(vi) Some machines can duplicate on to a wide range of paper sizes, from postcard-size upwards, and on to any quality of paper from airmail to pasteboard. The quality of reproduction on non-absorbent paper can be improved by interleaving the copy paper with sheets of absorbent paper.

(vii) Both sides of the paper can be used.

(viii) The most modern machines are almost completely automatic.

(c) **Disadvantages of Stencils**
On the other hand:

(i) If the stencil has to be specially typed, the extra care and different finger pressure needed, the flimsy nature of the stencil and the slow process of correcting mistakes can make this into rather a tricky job, and work must be very carefully checked.

(ii) Any creases in a stencil disfigure the finished result.

(iii) Duplicating ink tends to spread a little, so the outlines of letters are often slightly thicker than the original type. This makes duplicated work easy to recognize and some people feel it a disadvantage when a high standard of presentation is important.

(iv) Inking the drum can be a dirty job and, particularly with older machines, the ink may tend to come through unevenly, producing a rather patchy copy. (This problem is eliminated in modern machines.)

(v) Where only a few copies are needed, the additional effort involved in typing the stencil and preparing the machine is not usually worth while.

(vi) Changing the ink colour means running the work through twice and using separate stencils.

(d) Using Stencils
If you are using the ink duplicator, you should:

(i) Make sure that you are familiar with the contents of the operating instruction book for your particular machine.

(ii) Avoid creasing the stencil as you fix it round the drum.

(iii) Fan the sheets of paper so that they will go through the machine one at a time. (But don't stand over the paper tray as you fan, or dust from the paper will fall into the tray.) Then stack the duplicating paper carefully, so that it is properly lined up.

(iv) Run off one or two copies to assess the quality of duplication. If the copies are not dark enough or are patchy, check the ink, make sure that the stencil is properly cut, and if necessary adjust the speed of the machine. When you are satisfied with the quality, set the machine to produce the required number of copies.

(v) Stencils must be stored carefully, without creasing, if they are to be re-used. They should be allowed to dry thoroughly by placing them on large sheets of absorbent paper (blotting paper or duplicating paper, for instance). After drying, they are stored in a cool place, either suspended in a cabinet or in folders.

(vi) Keep the machine clean and free from fluff, and protect it with a dust cover when not in use.

9.3 Spirit Duplication

For spirit duplication (Fig. 9.3) a master copy must be prepared using paper coated in china clay and a special type of carbon paper—a *hectograph carbon*. The words written on the master are reflected, as in a mirror, by the hectograph carbon. They appear as a carbon impression, back to front on the reverse of the china clay paper. Inside the spirit duplicator the carbon is dissolved in alcohol

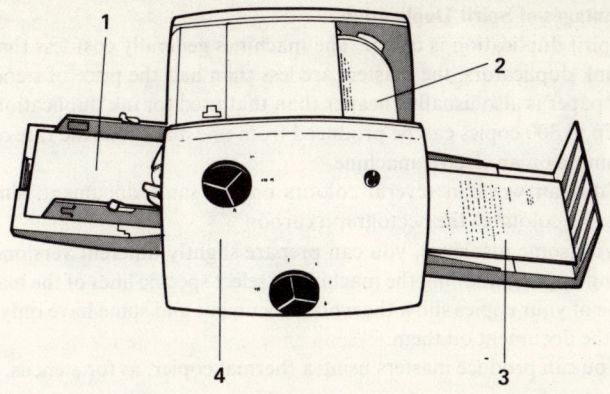

Fig. 9.3   A spirit duplicator. 1. Copy paper on feed tray. 2. Master drum with master, with mirror-image impression uppermost. 3. Duplicated copies. 4. Control panel

and the image of the words on the master is transferred, right way round, on to copy paper.

Spirit duplicating is sometimes called *hectography*; it is also known as *Banda-ing* and *Fordagraphing* after the names of particular spirit duplicating machines.

(a) Preparation
To make a spirit master:

(i) Put the hectograph carbon on the desk, carbon side facing up.

(ii) Put the china clay paper on top of it, with the shiny china clay side facing down.

(iii) Write or draw on the non-shiny side of the paper, using a hard pencil or a ballpoint pen. Or you can type on it, with a backing sheet behind the carbon to ensure an even surface. Leave an extra-wide margin along that side of the master which is to be attached to the drum of the machine, as lettering too close to the drum will not be reproduced.

(iv) If you make a mistake, gently separate the master from the carbon and erase the back (the shiny side) of the master sheet. For this you need a special knife to scrape off the errors. (Or you can use correction fluid specially made for spirit duplicating work.) You cannot, however, re-use the carbon when correcting the master, as hectograph carbon can be used only once. You must therefore slip a small square of new carbon over the spot, place paper and carbon sheet carefully back together, insert the correction on the side you have been writing on—perhaps in a different colour, to make proofreading easier—remove the slip of carbon, and carry on.

(*b*) **Advantages of Spirit Duplication**

(i) Spirit duplication is cheap. The machines generally cost less than comparable ink duplicators, the masters are less than half the price of stencils and the copy paper is also usually cheaper than that used for ink duplication.

(ii) Up to 300 copies can be produced from one master, at the rate of about 70 per minute on an electric machine.

(iii) You can work in several colours on the same document, simply by changing the colour of the hectograph carbon.

(iv) With some machines, you can prepare slightly different versions of the same thing by programming the machine to select specific lines of the master, so that some of your copies show the whole document and some have only certain parts of the document on them.

(v) You can produce masters using a thermal copier, as for stencils.

(*c*) **Disadvantages of Spirit Duplication**
On the other hand:

(i) The life of a spirit master is much shorter than that of a stencil. After about 300 copies it becomes unusable.

(ii) Correcting errors is fiddly and time-consuming.

(iii) The finished copies become blurred towards the end of a long run, fade if left in daylight and when kept a long time, and lack the professional presentation required for important documents.

(iv) The spirit used could present a fire hazard if it is not properly stored. Never keep more than 50 cm^3 (about one-third of a teacupful) in an open room. Larger quantities should be kept in a fireproof store.

(*d*) **Using the Spirit Duplicator**

(i) When you have prepared your master, remove the carbon and attach the china-clay-coated paper to the drum of the spirit duplicating machine, with the shiny side containing the mirror image of the words facing outwards.

(ii) Read the operating instructions and check that there is the right quantity of the special alcohol (spirit) on which the process depends.

(iii) Use the right non-absorbent paper, carefully fanned first and then stacked in the feed tray.

9.4 Offset Duplication

This is also called *offset lithography*. The machine contains three cylinders (Fig. 9.4). The first, the *plate cylinder*, bears the master with the image the right way round. The second, the *blanket cylinder*, comes into contact with the first, and picks up the image—in reverse. The third, the *impression cylinder*, which carries the copy paper, then receives the image and reverses it again. So the image is reversed twice and ends up the right way round.

The master used, called a *plate*, can be made of metal, plastic or paper. Metal plates last longest, produce most copies and can be re-used. The outlines of the

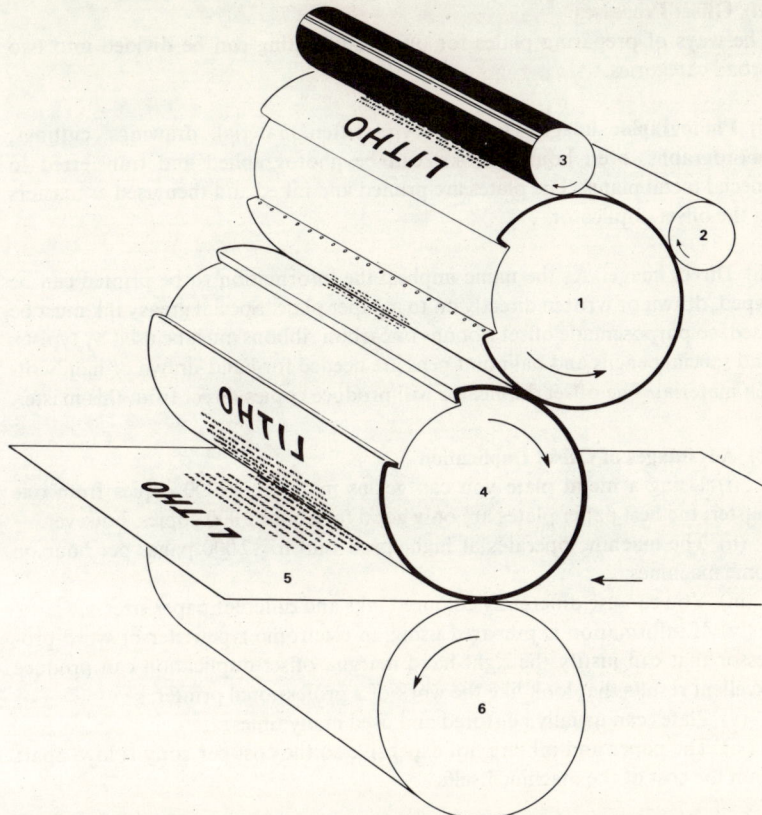

Fig. 9.4   The offset process. 1. Plate cylinder, with litho plate, carrying greasy image, curved and fixed around it. 2. Dampening roller, which damps the litho plate to prevent the spread of ink on to other (non-image) areas. 3. Inking roller, which applies a thin layer of ink to the plate, which is rejected by the damp areas of the plate but accepted by the greasy areas. 4. Blanket cylinder, carrying a rubber blanket—the image is printed (offset) off the litho plate on to the blanket surface. 5. Paper: the image is transferred from the surface of the rubber blanket on to the paper, which is held in close contact with the blanket cylinder by the impression cylinder. 6. Impression cylinder

letters, lines and figures on the master are produced in greasy ink. The rest of the master is damp. Grease and water don't mix, so that when the plate comes into contact with greasy printing ink inside the machine, the damp parts repel the ink while the parts that are already greasy accept it. This extra ink forms itself into the shape of the characters on the master, transfers to the blanket cylinder as the plate and blanket cylinders rotate past each other, and is then offset to the impression cylinder and the final copy.

(a) Offset Processes

The ways of preparing plates for offset duplicating can be divided into two broad categories.

(i) **Photographic image.** Ordinary typewritten material, drawings, cuttings, photographs, even bound books, can be photographed and transferred to special metal plates. The plates are primed and inked and then used as masters in the offset duplicator.

(ii) **Direct image.** As the name implies, the information to be printed can be typed, drawn or written directly on to a paper plate. Special greasy ink must be used, so purposemade offset ribbons or carbon ribbons must be used by typists, and special pencils and ballpoint pens are needed for hand-drawn or handwritten material. The offset duplicator will produce copies direct from this master.

(b) Advantages of Offset Duplication

(i) Using a metal plate you can get as many as 50 000 copies from one master; the best paper plates are only good for about 2 000 copies, however.

(ii) The machine operates at high speed—up to 17 000 pages per hour on some machines.

(iii) You can use differently coloured inks and different paper sizes.

(iv) If information is prepared using an electronic typewriter or word-processor that can justify the right-hand margin, offset duplication can produce excellent results that look like the work of a professional printer.

(v) Plates can usually be stored and used many times.

(vi) The paper and ink are not expensive so the cost per copy is low, apart from the cost of the machine itself.

(c) Disadvantages of Offset Duplication

On the other hand:

(i) The initial cost of the equipment can be two to three times as high as that of ink and spirit duplicating equipment.

(ii) It is uneconomic for runs of less than, say, 50 copies.

(iii) Although some machines are compact, others take up a lot of space.

(iv) Typing paper plates is a time-consuming and exacting task.

(v) The large capacity of the machine encourages people to ask for more copies than they need, which is wasteful.

(vi) The ink used takes a long time to dry, so jobs using several different coloured inks can take days, or even weeks, to process.

(vii) Operators of the equipment usually need to be trained by the manufacturer.

(d) Using the Offset Duplicator

(i) Follow the operating instructions for your particular machine.

(ii) Keep the machine clean; when the job is finished, the inking rollers must be washed and thoroughly dried, using special cleaning sheets, and left free of all trace of ink. (Some machines do this automatically.)

9.5 Copiers

Copiers produce an exact likeness or *facsimile* of an original document without changing the original itself, and without using plates, stencils or carbon paper. There are several different kinds of machine.

(*a*) Electrostatic Processes

These are now the most widely used methods of copying. They used to be known as *Xerox copiers* after the manufacturer who pioneered the original process. The copier contains a drum or plate charged with static electricity. When the paper to be copied is placed on the glass surface or *platen* of the copier, the light reflected from the white parts of the paper causes the electrostatic charge to disappear from the drum opposite. The charge pattern remaining on the drum corresponds to the dark-coloured shapes (writing or printing) on the original.

Special *toner* powder is then dusted over the drum, and sticks to those parts which are still electrostatically charged, forming an image of the original. When a piece of copy paper is passed over the drum, the particles of toner which form the image are attracted to it and fused into place by a short burst of heat.

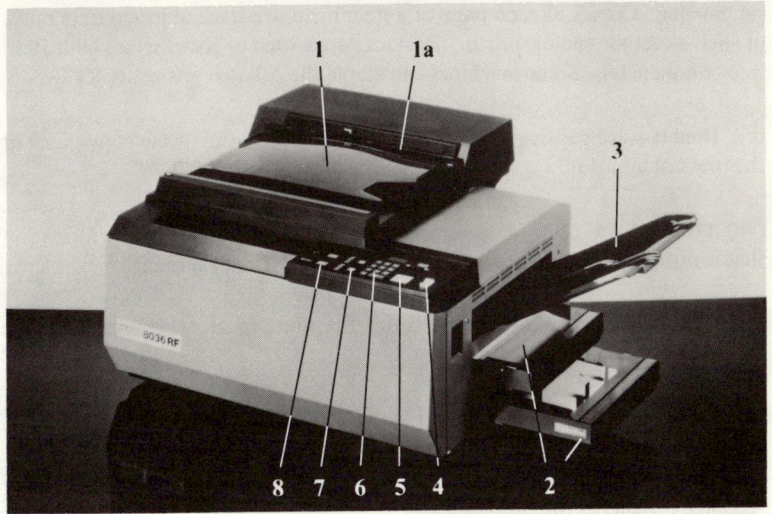

Fig. 9.5   Plain-paper copier. 1. Platen cover, under which the master is placed (or it can be fed in through the semi-automatic feed, 1a). 2. Paper trays (cassettes), which enable copy paper of different sizes to be used. 3. Exit tray for completed copies. 4. On/off switch. 5. Print key. 6. Keys to indicate the number of copies required. 7. Keys for selecting the size of copy paper to be used. 8. Reduction or full-size selector keys

The copy paper used in this process does not require any special treatment, and this form of copier is often called a *plain-paper copier*. A modification of this method, the *electrofax* or *direct electrostatic process*, uses rolls of zinc oxide-coated paper, which is cut by the machine to the required length for each document.

Speeds vary. The fastest machines produce copies at rates of 120 per minute or more. Smaller, less expensive machines give 20 to 30 copies per minute.

Some electrostatic copying machines can do much more than just reproduce the original. Your machine may have some, or all, of the following features.

(i) **Reduction.** This enables you to take a large document and produce a smaller copy of it. So an A3 original, for instance, can be reduced to A4 or even smaller.

(ii) **Enlarging.** A copy can be produced which is larger than the original.

(iii) **Cassette loading.** You can change from one size of copy paper to another, by pulling a lever or pressing a button.

(iv) **Automatic document handling.** The machine places the original on the platen automatically, and automatically removes it again.

(v) **Sorting.** Copies of each page of a document are stacked in separate racks or shelves. At the end of the run, the stacks are sorted or *collated* (see Unit 10.2) into complete sets. Some machines can staple the collated sets ready for use.

(vi) **Double-sided copying.** You can copy on to both sides of the copy paper at the press of a button.

(vii) **Overlays** are used for producing copies of business forms. Information that is not needed on all the copies is blanked off by the overlay.

(viii) **Automatic recording devices** count the number of copies made by the machine, and by each user.

(ix) **Adjustable contrast.** Copies can be made as dark or as faint as required.

(x) **Automatic power-saving devices.** If the machine has not been used for a few seconds, it switches off automatically.

(xi) **Automatic resetting devices.** When one user has finished with the machine, the resetting device makes sure that the next user deliberately selects the number of copies he or she wants. Without this facility, it is all too easy to prepare the same number of copies that the last user had, whether you want them or not, because you have forgotten to reset the machine.

(b) Light Processes or Photocopying

These are termed *wet processes*, because solutions of chemicals, rather than dry powder and heat, must be used to fix the image on to the copy paper and the copy comes out slightly damp.

The true photocopier uses the same photographic principles as a pocket camera. Special light-sensitive paper is used to prepare a negative. This is developed and fixed by chemicals and more special paper is needed for printing the finished facsimile. The process is rather expensive and the paper must be stored carefully as it deteriorates quickly if exposed to light.

(c) Heat Processes or Thermal Copying

These are called *dry processes*, as chemicals are not used. When infra-red light is passed through the original and special heat-sensitive copy paper, the latter retains the image of the carbon- or mineral-based ink used in the original. (The process may not work where vegetable-based inks, such as those in ballpoint pens, have been used to create the original.) It can prepare masters for spirit duplicating, stencils and overhead projector transparencies, although when used for paper copies the copy paper tends to be of rather poor quality.

Whichever kind of copier you are using, you should:

(i) Read the instruction book carefully before use.

(ii) Make sure that you are using the right kind of copy paper. Some so-called plain-paper copiers work better if the copy paper has a slight sheen on it. Heat and light processes can only function with special sensitized paper.

(iii) Make sure your original is suitable for the equipment. While some machines can make copies of overhead projector transparencies and can also produce transparencies from paper originals, not all can do this—and melted transparencies can wreck a machine.

(iv) Remember that not all copiers can copy on to both sides of the copy paper.

(v) If you are copying on to both sides of a page, without the help of a double-sided copying facility, take care to work out which way up the copy paper should be when you feed it back into the machine for the second time.

(vi) Take particular care with bound books. Thermal copiers are not suitable for copying from books. On some electrostatic machines you may need to adjust the height of the platen cover to allow a book to be placed underneath.

(vii) Remember that some photocopiers can produce only one copy at a time. If more are required, the negative may have to be inserted again. An electrostatic machine, however, can automatically produce the number of copies you want.

(d) Maintaining a Copier

(i) Familiarize yourself with the inner workings of the machine—*make sure it is switched off* when you do so. When you first open up a copier to add more toner, to clean the drum or to remove jammed paper, you will see that it is a

Table 9.1 Choosing a reprographic method

	Ink duplicator	Spirit duplicator	Offset litho	Electrostatic copiers	Photocopiers	Thermal copiers
Copying from:						
Handwritten originals				✓	✓	If ink has carbon content
Books				✓	✓	
Photographs				✓	✓	
Overhead projector transparencies + translucent material				✓		If ink has carbon content
Typed originals				✓	✓	If ink has carbon content
Specially prepared master copy	Can be prepared by machine from any of the above	✓	Can be prepared by machine from any of the above			
No. of copies:						
1 only						✓
2–10				✓	✓	
10–100				✓	Up to 20 with most types	
100–1000	Suggest minimum of 25 copies	✓ Up to 300	✓	✓		
More than 1000	Up to 10000		✓ Up to 50000			

{ Ink duplication or offset cheaper for longer runs }

Standard of presentation:

Impressive professional standard ✓

Good standard suitable for external use — Depends on machine and operator skills ✓

Internal documents ✓

Speed of output:

Less than 10 copies per minute ✓

10–20 per minute ✓

20–100 per minute   } Depends on model

100–200 per minute — Depends on machine ✓

More than 200 per minute — Doubtful ✓

Special capabilities:

Copies on to transparencies — Special overlays available with some machines ✓

Can produce sets of forms ✓

Copies in more than one colour — Some models ✓

very complex piece of equipment. It is vital to check you are using the correct materials and that you are putting them in the right places.

(ii) Keep the machine clean, particularly those parts which need to reflect light. The platen of an electrostatic copier must be kept free of scratches, so paper-clips and staples should be kept well away from the glass surface.

(iii) Keep adequate stocks of essential materials—toner for electrostatic processes, developer and fixer for wet photocopying—close to the copier.

(iv) Make sure copy paper is correctly stored. Heat- and light-sensitive paper must be kept out of direct sunlight. Copy paper for any type of machine is useless if it is dirty or ragged at the edges: always keep it wrapped until it is needed.

9.6 Facsimile Text Transmission

Facsimile text transmission, or *facsimile telegraphy*, is a copying process which is used with an office telephone.

If you have a *facsimile transceiver* or *remote copier* on your desk, you can telephone a business contact and, provided he or she has a transceiver which is compatible with yours, you can arrange to have copies of the same document in front of both of you while you talk. You simply insert the document into the machine and press the 'send' button. Your contact presses the 'receive' button and in as little as 30 seconds you can both be looking at the same letter.

Facsimile transmission equipment is very expensive; even so, the cost of transmitting an A4 letter from London to Aberdeen has been estimated as half the current cost of a first-class stamp.

9.7 Quick Questions

1. What do you understand by the term 'reprography'?

2. List four methods of cutting stencils.

3. What materials are needed in order to prepare a master for spirit duplication?

4. Give alternative names by which the following are sometimes known: (*a*) spirit duplication, (*b*) offset lithography, (*c*) electrostatic copying.

5. For what purpose would you use a direct image offset plate?

6. What is a facsimile?

9.8 Short Exercises

1. 'There is nothing that ink and spirit duplicators can do that electrostatic copiers cannot.' Do you agree? Write two sets of notes, one summarizing the case for copiers, the other in support of ink and spirit duplicators.

2. You have been made responsible for (*a*) a new plain-paper copier, (*b*) a new stencil duplicator. Both machines are to be used by staff from other departments. Write out a set of guidelines to be pinned up next to each machine, to remind users how to get the best results from the equipment.

Unit Ten

Paper Handling

10.1 Introduction

Whichever method of reprography you use, the appearance of the finished product can be improved by careful follow-up work. A single copy poses no difficulty. It can simply be sent or handed to the person requesting it, or used as a file copy. But let us look at what happens if you are asked to produce 10 copies of each page of a 24-page document. When you have finished copying, you will have 240 pieces of paper: how can you sort these out to produce 10 well-presented complete copies of the original document? The four main steps are discussed in this Unit.

10.2 Collating

As you copy or duplicate page 1 of your document, 10 crisp new copies will emerge from the machine. Place them, printed side upwards, in a neat pile on a large, clean table. Carry on copying pages 2 to 12, laying the piles out on the table following the pattern shown in Fig. 10.1(a). Lay out pages 13 to 24 on another table (Fig. 10.1(b)). You now have 24 piles, each containing 10 pages. But what you need is 10 piles each containing 24 pages.

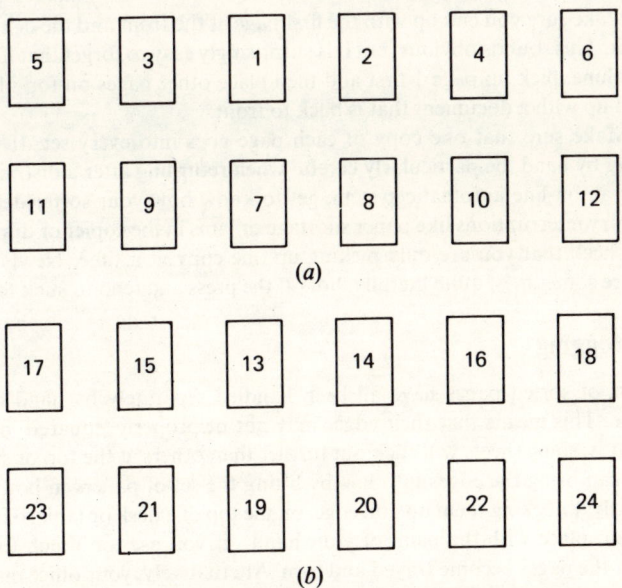

Fig. 10.1   Collation: (a) pattern for pages 1 to 12, (b) pattern for pages 13 to 24

Start at the end, at the second table. Wear a rubber thimble on your middle finger if you wish. Stand or sit in front of pages 19 and 20. Reach out with your right hand and pick up the top sheet from the page-24 pile, and with your left reach for the top sheet of page 23. Place page 24 face upwards on the table immediately in front of you and put page 23 on top of it, face up. Again, right hand for page 22, left for page 21 and put page 22 on top of page 23, then 21 on top of 22 and so on, always putting the lower page number on top of the higher. Carry on in this way, using your right hand for even-numbered pages and your left for odd-numbered. When you have collated the first set of pages 13–24, pick it up carefully, turn to the other table, and put the pile down in front of pages 7 and 8. Pick up page 12 with your right hand and 11 with your left and put 12 on top of 13, which is on the top of the pile you collected from the other table. Carry on as before until you have a complete set of 24 pages.

If there is space, you can leave this pile on one of the tables (keep it safely away from your working piles so that it doesn't get mixed in again by mistake). Alternatively, you can take the pile back to start collating the second set, placing its pages on top of the first document, but at right angles. Continue collating the sets in this way until all 10 are complete.

The layout we have suggested avoids wasted movement and therefore speeds up the collation process. In offices where sets of copies are regularly required, however, there is usually some form of collating equipment. This may be a very simple, non-mechanical system (an arrangement of trays, for instance), or a more complex automatic machine (Fig. 10.2).

Whether you are collating manually or by machine you should:

(*a*) Make sure you end up with the first page at the front and the last page at the back. This sounds obvious, but it is surprisingly easy to forget that if you, or the machine, pick up page 1 first and then place other pages on top of it, you will end up with a document that is back to front.

(*b*) Make sure that one copy of each page goes into every set. If you are collating by hand, be particularly careful when returning after a distraction. If there is an on-line automatic system, get to know how your sorter deals with temporary interruptions like paper shortage or jams in the copier or duplicator.

(*c*) Check that you are only picking up one copy at a time. Newly copied pages are sometimes, quite literally, hot off the press and tend to stick together.

10.3 Jogging

The sets of sorted pages have all been handled separately by hand or by a machine. This means that their edges may not be properly 'squared' or 'lined up', that is, some sheets will stick out further than others at the top or sides.

You can bring the edges into line by lifting the set of papers in both hands and gently 'knocking them up', on edge, on the top of a desk or table, or patting them into place with the palm of your hand—if you use too much force the edges of the pages become frayed and torn. Alternatively, your office may have an electric jogger which vibrates rapidly and shakes the pages into line (Fig. 10.3).

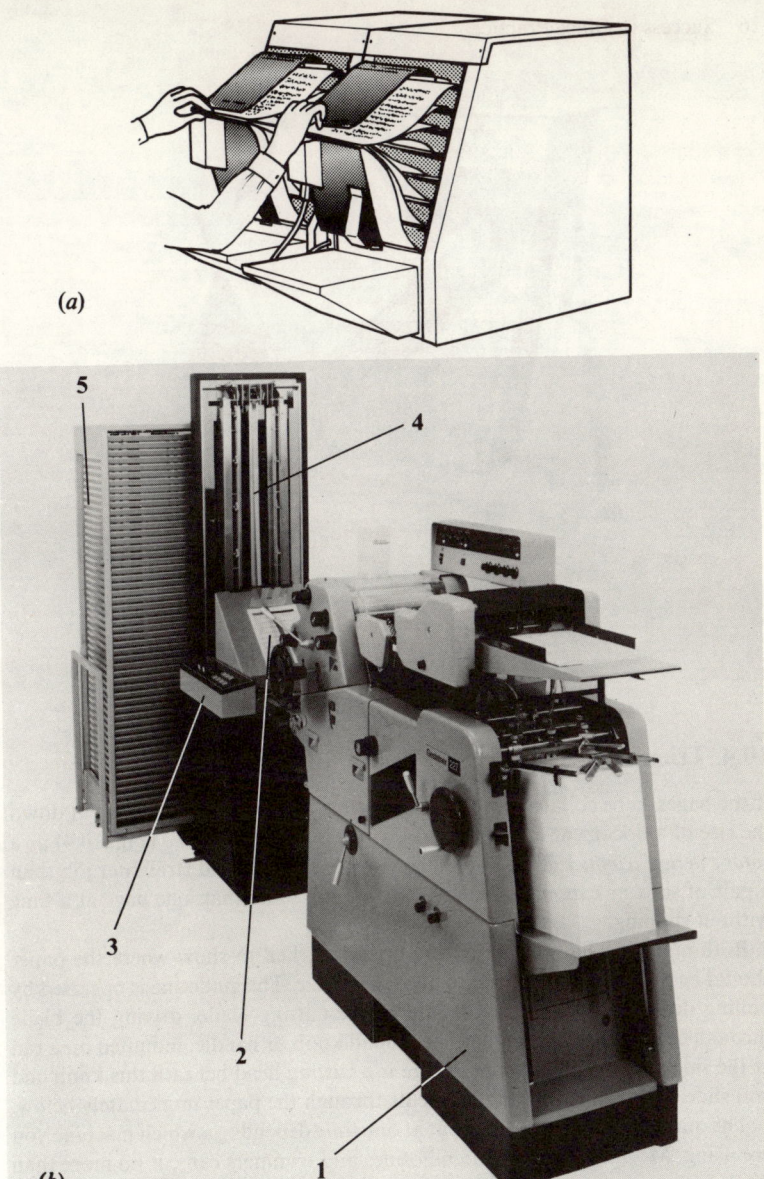

Fig. 10.2 Sorting and collating equipment: (a) a semi-automatic system, in which each pile of copies is placed on a separate shelf or 'station' and the machine gathers and presents the sets of sheets, (b) a fully automatic electronically controlled system. 1. Automatic offset duplicator. 2. Paper feed, linked directly to the duplicator (or, if required, to a copier). 3. Control panel. 4. Conveyor system to distribute copies. 5. Sorter bins—one copy of each page is automatically fed into each of the 104 bins

Fig. 10.3   Electric jogger

10.4 Trimming

If the pages to be collated are not all the same size, or if you need to cut down the size of a document for any reason, you can use a *guillotine* (Fig. 10.4) or a *rotary action trimmer* (Fig. 10.5). These make a neater and straighter job than a pair of scissors can, and can also cut through more than one page at a time without slipping.

Both machines have a flat cutting board marked to show where the paper should be positioned to produce a given page size. The guillotine is operated by pulling down sharply on the handle of the cutting blade, driving the blade through the paper. The trimmer has a small knob or handle, mounted on a rail at the side of the cutting board. There is a cutting head beneath this knob and you slide it along the rail; the head cuts through the paper immediately below.

The number of sheets you can cut at one time depends on which machine you are using. Most hand-operated guillotines and trimmers can cut no more than 20 sheets at once, although some can cope with 30. Very large machines, with a capacity of half a ream (250 sheets) are available, and electric guillotines can cut 500 sheets at once.

If you are using cutting equipment of any sort, you should:

(*a*) Make quite sure that your fingers are out of the way of the blade. Employers are required by law to ensure that the cutting edge is properly guarded, but thoughtlessness and stupidity can still lead to injury.

(*b*) Check that you are only cutting off parts of the paper which are not

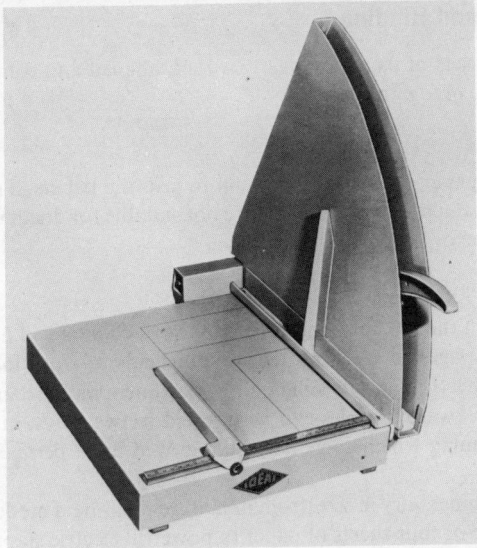

Fig. 10.4   Guillotine

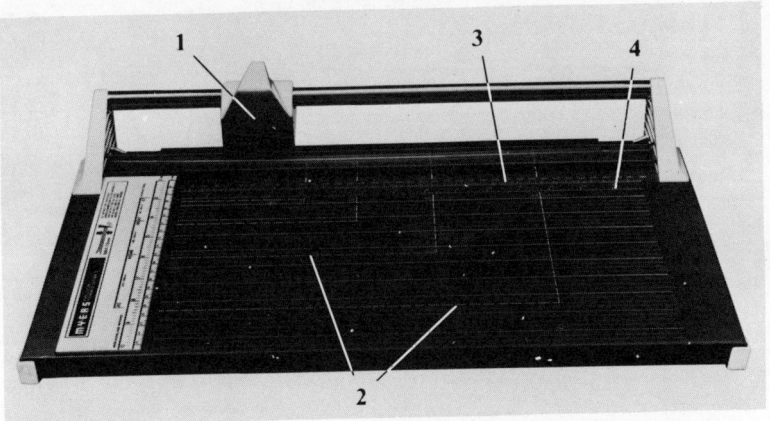

*Fig. 10.5   Rotary action trimmer. 1. Cutting head and guard. 2. Paper guides.
3. Millimetre scale. 4. Inch scale*

needed, and that all the pages are the right way up and properly aligned before
you cut them.

(*c*) Do not try to cut too many pages at once, or the paper will slip as the
cutting edge passes through it, leaving the pages out of line.

(*d*) Make sure the paper is correctly and securely positioned. Use the guidelines and the position of the other three edges of the paper to judge this
accurately; don't just guess where the cutting edge will fall.

10.5 Fixing and Binding

Now that your sets of pages are neatly sorted, aligned and trimmed, the final stage is to fix them together.

(a) Clips
You can use a paper-clip or foldback clip to grip the papers. These are cheap and easy to use, but may slip off. They are not suitable for documents that must be well presented or kept a long time.

(b) Staples
A staple through the top left-hand corner of the document will hold it together and enable the pages to be turned easily, but tends to work loose. A row of staples down the left-hand side will hold the document more securely, but make page-turning awkward. Staples can be inserted in two ways, making either a temporary fastening which can easily be removed, or a permanent fastening (Fig. 10.6).

Stapling machines vary in size, from miniature hand-held models suitable for fixing only three or four sheets of paper to powerful electric staplers which can hold 100 pages.

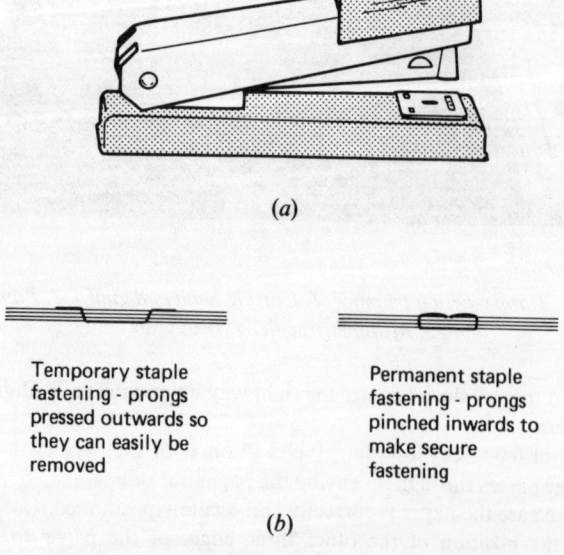

(a)

Temporary staple
fastening - prongs
pressed outwards so
they can easily be
removed

Permanent staple
fastening - prongs
pinched inwards to
make secure
fastening

(b)

Fig. 10.6   (a) Stapler and (b) staple fastenings

(c) Binders

The look of a stapled document is improved if it is given a cover of thick card; important documents, such as reports, agendas, scripts and stock lists, look more impressive if the pages are bound. Where only a few documents are produced, card covers with slide bindings (Fig. 10.7) are available, which will grip 30 to 40 sheets of A4 paper, while punchless binders (Fig. 10.8) can be used for documents of up to 150 sheets.

Fig. 10.7   Slide bindings, showing how documents are inserted into them

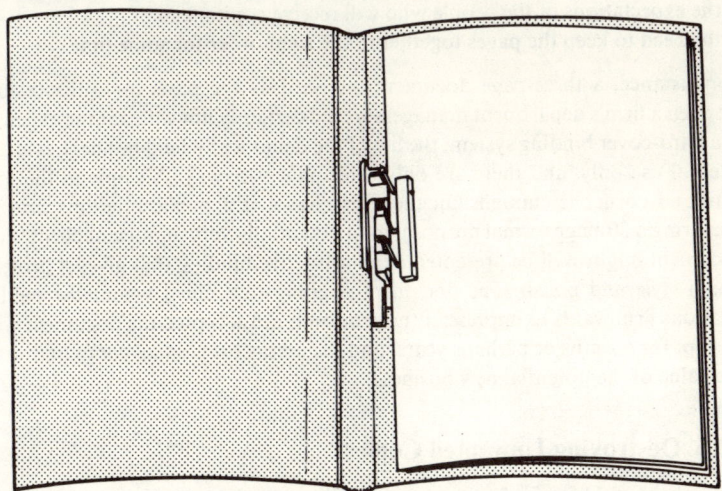

Fig. 10.8   Punchless binder

If your company regularly needs to produce well-presented documents, it may use a special binding machine (Fig. 10.9). For an even more impressive presentation, a hard-cover binding system can be used: the covers can have simulated leather or suede embossed finishes and can be put on in under two minutes to make a report look like a bound book.

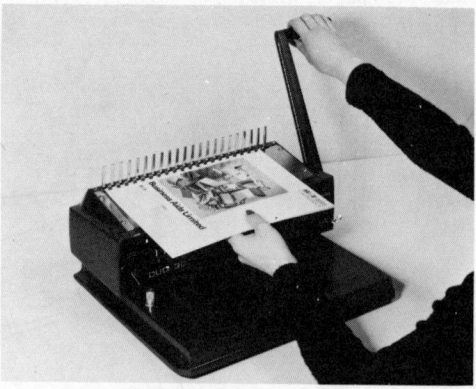

Fig. 10.9   Binding machine: the sheets and covers to be bound are slid into the front of the machine against a side-lay and the handle is moved forward to punch; a plastic 'comb' is then placed on the binding mechanism and the handle is moved backwards to receive the punched sheets

Choosing a method of fixing or binding involves taking into account

cost
the importance of the document
the expectations of the people who will receive copies, and
the need to keep the pages together in the right order for some time.

For instance, a three-page document intended as the basis for a discussion between a firm's department managers would certainly not warrant the expense of a hard-cover binding system: the life of the document would be short, it is for internal use only, and there are only three pages anyway. A staple in the top left-hand corner is enough. On the other hand, if a public relations firm is preparing a 30-page formal proposal for a potentially very important client, this document might well be presented in an attractive binding that gives it professional style and polish. The document is going to a client whom the public relations firm wants to impress; if the proposals are accepted the document will be kept for months or perhaps years, and the extra cost is small compared with the value of the potential new business.

10.6 Destroying Unwanted Copies

Once the useful life of a document is over, it need be kept no longer. It will take up space which could be used for other purposes. If it has been superseded by a new document, the continued existence of the old one can create confusion. And if you find you have accidentally taken too many copies of a confidential document or if you have spare pages left over after collating one, these must be destroyed.

The decision to destroy documents is usually taken by a manager. But you might be asked to get rid of them for him or her. Traditionally, waste paper from the office is thrown into a waste-paper basket, emptied into central refuse points by cleaners and collected by the refuse collectors. If the information handled by your office is of a particularly confidential nature and should not be seen by any unauthorized person, you should get into the habit of tearing up all the papers you throw into the bin or basket. (This also reduces the bulk, so that more waste can be accommodated in a limited space.) Where waste paper comes in large quantities, however, mechanical help is needed.

Many offices now use an electrically operated *shredder* to dispose of paper that outside people must not see. Unwanted paper is fed into the machine through a slit, and shredded into strips (usually 6 or 8 mm wide, though narrower cuts are available for top security work) by power-driven blades. As with

Fig. 10.10   Heavy-duty shredder

other types of office equipment, the range of sizes, prices and capacity is wide. The smallest models can sit under a desk in place of a traditional waste-paper basket. Where larger amounts of shredding must take place, a heavy-duty shredder (Fig. 10.10) can accept 50 or more sheets of paper at once, and can cope with paper-clips and staples.

If you are working in an office where there is a shredder, remember that:

(*a*) A shredded document cannot be put together again: only papers that are definitely not wanted should be disposed of in this way.

(*b*) A shredder is designed to cut certain materials only. Never attempt to put anything other than the specified materials through it.

(*c*) Do not overload the shredder through trying to feed in more sheets of paper than it was designed to accept.

(*d*) If the shredder jams, switch off the electricity before you investigate.

10.7 Quick Questions

1. What do you understand by the word 'collating'?

2. What (in the context of paper-handling) is meant by 'jogging'?

3. What would you use a guillotine for?

4. What factors should be taken into account in deciding what form of binding to use for a finished document?

5. Name two methods of getting rid of unwanted paper in the office.

6. List four points to watch when using an electric shredder.

10.8 Short Exercises

1. Make brief notes about the ways in which the finished presentation of a document can affect the reactions of those who receive it.

2. How would you persuade your office manager that (*a*) automatic collating equipment and (*b*) a shredder are needed in your office? Make notes to support the arguments you would use.

Unit Eleven

Handling the Mail

11.1 Introduction

The documents flowing into and out of the office are referred to collectively as the *post* or the *mail*. The local post office plays an important part in the movement of mail from one person to another and from one business to another, and in Unit 12 we shall consider the various means provided by the Post Office in the United Kingdom for the dispatch of letters and parcels to other parts of the country and overseas.

In addition, large organizations operate their own internal mail system, which deals with the correspondence passing from department to department within the firm. Sometimes the internal mail system simply involves the movement of paper round a single building. But if the organization operates from several separate buildings, a more complex system is needed.

Both the internal and the external mail of a large organization enters and leaves the building via the *post room* (Unit 22.6), which is the department responsible for the receipt and dispatch of all correspondence and parcels. Your role in handling the office mail will depend on whether or not your organization has a post room.

11.2 Handling Incoming Mail

Incoming mail must be dealt with efficiently and systematically, so that it can be distributed to the addressees as quickly as possible.

(*a*) Collect the mail from the post room, postman or messenger, whichever is the procedure in your organization.

(*b*) Set aside all envelopes marked 'Personal', 'Confidential' or 'Private', as these must be passed unopened to the addressees.

(*c*) Open the remaining envelopes carefully. Using a letter-opener or a letter-opening machine speeds up the task and reduces the risk of damage to the contents (see Unit 22.6(*a*)(vi)). Keep empty envelopes for several days in case any query arises.

(*d*) Remove the contents. If there are enclosures, fasten them together, making sure that nothing is left in the envelope.

(*e*) If your firm keeps an *incoming mail register*, enter details of every letter or document received.

(*f*) Record the amount and method of payment for incoming remittances (see Unit 13.3). Some organizations use a *remittances book* for recording these payments and for registered mail. Any discrepancies between the amount stated on the documents and the amount actually enclosed should be reported.

(*g*) Stamp each paper with a date stamp (Fig. 11.1), taking care not to stamp over anything important.

Fig. 11.1　Date stamp

(*h*) Sort the correspondence, separating out the mail for each person, department or section. A series of folders, trays or pigeon holes will speed this up. If more than one person needs to see an item, either take extra copies or prepare a circulation slip (Fig. 22.4).

Remember to include the unopened envelopes (paragraph (*b*) above) before delivering the mail to the addressees.

11.3　Handling Outgoing Mail

Outgoing mail must be dealt with regularly and promptly by the clerk concerned, so that important documents are not delayed by missing the postal collection.

(*a*) Make sure that each letter has been signed and that any enclosures mentioned in it are attached.

(*b*) Check the address on each envelope with the address on the letter, and see that the envelopes are large enough for any enclosures.

(*c*) Fold papers carefully before inserting them in the envelopes. (Fig. 5.3 shows how the most common paper sizes should be folded for insertion into different sizes of envelope.) If window or aperture envelopes (see Unit 5.2(*i*)) are used, make sure the full address can be seen. Seal the envelopes.

(*d*) Keep letters that are to be delivered by internal messenger separate from the rest.

(*e*) Separate out letters, packets and parcels that require special treatment (overseas mail, recorded delivery and so on) and deal with them as outlined in Unit 12.

(*f*) Weigh each letter or packet, and check whether it is to go first class (delivery next working day) or second class (delivery up to three working days after posting). Your organization probably has a general policy on when each service should be used.

(*g*) Check the amount of postage to be paid, consulting if necessary the label on the scale or the *Compendium of Inland Postal Rates*. Electronically controlled scales automatically show the correct charge.

(*h*) Stick on postage stamps of the correct value, or use a franking machine (see Unit 11.5).

11.4 Stamps and the Postage Book

(*a*) Sheets of Stamps
Where only a few letters are sent out each day, sheets of stamps bought over the counter at the local post office are usually used. You can buy a sheet of first-class and a sheet of second-class stamps and additional sheets for other values. The stamps should be kept in a folder, with a separate section for each value.

(*b*) Stamp-emitting Machines
Rolls of stamps can be bought from the post office and inserted into a machine. A separate machine is needed for each value of stamp. The machine has a meter to keep count of the number of stamps used, but you still need to stick the stamps on to the envelopes by hand.

(*c*) The Postage Book
Stamps are paid for out of petty cash (the money available for minor office expenses – see Unit 13.2). The value of the stamps you buy is entered in a *postage book*, in the left-hand column of the page (Fig. 11.2). In this example, on Monday 4 April there were £2.00 worth of stamps left over from the previous week and another £20.82 worth has been bought for this week. The address to which each letter or parcel is sent is listed briefly in the 'item' column. The 'stamps used' column shows the value of stamps used, and any item that was not sent at standard letter rate is explained in the 'remarks' column. At the end of the day, the total value of stamps used is added up; the value of the remaining, unused stamps is also added up and entered as the balance to be *carried forward* (c/f) to the next day. This balance is added to the value of the stamps used, and the result should equal the total value of stamps held at the start of the day's business. On Tuesday 5 April the balance carried forward from the Monday is entered in the left-hand column and the same procedure is followed.

When you have stuck the appropriate value of stamp on each letter or packet and entered it in the postage book, you can put the letters in the local pillar box or post them at the post office. Recorded delivery, registered mail and certain other types of mail cannot be dealt with in this way: you have to hand them in at the post office (see Unit 12.2).

(*d*) Prepayment at the Post Office
Your organization can avoid the use of stamps, by arrangement with a main post office. The firm must pay the cost of postage in advance and state at which post office mail will be handed in, the date(s) of posting and the number of items involved and their postal rates. Not fewer than 20 parcels or 120 letters can be

Stamps bought (Dr)		Date	Item	Stamps used (Cr)		Remarks
£	p	19..		£	p	
2	00	4 April	balance b/f			
20	82		cash received			
		4 April	Costalot, Wigan	0	18	
			Tinkast, Crewe	0	76	1st class packet
			Nepos Inc, New York	0	24	
			Righteways, Birmingham	1	89	Registered packet
			Schmidt, West Berlin	0	38	Packet
			Le Blanc, Paris	0	38	Packet
			Willis Co, Ontario	0	28	
			Norris Bros, Hartlepool	0	18	
			Westons, London	0	18	
			Sobers Ltd, Brighton	2	93	Recorded delivery
			Preview invitations	3	60	20 @ 18p
				11	00	
			balance c/f	11	82	
22	82			22	82	
11	82	5 April	balance b/f			

Fig. 11.2   Entries in a postage book

sent at a time, the letters must be tied in bundles of 50, with the addresses all facing the same way.

The other main alternative to stamps, the franking machine, is discussed in Unit 11.5.

11.5 Using a Franking Machine

Sticking on postage stamps is a time-consuming and sticky business. Where a dozen or more letters are sent out through the post every day, the office manager may decide to invest in a *franking machine* or *meter* (Fig. 11.3).

When you have determined the postal charge for a letter or package, you set the machine to the required rate and the day's date by operating a lever or knob. The envelope (or a strip of gummed label for a parcel) is passed through the machine and emerges stamped with the date, the postal district and the value of

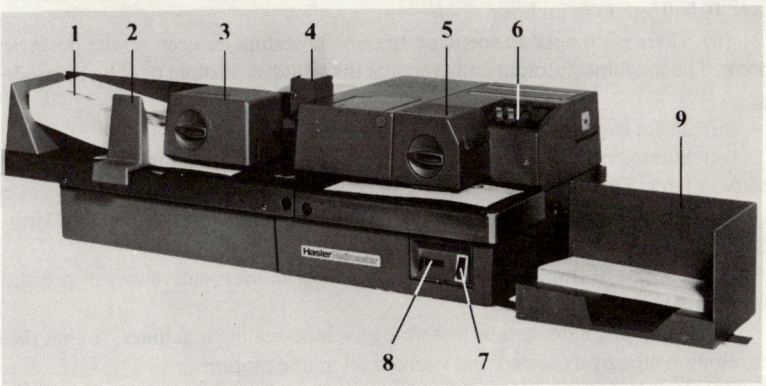

Fig. 11.3   Franking machine. 1. Unfranked envelopes. 2. Guide. 3. Feed-in and sealing device. 4. Label franking. 5. Date setting and slogan stamp. 6. Franking setting levels. 7. Power switch and indicator light. 8. Item counter. 9. Collecting tray for franked envelopes

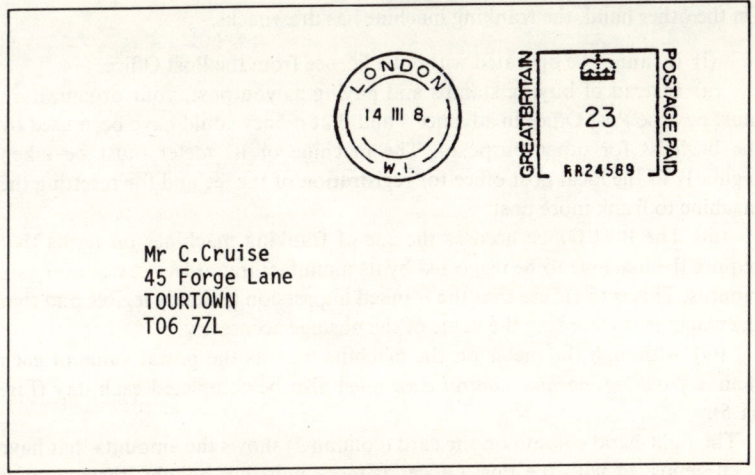

Fig. 11.4   Franked envelope

postage paid (Fig. 11.4). If the organization wishes, an advertising slogan or name and address of the firm can be printed on it at the same time.

A franking machine is not a licence to print stamps. The company pays a fee to the Post Office at intervals, and this buys the right to frank letters up to the value of the fee.

(a) Advantages
The franking machine has several advantages.

    (i) It is much quicker than sticking on stamps. Some machines can frank over 10 000 letters in an hour.

    (ii) There is no need to spend petty cash on stamps or keep up the postage book. The machine automatically records the value of postage passing through it.

    (iii) There is no danger of running out of stamps.

    (iv) Stamps need not be left lying about where they are an invitation to the petty pilferer. The franking machine can be locked when not in use.

    (v) All types of mail can be franked, including registered letters (see Unit 12.2(a)).

    (vi) The use of franked advertising slogans is an inexpensive way of getting the company's name known.

    (vii) Some machines can be linked to envelope-sealing machines, so that the envelope is effectively sealed and franked all in one motion.

    (viii) Franked material should pass through the Post Office's sorting system more quickly than stamped mail. Stamps on letters have to be cancelled by stamping a postmark across them to show that they had been used. With franking this is not necessary.

(b) Disadvantages
On the other hand, the franking machine has drawbacks.

    (i) It cannot be operated without a licence from the Post Office.

    (ii) Instead of buying stamps and paying as you post, your organization must pay the Post Office in advance – and that money could have been used by the business for other purposes. The machine or its meter must be taken regularly to the local post office for registration of the fee and for resetting the machine to frank more post.

    (iii) The Post Office licenses the use of franking machines on terms that require the machine to be inspected by its manufacturer at least twice every six months. This is to ensure that the franked impression is clearly legible and that the machine is recording the value of the postage accurately.

    (iv) Although the meter on the machine records the postal value of each item, a *franking machine control card* must also be completed each day (Fig. 11.5).

The right-hand column on the card (column 3) shows the amounts that have been deposited with the Post Office; as more units are bought, their value is added to this figure to produce a total. Column 1 shows the figure displayed on

FRANKING MACHINE CONTROL CARD

Licensee . . . .

Machine
(or Meter No.) . . . .
Setting or
Recording Unit . . . .

Meter Office
(as shown on Record Card) . . . .

I certify that the following entries for the above machine for the week

ended . . . . .are correct

and that the correct date has been shown on each day's posting

**CHECK
DATE
DAILY**

Put initials in column below to show date has been changed		ALL MACHINES Reading of Ascending Register (Totalisator)	LOCKING MACHINES Reading of Descending Register (Credit Meter)	ALL MACHINES Last entry in col. "Total Deposits" or "Total Settings" on Record Card
	Mon.			
	Tue.			
	Wed.			
	Thur.			
	Fri.			
	Sat.			

NOTE 1 Whether or not the machine has been used, this card must be posted on Saturday, or on Friday if no postings are made on Saturday.

NOTE 2 The daily entry must be made on completion of each day's postings.

Signed. . . . .

. . . . .19 . . . .

Post Office Examining Officer's initials . . . .

Fig. 11.5   Franking machine control card

the ascending register of the machine – the postage franked so far. Column 2 shows the amount of money left, that is, the figure shown on the descending register of the machine. Column 1 plus column 2 must always equal column 3, because as the figure on the ascending register rises to show the value of additional postings, the descending register shows the difference between this figure and the total available. The card must be completed daily, whether or not the machine has been used that day, and each week the control card must be sent to the post office.

(v) Although anyone can go to the post office to buy stamps for urgent mail that is to be posted that evening, not everyone can be authorized to operate the franking machine. For security reasons it must be locked away after the bulk of the day's post has been dispatched, so late items still have to be stamped by hand.

(vi) Special handling is necessary after the letters have been franked. They must be *faced* – that is, tied in bundles, with all the names and addresses facing the same way.

(vii) Franked mail cannot usually be posted in a pillar box. Normally it must be handed in at a specified post office; if that office has closed, however, the mail can be put into a special envelope and posted in a pillar box.

(viii) The franking machine records only the amount of postage paid, not the name of the person to whom the letter was sent. The date of dispatch of a letter thus cannot be checked, as it can with the postage book system (see Unit 11.4).

(ix) Although the machine is generally more secure than loose stamps, staff may lose sight of the real cost of sending each letter; they may even allow personal letters to be franked. Genuine errors can also be costly. Incorrectly franked envelopes should be put aside and a refund claimed from the Post Office from time to time.

11.6 Internal Mail

Internal mail, unlike external mail, does not need franking or stamping. Indeed it may not even need a new envelope (see Unit 5.2(*i*)(vii)). This mail should be handed to the office messenger or taken to a central point for collection by the organization's mail van.

Where there is no internal mail service, the letters, memoranda and other items may all have to be put together in one large envelope or package and sent through the external post to head office. There the contents are sorted and distributed to head office departments, or forwarded to other branches.

11.7 Quick Questions

1. Where will you find up-to-date information about postal rates?

2. If you were responsible for opening the department's mail, what would you do with (*a*) letters marked 'Private', 'Confidential' and 'Personal', and (*b*) old envelopes?

3. Describe the main steps that have to be taken to get a department's mail from out-trays to envelopes.

4. What is 'petty cash'?

5. One way of paying the postage on outgoing mail is to use postage stamps. What is the other?

6. Name two factors that affect the cost of sending a letter or packet.

11.8 Short Exercises

1. Prepare brief notes about the advantages and disadvantages of the use of a franking machine in your office.

2. You have been asked to explain to a junior new to your office the procedures for handling incoming and outgoing mail. Write down the main points you would wish to make.

Unit Twelve

Using Post Office Services

12.1 Introduction

Much of the mail you handle will be straightforward letters and packets, but some requires special treatment. A packet may be of particular value or may need to be delivered quickly, or it may be addressed overseas. The range of services offered by the world's postal networks is constantly changing, and choosing an appropriate service can be a complex task.

In the United Kingdom, there is invaluable help in the *Post Office Guide*, with its comprehensive index of services. Copies are held in your local post office and library, or you can buy one from a main post office. The *Guide* is published annually, and is updated by the issue of regular supplements. Current postal charges are listed in separate *Postal Rates Compendia, Inland and Overseas*. The Post Office also publishes a *Code of Practice for Postal Services*, which details the most commonly used services, and tells you how to obtain further information and what to do if things go wrong.

The Post Office's banking services are discussed in Unit 14.8.

12.2 Items of Value: Inland

(a) Small Items of Value

Letters and packets containing items of value—money, unused postage stamps and other such negotiable items (see Unit 13.1)—should be sent by *registered post* in a special envelope available from a post office (Fig. 12.1(*a*)). As well as the normal first-class postage charge, an additional fee is payable.

Registered mail goes by first-class letter post, but gets special security handling. If an item does get lost or damaged, the Post Office will pay compensation.

For an additional fee, it is possible to take out *consequential loss insurance*. This means that extra compensation will be paid for other losses arising from ('consequential to') the loss or damage of the packet itself.

(b) Large Items of Value

Parcels cannot be sent by registered post, but the *compensation fee parcel service* provides compensation for loss or damage, if you pay the required fee at the time of posting.

(c) Important Documents

Some business papers (legal documents and contracts, for instance) have no value in themselves but could cause great inconvenience if not delivered on time or if they were lost in the post. These can be sent by the *recorded delivery service* (Fig. 12.1(*b*)); a small additional fee is charged at the time of posting. A receipt is given as proof of posting, and proof of delivery can also be supplied if

For official Registration label.

REGISTERED LETTER RECOMMANDÉ

This letter must be handed to a Post Office official and a receipt obtained

£1·16

Royal Mail

See note on back for details of compensation

Postcode_____

(a)

B571201 **Recorded Delivery**

Certificate of Posting for Recorded Delivery

How to post

1 Enter below in ink the name and address as written on the letter or packet.
2 Affix the numbered adhesive label in the top left-hand corner of the letter (or close to the address on a packet).
3 Affix postage stamps to the letter for the correct postage and Recorded Delivery fee.
4 Hand this certificate, together with the letter, to an officer of the Post Office.
5 This certificate will be date-stamped and initialled as a receipt. Please keep it safely, and produce it in the event of a claim.

Name

Address

Postcode

No compensation will be paid in respect of money or jewellery sent by this service.

For Post Office use

Date stamp

Accepting Officer's initials

Recorded Delivery no. **B571201**

P2297 Oct 82

(b)

Fig. 12.1 (a) Registered envelope, (b) sticker to be applied on a recorded delivery letter, (c) Datapost label

datapost
A ROYAL MAIL SERVICE

Contract No **D/**	**/INT**
To	Date

From

(c)

requested. If a packet is lost or damaged, a small amount of compensation is paid.

(*d*) Regular Consignments of Value

Where urgently needed items, like medical samples and supplies, spare parts and equipment, must be delivered promptly, they can be sent by *Datapost* (Fig. 12.1(*c*)). For regular consignments to particular destinations, a special Datapost contract can be arranged with the Post Office and packages are collected at regular times; individual items can be handed in at a post office. Consignments are normally delivered by 9.30 a.m. on the day after they are collected or handed in.

Datapost consignments are supervised by Post Office staff throughout their journey and are signed for on delivery, though no compensation is payable if they are lost or damaged. The various types of Datapost are outlined in Tables 12.1 and 12.2, at the end of this Unit.

12.3 Items of Value: Europe and Overseas

(*a*) Small Items of Value

These can be sent overseas by registered post, but only a small amount of compensation is payable in the event of loss or damage.

(*b*) Large Items of Value

These cannot be sent by the compensation fee parcel service, which has no overseas equivalent. Instead, parcels and letters of high value can be insured, provided they are properly packed. A fee or *premium* must be paid and a certificate of posting obtained from the post office clerk.

(c) Important Documents and Regular Consignments

These are both best dealt with through *Datapost International*, which works in much the same way as the inland service, and which operates to many overseas countries.

There are other differences between sending mail inland and sending it overseas which you should note.

(d) Customs Declarations

Most countries have rules about the kind of items that can and cannot be imported, and certain kinds of goods may be liable to taxation or special *duty*. If you have travelled abroad you will be familiar with the customs procedures at ports of entry, airports and frontiers. Wrapping up a watch or a camera and sending it through the post does not mean that you can avoid paying the duty that would be charged if you carried it into or out of certain countries yourself.

So for overseas parcels, whether sent by air or surface mail, you must complete a *customs declaration form*, obtainable from a post office. On the form you should enter a description of the contents of the parcel and, as the addressee may be asked to pay duty on them, their approximate value. False declarations can result in the parcel being seized or the addressee being punished. Different countries have different requirements as far as customs declarations and dispatch notes are concerned. Full details are published in the *Post Office Guide*.

(e) Franc de Droits

It is possible for the duty on some parcels to be paid at the time of posting. The item should be clearly marked 'To be delivered free of charges' or 'Franc de droits' (FDD). When you hand it in to the post office clerk you will be asked to pay a deposit to cover the customs charges. Any overpayment is refundable.

12.4 Urgent Items: Inland

The Datapost service (see Unit 12.2(*d*)) provides a fast, as well as safe, link with customers and clients. Datapost is fairly expensive, however, and is not available to every destination. There are other ways of sending urgent items, which can be cheaper.

(a) Items for Same-day Delivery

For really urgent items for delivery in the same city or to another major town, the *Expresspost* service can be used. The consignment is collected by messenger and items for local delivery are delivered direct; those for other towns are forwarded by train and collected by another messenger. (Similar messenger services are operated by private contractors in most towns; they are listed in the

Yellow Pages telephone directory under 'Delivery and Collection Services'. British Rail also offers an express service, called *Red Star*, for which items must be taken to the parcels office at certain stations.)

It can be slightly less expensive to take the item to the railway station yourself, and send it as a *railway letter*. It can either be collected by the addressee from his local station or be transferred to the local postal service.

Parcels can travel by the *railway parcel* service and should be handed in at an express delivery post office, rather than at the station. A Post Office messenger will take the parcel to the station and put it on the train to its destination. Over longer distances, the *airway letter* service is usually quicker. Items should be taken to a British Airways terminal and travel by air.

(*b*) Next-day Delivery Guaranteed
Although first-class letters and packets are usually delivered on the next working day after posting, this is not guaranteed. Arrival on time can be ensured by using the *Royal Mail Special Delivery*, by which items are delivered by special messenger from the sorting office at their destination. Registered and recorded-delivery packets can also be sent by this service. The special delivery fee is refunded if the packet does not arrive next day.

(*c*) Late Posting
Letters and packets posted after the last collection at the post office are delayed, because they will not be sorted until the following working day. If you have missed the last post you can take items, including recorded-delivery and registered letters, to a station where there is a *travelling post office*, which is a mail train with a sorting office attached. Items are accepted until five minutes before the train is due to leave.

12.5 Urgent Items: Europe and Overseas

Where there is no hurry, letters and parcels can be sent overseas by surface mail, travelling by sea and rail. Delivery time depends on the distance to the destination, but can be several weeks. Where speedy delivery is needed, the Datapost International service (see Unit 12.3(*c*)) can be used. The service is not available to every country, however, and to some a limited service is offered, for business papers only. There are several other options.

(*a*) Accelerated Treatment
An urgent letter or packet, including one that has been registered or insured, can be sent by the *Swiftair* service. It will be speeded through the British sorting procedures and put on the earliest possible plane. On arrival in the addressee's country it may be delivered by messenger if this will be quicker than normal postal delivery.

Parcels requiring accelerated treatment can be sent by the *Express Delivery* service.

(b) Less Urgent Items

Letters and parcels that only need to arrive without undue delay can be sent by ordinary airmail. Items sent to European addresses from the United Kingdom automatically travel by air, but for other destinations you must specify that the airmail service is to be used by attaching a blue airmail sticker close to the address. Airmail is generally more expensive than surface mail.

12.6 Special Services for Business

(a) Cash on Delivery

The *Cash on Delivery* (COD) service operates for both inland and overseas transactions. For a flat fee in addition to normal postage charges, the Post Office delivers the item and collects what is known as the *trade charge*, that is, the payment for the goods. The trade charge must not exceed £100 in the United Kingdom, but there are different limits in other countries. The money collected is then remitted to the sender of the goods.

(b) Freepost and Business Reply Services

There are four ways in which an organization can encourage customers and clients to communicate with it at no cost to themselves. The choice between them depends upon the firm's requirements and the type of mail concerned.

(i) **Freepost.** The organization obtains a licence from the head postmaster of the district, and it is allocated a *Freepost address.* A fee is payable for the licence and a monthly sum is also payable to cover the number of letters and packets that are likely to be sent to the organization by Freepost. When this amount is used up, an additional payment must be made. Each item is charged at second-class postal rates plus a small additional charge. When the firm advertises its products and invites people to write in for more information about them, it can quote the Freepost address, which is used by interested readers on their own envelopes. No stamp is needed on the envelope, and no specially printed stationery is required.

(ii) **Business reply services.** This is a restricted method of enabling clients and correspondents to write to an organization without paying postage. As with Freepost, a licence must be obtained from the postmaster. Envelopes and cards are specially printed, showing the firm's address and the licence number (Fig. 12.2). When statements of account are sent out, for instance, they can be accompanied by a reply-paid envelope which customers can use when sending back their payments, costing them nothing. The firm is charged for each envelope or card sent through the mail, at a rate slightly above the normal charge for first- or second-class postage. An annual licence fee is also payable.

The fact that the firm's address is clearly printed on the envelope eliminates the chance of letters being wrongly addressed. (Where a firm needs to prepay the postage on incoming mail only occasionally, it can send out envelopes already stamped and carrying the firm's address already typed in.)

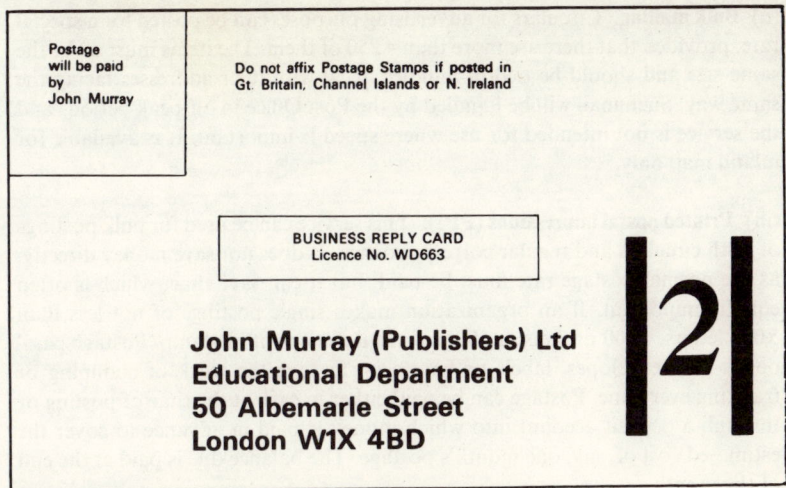

Postage
will be paid
by
John Murray

Do not affix Postage Stamps if posted in
Gt. Britain, Channel Islands or N. Ireland

BUSINESS REPLY CARD
Licence No. WD663

**John Murray (Publishers) Ltd
Educational Department
50 Albemarle Street
London W1X 4BD**

2

Fig. 12.2   Reply-paid card

(iii) **Postage forward parcel service.** This is particularly useful for organizations like mail order shopping firms which regularly send parcels of goods to people *on approval* (that is, the customer can send them back if they are unsuitable). With the postage forward parcel service, the customer can return unwanted goods without paying postal charges. The firm is issued with a licence and pays the postage for incoming parcels.

(iv) **International reply coupons.** The business reply service does not operate for your correspondents abroad. Instead, you can send an *international reply coupon*, which can be bought from a post office. When the recipient replies, he exchanges the coupon for postage stamps at his local post office and affixes these to his letter to you.

(c) Household Delivery and Bulk Mailing

Extra large mailings can cause problems for an organization because normal postal services may be expensive in relation to the return—many of the people who receive your organization's circulars and promotional material will put them straight into the waste-paper basket. The Post Office has three services which can reduce the cost of this kind of distribution.

(i) **Household delivery service.** This service can help a business to bring its goods and services to the attention of people in a given area of the United Kingdom by arranging for the postman to deliver leaflets and other advertising material to every house. Items of identical shape, content and weight, unaddressed and without envelopes, can be delivered to all the addresses in any district that is at least as large as a postman's round.

(ii) **Bulk mailing.** Circulars for advertising purposes can be posted for a special rate, provided that there are more than 4 250 of them. The items must all be the same size and should be tied in bundles of 50 with their addresses facing the same way. Such mail will be handled by the Post Office in off-peak periods and the service is not intended for use where speed is important. It is available for inland mail only.

(iii) **Printed postal impressions (PPI).** This service can be used for bulk postings of both circulars and regular correspondence. It does not save money directly, as the normal postage rate must be paid, but it can save time, which is often equally important. If an organization makes single postings of not less than 5 000 letters, 1 000 packets or 100 parcels, it may print or stamp 'Postage paid' on its own envelopes, labels or wrappers, to save the work of stamping or franking every one. Postage can be paid either in cash at the time of posting or through a deposit account into which money is paid in advance to cover the estimated cost of, say, one month's postage. The balance due is paid at the end of the month.

The PPI service is available for all inland and overseas letters and for inland parcels, but not for overseas parcels.

12.7 Intelpost

Intelpost is a *facsimile text transmission service* (see Unit 9.6). Instead of investing in expensive transmission equipment, organizations can use this service, on certain routes within the United Kingdom and to some other countries, to send high-quality black-and-white facsimile reproduction of documents, line drawings and pictures of up to A4 size. Documents for copying can be collected by special messenger or handed in at a post office that has an Intelpost facility. They can be collected from the receiving Intelpost centre or delivered to the addressee by messenger.

Table 12.1 Inland postal services

Service	Weight limits	Size limits (mm)	Delivery (approximate)	Payment/special requirements
First-class letters	None	Max: 610 × 460 Min: 100 × 70	First working day after collection	Payment, related to weight, affixed in postage stamps before posting in post box
Second-class letters	750 g	As for first class	By third working day after collection	As above, but slightly cheaper
Registered letters	None	As for first class	As first class	First-class postage, plus registration fee; hand to post office clerk; special envelopes available

Service	Weight limits	Size limits (mm)	Delivery (approximate)	Payment/special requirements
Recorded-delivery letters	None	As for first class	First or second class	Postage plus small fee; hand to post office clerk; special sticker affixed; parcels, railway and airway letters and COD items cannot be sent recorded
Airway letters	450 g	As for first class	Usually same day	First-class postage plus flat fee; handed in at British Airways terminal, collected at destination or transferred to special delivery or normal post
Railway letters	450 g	As for first class	Usually same day—depends on train times and distance	First-class rate plus railway carriage fee; hand in at station but check an appropriate service is available
Royal Mail special delivery	None	As for first class	Delivery next working day guaranteed—by messenger if necessary	First-class postage plus fee; hand to post office clerk before last posting time
Late posting facility	None	As for first class	Next day	First-class postage plus additional fee affixed in postage stamps before handing in at travelling post office
Parcel post	10 kg (or more for franked mail by special arrangement)	1070 × 2000 (length and circumference combined)	Parcel post 3 or 4 days, or items can go first class for next-day delivery	First- or second-class postage, amount related to weight
Compensation fee parcels	10 kg	As for parcels	As for parcel post	Postage, related to weight plus small fee; hand to post office clerk; negotiable items not accepted
Expresspost	Approx. 10 kg inter-city; approx. 20 kg central London; heavier packages can be accepted in many areas	Depends on whether van, moped or motor cycle is used	Same day inter-city or in same city	Payment at time of ordering, or by account for regular users; hand to messenger

Service	Weight limits	Size limits (mm)	Delivery (approximate)	Payment/special requirements
Datapost—contract pick-up	27½ kg	As for first-class letters	Usually by 9.30 a.m. next day	Contract agreed in advance; regular schedule of postings; consignment collected by Post Office; Datapost labels; payment by account
Datapost on Demand (account)	27½ kg (if post office has suitable scales)	As for first-class letters	Next working day, mostly before noon	Account for items sent; hand in at nominated post office; Datapost posting document pad; authority card
Datapost on Demand (over-the-counter)	27½ kg (if post office has suitable scales)	As for first-class letters	As above	Payment at time of posting; hand in at main post office or sub-post office with Datapost sign; Datapost posting document pad
Railway parcels	10 kg	As for parcels	Same day—depending on train times and distance	Railway charge plus additional charge per mile travelled by messenger, plus waiting time for messenger; hand in at Express Delivery post office

Notes

1. Most letter and parcel services are available on a contract basis for the larger user. Special terms are agreed with the head postmaster; items need not be weighed or stamped individually; bulk collection can be made from the firm's premises and a regular account, rather than stamps or franking, can be used for payment.

2. Not all the services listed in this table are available at every local sub-post office. Some are only obtainable at main post offices or designated centres.

3. The sender's name and address should appear on the reverse of all mail.

Table 12.2 Overseas postal services

Service	Weight limits	Size limits (mm)	Delivery	Payment/special requirements
European all up	2 kg	Max: 900 width, length and depth combined, 600 for greatest dimension	Airmail, within a few days	No special charge or markings, European letters, cards, packets and newspapers automatically use this service (hence the name)

Service	Weight limits	Size limits (mm)	Delivery	Payment/special requirements
Overseas airmail letters	2 kg	As for Europe	Few days, depending on distance	Postage, airmail sticker
Overseas airmail small packets, printed paper	1 kg	As for Europe	Few days	Postage, airmail sticker
Overseas airmail parcels	10 kg usually, 20 kg to some countries	1050 × 2000, length and girth combined	Several days, depending on distance	Postage, airmail sticker
Overseas surface mail letters	2 kg	Max: 900 width, length and depth combined, 600 for greatest dimension	A week or more, depending on distance by sea and land	Surface postage
Overseas surface packets and printed paper	1 kg, but 5 kg for packets of books and pamphlets	As for overseas letters	As for overseas letters	Surface postage
Overseas surface parcels	Usually 10 kg but 20 kg for frequent users	1050 × 2000 length and girth combined	A week or more, depending on distance	Surface postage
Swiftair	2 kg	Max. 900 width, length and depth combined, 600 for greatest dimension	Airmail with accelerated treatment at either end	Postage plus additional fee; airmail and Swiftair stickers; hand over separately; items can be registered or insured
Express delivery	As for parcels	As for parcels	Airmail with accelerated treatment at receiving end	Postage plus additional fee; write EXPRESS in red
Overseas registered post	2 kg	As for letters	As for letters	Postage plus registration fee
Insurance for letters and parcels	As letter or parcel	As letter or parcel	As letter or parcel	Postage plus fee; insured value must not exceed market value
Datapost International	15 kg	900 length, width and depth combined, 600 for greatest dimension	Overnight to Europe, 2 or 3 days to most other places	Contract agreed in advance; regular schedule of postings; Datapost posting document pad; some restrictions on merchandise

Service	Weight limits	Size limits (mm)	Delivery	Payment/special requirements
Datapost International on Demand (account)	15 kg to most countries	As Datapost International	As Datapost International	Contract agreed in advance; hand in at nominated post office; pay by account; Datapost posting document pad; available to all countries operating a scheduled service; authority card for posting
Datapost International on Demand (over-the-counter)	15 kg to most countries	As Datapost International	As Datapost International	Hand in at any main post office or sub-post office with Datapost sign; Datapost posting document pad; payment at time of posting

Notes

1. A customs declaration form is required for all overseas mail except current personal correspondence and most printed paper. Items to be treated as packets rather than parcels should have the words 'small packet' written on them.

2. The sender's name and address should appear on the reverse of all mail.

12.8 Quick Questions

1. List three ways of sending things of value through the post.

2. What are (a) a certificate of posting, and (b) a certificate of delivery?

3. What is the business reply service?

4. What is bulk mailing?

5. In what circumstances would you be required to complete a customs declaration form when posting a packet or parcel?

6. What do the letters FDD stand for, and what do they mean?

12.9 Short Exercises

1. Choose three inland and two overseas postal services. Check the current details of each in the *Post Office Guide*. Prepare brief notes for a new member of staff, explaining the purpose, cost and other key features of each of your chosen services.

2. Describe briefly, giving your reasons, the Post Office services you would use for each of the following:

   (a) to send a legal document for which proof of delivery may be required in a court of law;

(b) to dispatch an urgent letter after the last post has been collected from the post office;

(c) to send a gold ring, valued at £100, to another part of the country;

(d) to enable a customer abroad to reply to you without having to pay postage;

(e) to collect money from customers for mail order transactions.

Unit Thirteen

Handling Money

13.1 Introduction

Organizations buy and sell goods and services at a price. Employees offer to work—at a price. Governments provide the framework within which business operates—at a price.

In the simplest form of trading, *barter*, the 'price' is expressed in kind—one horse for three goats, perhaps. In most countries, though, trade relies on money. One horse may fetch £200, which in turn will buy three goats.

Sometimes money takes the form of cash, whether coins or bank-notes—the *legal tender* of the country. The *denomination* of the coin or note—50p, £5 and so on—is stamped or printed on it, so that no one can argue over what it is worth. Such coins and bank-notes are *negotiable*. This means that when you are given, say, a £5 note which you accept in good faith for work you have done, you become the owner of that note, even if the person who gave it to you had stolen it from someone else. Whoever has the £5 note may spend it as he or she thinks fit.

Sometimes money takes other forms, which are not so readily passed from person to person, that is, which are *non-negotiable*. Cheques, postal orders and credit transfers (see Unit 14) are examples.

Whatever its form, all the money flowing into and out of your organization must be accounted for, so that management knows where it has come from and where it has gone. In some organizations the handling of money is restricted to the cashier's department or the cash office; in others, like banks and building societies, many staff are involved. Small items of daily expenditure are normally dealt with out of the office *petty cash*.

13.2 Petty Cash

Postage stamps, cleaning materials, labels, notebooks, flowers, bus fares, magazines, tea and coffee—these are just some of the many incidental expenses which have to be met from time to time. Most of them call for a cash payment—putting a cheque in the slot of a parking meter will not stop the needle moving round to the 'penalty' zone. So a small ('petty') supply of cash is kept in most offices, a system that is quicker and simpler than troubling the cash office for every small payment.

(a) The Cash Box

Petty cash should be kept in a lockable box to reduce the risk of theft. Bank-notes are kept in the bottom of the box, and coins are kept in a tray in the top. The box itself must be locked away when not in use. The key to the box, and that of the drawer or cupboard where it is kept, are held by the person in charge of petty cash.

(b) Petty Cash Vouchers

Even though the sums involved are small, money can only be taken out of the cash box for expenditure which has been authorized by a senior member of staff. Petty cash vouchers (Fig. 13.1) are completed and signed by the person to

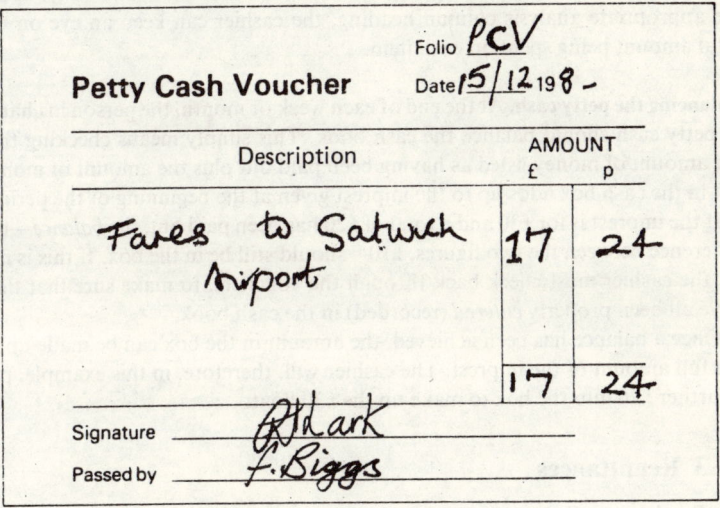

Petty Cash Voucher	Folio *PCV* Date *15/12* 198 –		
Description		AMOUNT £	p
Fares to Saturch Airport		17	24
		17	24
Signature	*R H ark*		
Passed by	*F. Biggs*		

Fig. 13.1   A petty cash voucher

whom payment is to be made. They must also be signed by the person authorizing the payment.

The voucher is handed to the person in charge of petty cash, who keeps it as a record of where the money has gone. The amount stated on the voucher is paid over to the person claiming it.

(c) Receipts

When you are buying things for which petty cash is used, you should ask for a receipt from the shop. Such receipts should be handed in to the person in charge of petty cash, as proof that the money was used for the purpose stated.

Sometimes you may be expected to pay out of your own pocket when making a purchase, and you may only be reimbursed (paid back) out of the petty cash if you produce both a receipt and an authorized petty cash voucher.

(d) The Petty Cash Book

Each week or month, the person who holds the petty cash is given an *imprest*— a loan, advance or *float*. This is a sum of money which is estimated to be enough to cover the expenses for the period. The amount is recorded in the 'cash received' columns of a cash book (Fig. 13.2), together with the date on which the payment was made.

When a properly authorized petty cash voucher is received, the details are recorded in the petty cash book, showing in the appropriate columns the nature of the expenditure, the number of the voucher and the amount paid out. Sometimes the amount is shown again in an *analysis column*. There may be one analysis column for postage, one for cleaning, one for fares, and so on through all the types of item for which petty cash is used. By listing the amounts under the appropriate analysis column heading, the cashier can keep an eye on the total amount being spent on each item.

Balancing the petty cash. At the end of each week or month, the person in charge of petty cash should balance the cash book. This simply means checking that the amount of money listed as having been paid out plus the amount of money left in the cash box adds up to the imprest given at the beginning of the period.

If the imprest is for £30 and a total of £20 has been paid out, the *balance*—the difference between the two figures, £10—should still be in the box. If this is not so, the cashier must check back through the vouchers, to make sure that they have all been properly *entered* (recorded) in the cash book.

Once a balance has been achieved, the amount in the box can be made up to the full amount of the imprest. The cashier will, therefore, in this example, put a further £20 into the box to make up the £30 float.

13.3 Remittances

(a) Remittances Outwards
Whenever one organization buys goods or services from another, it must pay for them. Cash, cheques or other forms of payment may be sent—*remitted*—in settlement of the debt. These outgoing payments are *remittances outwards*.

The organization making the remittance must record the amount and the reason for the payment, and the name of the supplier of the goods. This enables management to see which of its debts have been paid and which are still outstanding, and it also avoids the danger of paying for the same item twice.

The remittance is normally made through the firm's cashier. If a cheque or postal order is to be sent, it is generally accompanied by a *remittance advice*, explaining what the payment is for (see Fig. 19.1 on page 211). The remittance advice may be a portion torn off the invoice or request for payment submitted by the supplier, or it may be the organization's own remittance advice slip. If you are responsible for the dispatch of remittances outwards, check to make sure that both the payment and the remittance advice are enclosed, and that the amounts agree (are the same on each).

(b) Remittances Inwards
Whenever one organization sells goods or services to another, it must collect payment for them. These incoming payments are *remittances inwards*.

Envelopes containing remittances must be opened with care, and the contents

Left-hand page   Right-hand page

Dr.	CASH RECEIVED						CASH PAID												Cr.
		1	2						3	4	5						6			
Date	Details	Details	F	£	p		Date	Details	Details	PCV	Total £	Total p	Postage £	Postage p	Cleaning £	Cleaning p	Fares £	Fares p	Sundries £	Sundries p
198– 15 May	Imprest		CB1	30	00		198– 15 May	Stamps		111	3	20	3	20						
							18 May	envelopes		112	2	15							2	15
								cleaner		113	8	15			8	15				
								rail fare		114	4	00					4	00		
							20 May	Stamps		115	2	50	2	50						
										7	20	00	5	70	8	15	4	00	2	15
								8 balance	c/d		10	00								
		9	30	00						10	30	00								

Fig. 13.2 Petty cash book. 1. Where the cash was received from. 2. The page in the cash book on which the petty cash total is recorded. 3. What the money was spent on. 4. Petty cash voucher number. 5. Amount spent on each petty cash voucher. 6. Analysis columns, totalled separately. 7. Total spent (must be the total of all the figures above it, and will also equal the total of all the analysed column totals). 8. Amount left in cash box is carried down (c/d). 9. Total cash received. 10. Sum of total spent (7) and balance in cash box (8), which must equal the total cash received (9)

checked. In some organizations the remittance is initialled by the clerk who opens the envelope. The amount of the remittance and the sender's name may be entered in a remittances book, before the remittance and remittance advice are passed on to the accounts section. If money is later found to be missing, such records can help to trace it.

13.4 Security

Since cash is negotiable, it may be very difficult to recover it if it is stolen. So when you first start dealing with money, find out what your organization's cash handling procedures are, and stick to them at all times. Remember, if money for which you are responsible goes missing, your own honesty may be called in question. Here are a few basic rules.

(a) Never keep cash on a desk or counter where visitors or other staff can reach it.

(b) Never leave cash unattended, even for a few seconds. If you have to leave your desk, lock all money away securely first.

(c) Keep accurate records of all money paid in or out.

(d) Never 'borrow' money from your cash—even a few pence for the telephone. If you are caught, you may be dismissed on the spot.

(e) Never mix up your own money with the firm's. It's tempting, when you are short of change in your cash box, to take coins out of your own pocket, with the idea of recovering them later. If you are seen 'recovering' them, you could find it hard to prove that the money is rightfully yours.

(f) If you are receiving or paying out money to customers or staff, always count it out carefully in their presence so that no one can claim that you took or gave out the wrong amount.

(g) If you are giving change, always leave the cash that you have been given on top of your box, drawer or till, until you have counted out the right change. You cannot then be caught out by the customer who claims that it was £10, not £5, that he gave you.

(h) If you are handling remittances inwards, check amounts carefully. If the cash doesn't match the amount on the remittance advice slip, tell your supervisor immediately.

(i) If you are handling remittances outwards, avoid sending cash or other negotiable forms of payment through the post if at all possible; if this is absolutely unavoidable, make sure it goes in a registered envelope (see Unit 12.2 (a)). Wherever practicable, use one of the non-negotiable forms of payment (see Unit 13.1) available through the organization's bank.

13.5 Quick Questions

1. What do you understand by the words (a) legal tender, (b) denomination?

2. What does 'negotiable' mean?

3. Name two documents necessary for efficient handling of the petty cash.

4. What is an imprest? By what other names is it also known?

5. What are (*a*) remittances outwards, (*b*) remittances inwards?

6. List six things you should do to ensure security when you are responsible for money in the office.

13.6 Short Exercises

1. Find out the procedure for dealing with petty cash claims in your organization. Compare it with that described in Unit 13.2.

2. A new colleague seems to think that your office's security measures are a waste of time and an insult to his integrity. Prepare a list of points you would make in order to persuade him to change his mind.

Unit Fourteen

Methods of Payment

14.1 Introduction

Where does your organization keep the money that people pay into it? One possibility is to store all the notes and coins in a huge strongroom and leave it there until it is needed. Another is to pay it into a bank, and draw it out when wanted. Most business organizations choose this second method, for four main reasons:

(a) Money is safer in a bank.

(b) No storage space is needed on the firm's premises.

(c) When money has been paid into a bank account, it is no longer necessary to trade in cash: cheques and bank transfers can be used instead. This is quicker and safer than carrying stocks of cash.

(d) Banks offer a range of other services which can assist the organization, such as lending it money and providing financial advice, and the payment methods discussed in Units 14.5 and 14.6.

You will find full details of how the banking system works in *Success in Elements of Banking*. Here we are concerned with the range of services offered to current account holders (as opposed to people saving money on deposit), at the high street banks or *clearing banks*.

14.2 Cheques

When an individual or an organization opens a bank account, the bank issues a cheque book. Each cheque bears a *serial number* in its bottom left-hand corner. A missing cheque can be identified by looking for the missing serial number. The bank's *branch code number* and the account-holder's own *account number* also appear along the bottom of the cheque.

When the account-holder wishes to make a payment to someone, he or she writes out and signs a cheque. The person to whom the cheque is made payable is the *payee*. The account-holder is the *drawer* of the cheque. When the payee presents the cheque to a bank, the bank will accept it as authorization to transfer money out of the drawer's account—provided

(a) that there is enough money in the drawer's account to cover the amount of the cheque,

(b) that the cheque has been properly completed and is signed, and

(c) that the cheque is current. If it is dated more than six months ago, it is said to be *stale* and the bank will not accept it. Nor will it accept a *postdated* cheque, that is, a cheque that carries a date some time in the future.

If these conditions are not met, the cheque will be *referred to drawer*—that is, sent back to the drawer, so that the situation can be clarified.

There are various kinds of cheque.

(i) **Open cheques.** Fig. 14.1 shows an *open* or uncrossed cheque, properly completed: it bears the payee's name, the amount of money to be paid over (in

Fig. 14.1   Open cheque, with counterfoil

figures and in words), the date and the signature of the drawer. This cheque can be *encashed* (exchanged for cash) by the payee at the drawer's bank: it does not have to be paid into the payee's own bank account.

(ii) **Crossed cheques.** The cheque in Fig. 14.2 cannot be encashed at a bank. The two parallel lines across it mean that it must be paid into a bank account.

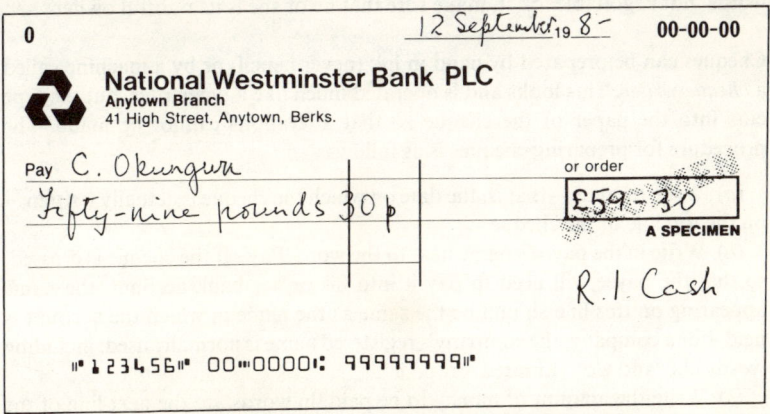

Fig. 14.2   Cheque carrying a general crossing

If the payee does not have a bank account, he or she can *endorse* the cheque, by signing it on the back, and can then pass it on to someone else in exchange for cash. A cheque with a *general crossing* can change hands in this way several times, so long as it is endorsed each time. But unless it comes to rest in someone's bank account within six months of its date of issue, it becomes stale.

The crossing on the cheque may be printed by the bank or drawn by hand by the drawer. Sometimes the words 'and Company' or '& Co' appear between the lines (Fig. 14.3).

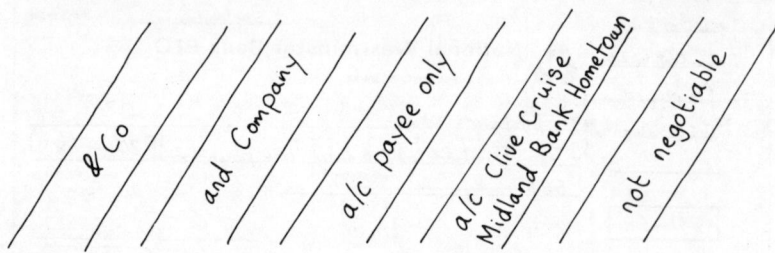

Fig. 14.3   Other cheque crossings

(iii) **Special crossings.** The words 'a/c payee only' may be written between the crossing lines to indicate that the payee cannot endorse the cheque and pass it on. It must be paid into his or her own bank account; alternatively, the drawer must be asked to use a different method of payment. The words 'a/c Clive Cruise at Midland Bank, Hometown' mean that the payee, Clive Cruise, can only pay the cheque into his account at the specified bank—Midland Bank, Hometown branch.

'Not negotiable' indicates that although the cheque can be endorsed and passed on, the person receiving the cheque has no more claim to the money than the person who passes it on. So if someone transfers to you a cheque with the words 'not negotiable' on it, make sure that he or she is its rightful owner.

Cheques can be prepared by hand in ink (never pencil) or by a machine called a *cheque-writer*. This looks and is operated much like a typewriter, but the type cuts into the paper of the cheque so that alterations cannot be made. The procedure for preparing cheques is as follows.

(*a*) Write the date—that is, the date on which the cheque is actually written—on the top line of the cheque.

(*b*) Write in the payee's name next to the word 'Pay'. If the cheque is crossed, so that the payee will need to pay it into his or her bank account, the name appearing on this line should be the same as the name in which the account is held. For a company, the company's registered name is normally used, including words like 'and Co', 'Limited' or 'p.l.c.'.

(*c*) Write the amount of money to be paid, in words, on the next line of the cheque, extending into the third line if necessary. The number of pounds is written out in full, followed by the number of pence as a figure: 'Two hundred and ninety-one pounds–68p', for example, as in Fig. 14.1. The word 'only' or 'stg' (sterling) may be added, to indicate that this is the full amount and to prevent anything being inserted; alternatively, a line can be drawn after the words.

(*d*) Enter the amount of money in figures in the box at the right-hand side of the cheque. Start writing close to the £ sign, so that no alterations are possible.

(*e*) Complete the counterfoil of the cheque, recording the amount of money that has been paid, to whom it was paid and on what date. Some cheque books have perforated counterfoils, ready-printed with the number of each cheque. Others have a separate section at the front in which you can keep a record. Make sure to keep a note of the number of each cheque.

(*f*) Submit the cheque for signature to an *authorized signatory*—someone who has the authority to sign cheques or to use the firm's cheque-signer machine to imprint the signature required by the bank on the cheque.

If you make an error while preparing a cheque, never erase it as this invalidates the cheque. Instead it should be altered or crossed out neatly, and the correction should be signed or initialled by the authorized signatory. If a cheque has been prepared by mistake, or if it contains several errors, it should be marked 'void' and a note should be made on its counterfoil to this effect. As the cheques in a cheque book are numbered consecutively, a missing cheque will be noticed and queried by your manager, so the void cheque may be either left in the cheque book or filed separately.

14.3 Paying-in

If your job involves handling remittances inwards, you may be asked to pay the amounts into a bank. You will need to use a *paying-in book* (Fig. 14.4), which consists of bank giro credit slips. Paying-in slips are provided in a variety of styles. Sometimes the bank giro credits are in duplicate or triplicate; carbon paper should be used to make the number of copies required. Alternatively, there may be a counterfoil attached to the voucher with a perforation for separation by the bank cashier: you keep the counterfoil as a record of the transaction. The procedure for completing the form is as follows.

(*a*) Write the date on the line at the top of the page.

(*b*) Enter your name and office reference number (if you have one) in the section marked 'Paid in by'.

(*c*) Check that the name and number of your organization's bank account is already stamped on the paying-in slip next to the words 'Account to be credited': if they are not, write them in. (The account number is stamped on the bottom line of your firm's cheque book. It is the last of the three groups of numbers at the bottom of the cheque, reading from left to right.)

(*d*) Count any £50 notes carefully and enter their total value on the top line of the *cash analysis*, the ruled part of the top right-hand section of the paying-in

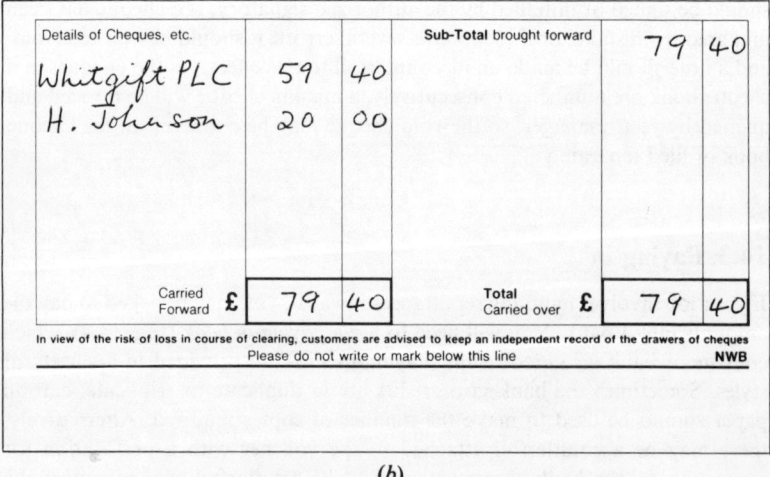

Fig. 14.4   Bank paying-in slip: (a) front, (b) back

slip. Thus, if there are four £50 notes, write in the figure £200.00. Then count the £20 notes and enter the total amount, followed by the £10, £5 and £1 notes, and any Scottish and Irish notes, and the various denominations of coin as specified in the analysis. After counting, make sure that the notes are stacked neatly in bundles with the Queen's head uppermost on all of them, and secured with the appropriate bank wrapper (supplied by the bank). Put the coins in bags as shown in Table 14.1.

(e) Add up the columns of the analysis and write in the total on the line marked 'Total cash'.

Table 14.1 How to divide up coins for bank paying-in

Coin denomination	Bags	Number of coins in each bag
£1	£20	20
50 p	£10	20
20 p	£10	50
10 p	£5	50
5 p	£5	100
2 p	£1	50
1 p + $\frac{1}{2}$ p (mixed)	50 p	50–98
$\frac{1}{2}$ p	25 p	50

(*f*) Check that this figure is the same as the total amount of cash you are paying in, by counting the money through again. If there are any discrepancies you must identify and correct them. You may have miscounted one group of notes when you were filling in the slip, or you may have written down a wrong number.

(*g*) On the back of the paying-in slip (or in the lower section of duplicate sheets) you will find space to list the names of the drawers of the cheques and postal orders you are paying in—that is, the people and companies from whom they have come. Usually the name appears in the lower right-hand corner of the cheque, above the signature. Large organizations often have their name printed across the top of the cheque.

(*h*) Write the name of the first drawer in the wide column; in the two narrower columns, write the amount of the cheque, as entered in figures in the box above the signature and in words on the body of the cheque. If the amount in words is different from the amount in figures, the cheque must be referred to the drawer, that is, the person who wrote it must be asked to say which of the two amounts he intended to pay.

(*i*) Carry on entering all the cheques you wish to pay in, making sure that it is clear which amount relates to each name.

(*j*) When you have filled in as many names as you can get in the first column, add up the value of the cheques and write the total against the words 'carried forward'.

(*k*) Enter the amount carried forward again at the top of the next column, as the amount brought forward.

(*l*) Carry on listing any remaining cheques on the right-hand side of the form.

(*m*) Add up the value of this second list of cheques, making sure to add in the amount brought forward at the top.

(*n*) Write the total where it says 'total carried over', and then enter that amount in the analysis section on the front of the credit, beneath the total of the cash, where it says 'cheques, etc'.

(*o*) Check this total against the total value of cheques, working quickly through the cheques and adding up the values. Investigate any differences.

(*p*) If you are using a paying-in book with a perforated counterfoil, enter the information from the summary columns again on the counterfoil. Use the back of the counterfoil to record, in shortened form, the names of the drawers of cheques and postal orders. (This procedure is not necessary if your book allows carbon copies to be made and retained by the account-holder.)

You can then hand the form and the money to the bank's cashier. He or she will count the money and check the value of the cheques against your entries on the paying-in slip and, when satisfied, will stamp and initial the counterfoil or carbon copies as proof that the money has been received. These must be kept in your office so that there is a record of what has been paid in. The amounts will be entered in the firm's own accounts ledgers (see Unit 19.2) and, in due course, will be checked against the *bank statement* issued to each customer by the bank.

14.4 Safeguarding Transactions

If your organization receives a cheque in payment for goods, it needs to be certain before the goods are dispatched that the cheque it has been given will be *honoured* by the bank.

(*a*) Cheque Cards
If the amount is relatively small, a bank will honour the cheques of those customers to whom a *cheque card* has been issued (Fig. 14.5). This is a small

Fig. 14.5 Cheque card

plastic card which bears the bank code number, the number of the cheque card itself and the date when it expires. Provided the cheque is correctly completed and is for less than the amount shown at the top of the cheque card, the bank will honour the cheque even if the drawer does not have enough money in his account to cover it, as long as the regulations printed on the back of the cheque card have been observed. The regulations require:

    (i) that the cheque is completed in the payee's presence;

    (ii) that the signature and the code number on the cheque correspond to those on the card;

(iii) that the cheque is dated before the card's expiry date;
(iv) that the card number is written on the back of the cheque by the payee.

(b) Special Clearance

Several days usually elapse between a cheque being paid into the bank and the amount being *credited* (added on to) to the payee's account. This is because the cheque must first be *cleared* through the drawer's bank, to ensure that there is money in the account to cover it. Only then is the payment transferred into the payee's bank account. Where the goods or services must be supplied before this clearing process is complete, the payee faces the risk that he may part with the goods, only to find that the cheque he has been given has 'bounced' – that is, that it has not been honoured by the drawer's bank, or that it has been stopped or cancelled by the drawer.

The special clearance facility allows the speeding up of the clearing process. On payment of a fee, the payee can find out whether or not a cheque will be honoured, usually within a day of presenting a cheque to his bank.

(c) Bank Drafts

A bank draft is a cheque drawn on a bank itself. The customer pays the amount to the bank, or it is *debited* to (deducted from) his account, and the cheque is issued for the required amount. Because it is drawn on a bank the cheque is acceptable to any person or organization: there is thus no need to allow time for clearance to ensure that the cheque will be honoured.

14.5 Bank Giro: Payment without Cheques

Cheques are not the only means of making payments through the clearing banks. With the bank giro credit system, individual cheques are unnecessary and there are none of the delays, risks and postage costs that arise when cheques are sent from one person to another.

The person making a payment authorizes the transfer of a specific sum on a

From National Westminster Bank		bank giro credit	
Branch WESTTOWN		Date 15/4/8-	
Destination Branch Sort Code	Bank and Branch	Account and Account Number	Amount
99 99 99	National Westminster Bank 41 High Street Anytown	Costalot Ltd 99999999	£ 444-44
By order of Live Wire Electrics Ltd			
NWB1814 Rev May 81-1			

Fig. 14.6 Bank giro credit slip

particular date to the accounts of the payees (or *beneficiaries*), whether or not the beneficiaries have their accounts at the same bank or branch. To make a payment using the bank giro credit system you need:

(*a*) cash or a cheque for the total amount to be transferred;
(*b*) a *bank giro credit slip* for each payment (Fig. 14.6).

Payments can be made singly, or to several beneficiaries at once.

(i) **Single payments.** Where payment is being made to one person, the procedure is similar to that for paying in cash or cheques to the firm's own account. You need to know the name, address and branch sort code of the payee's bank, the name in which the payee's account is held and the account number. These must be written or typed on a bank giro credit slip. The credit slip, together with cash or a cheque, should be handed to the bank cashier. (If you use cash, you can make bank giro payments without having a bank account.) The bank will pass the details to the payee's bank and the amount will appear on his or her next bank statement. The sum paid is deducted from the drawer's account. The beneficiary can be notified that payment has been made by sending a separate *advice slip*.

(ii) **Multiple payments.** Many firms use the credit transfer system to make several payments at once. Salary payments are an example. Management instruct the bank to make payments from the firm's account to the accounts of their employees on a monthly or weekly basis. This can be done even if the employees bank elsewhere. The firm asks staff for the name, address and sort code number of their bank, and for their account number. Individual bank giro credits and a list of beneficiaries are then prepared, together with one cheque for the total amount, which is to be charged to the firm's account, and the bank does the rest.

The system can also be used for payments to any other firms or individuals to whom the organization owes money, provided the relevant information about their banks and accounts is known.

(iii) **Electronic funds transfer.** Where very large numbers of payments have to be made, the computerized system operated by *Bankers' Automated Clearing Services Ltd* (BACS) can be used. Instead of providing the bank with individually prepared bank giro credits, all the information for the payments is supplied to BACS in the form of a magnetic tape, cassette or diskette produced by the firm's computer section. It is processed electronically through the banks' computers.

14.6 Other Payment Methods

There are other ways in which money may be transferred from one account to another without the use of cheques. These include the standing order system, the direct debit system and the use of credit cards.

(a) The Standing Order System

The bank, if authorized by the account-holder, transfers a fixed amount regularly on a specified date, to another account.

(b) The Direct Debit System

The bank, again if authorized by the account-holder, transfers differing amounts to another account, at the request of the payee. (Both these methods are described in more detail in *Success in Elements of Banking*.)

(c) Credit Cards

These are issued by the major banks to their customers: in the United Kingdom the two best-known cards in use are Barclaycard and Access. The card-holder is given a small embossed plastic card (Fig. 14.7), and assigned a credit limit.

Fig. 14.7   Access card

The card-holder may use the card to make purchases up to the value of this credit limit, without writing cheques or paying cash. He or she simply gives the credit card to the seller, who uses a hand press to transfer an impression of the card on to a pad of triplicate record slips. A description of the items purchased, and their value, is entered on the slip by the seller, and the purchaser signs the slip. The seller must make sure that this signature matches the one on the credit card and that the card has not expired. The purchaser is given one copy of the record slip and the seller keeps the other two.

From time to time, the seller sends off the record slips to the company operating the credit card scheme, and in due course receives a cheque for the value of the goods he has sold to credit card-holders, less 5 per cent commission. The purchaser is sent a statement from the credit card company each month showing him how much he has spent and requesting payment of at least part of the amount.

For the seller of goods and services, credit cards have three main advantages.

(i) The risk of fraud and non-payment is reduced. Once the seller has accepted payment by credit card the credit card company is bound to pay him for the goods.

(ii) Credit card transactions reduce the security problems that arise when large sums in cash have to be looked after.

(iii) Sales rise—customers are able to buy even when they are short of cash.

On the other hand, the clerical procedures required can be more time-consuming than with payments by other methods, and the seller must pay commission on each sale.

14.7 Making Payments Abroad

(a) Personal Payments
People who travel abroad on company business can pay for the goods and services they require in several different ways.

(i) **Cash.** Limited amounts of foreign currency can be obtained through banks and foreign exchange offices. The price of this money depends on the current *rate of exchange*, that is, the value of one currency in relation to another. Some governments restrict the amount of currency that may leave the country and some will not allow any to circulate outside their borders.

(ii) **Travel cheques.** These are a form of bank draft (see Unit 14.4(c)), obtainable in one country for use in another. You can buy travel cheques in sterling, US dollars, Japanese yen, Swiss francs and various other currencies. Fig. 14.8 shows a £20 travel cheque. The cheque must be signed when it is issued and again when

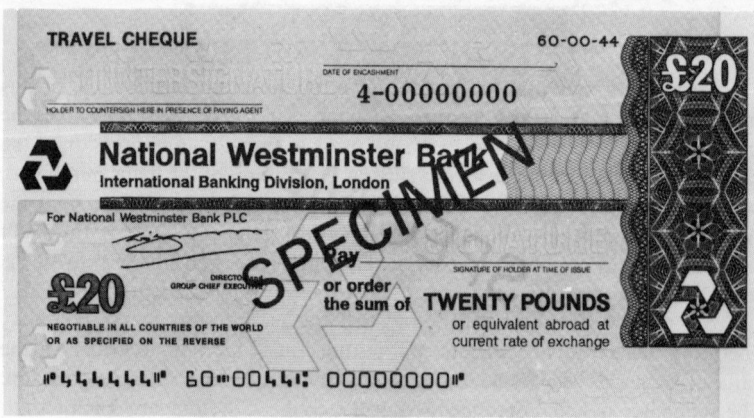

Fig. 14.8   Travel cheque

it is exchanged for goods, services or cash in another country. These cheques provide a secure method of payment for the traveller, as lost cheques can be cancelled and replaced by the issuing bank.

(iii) **Cheques with a Eurocheque encashment card.** Although the cheque cards issued by the banks to their United Kingdom customers cannot be used abroad, a special cheque card, the Eurocheque encashment card, is available to customers on application. Cheques drawn on the account for which the card was issued can be cashed at any European bank displaying the blue and red EC symbol. The amount cashed must not exceed £100 per day—£50 on one cheque, but two cheques can be drawn together.

(iv) **Credit cards.** Some credit cards, particularly the American Express card, are internationally acceptable. Access and Barclaycard, too, can be used to obtain cash from some banks abroad or, for example, to pay hotel bills.

(v) **International Giro.** National Girobank (see Unit 14.8) can also be used for making and receiving payments to and from other countries. Payment can be arranged even if the country to which you wish to send money has no Giro system of its own, but it is quicker where there is a Giro system at both ends. The payments can be made in the currency of either country, and the system can be used for both personal and trade payments.

(b) **Trade Arrangements**
When a firm wishes to buy raw materials or finished goods from abroad, the goods are *exported* from their country of origin and *imported* into the purchaser's country. *Customs duties* (see Unit 12.3(d)) may be payable; there may also be limitations on the type or quantity of materials that can be imported or exported.

There are four main ways of paying for goods and materials imported from other countries or of receiving payment for goods that have been exported to other countries.

(i) **Payment with order.** This is the simplest method of payment. The purchaser sends the amount due when he orders the goods. Instead of cash, he can send an *international bank draft* or *transfer*, which operates on broadly similar principles to the drafts and transfers we discussed in Unit 14.4(c).

(ii) **Open accounts.** If the exporter and the importer frequently have business with each other, they can trade on credit in the same way as local customers do. A statement is sent out at regular intervals, and payment is usually made by means of a bank draft or transfer.

(iii) **Bills of exchange.** A document, the *bill of exchange*, is drawn up by the seller of the goods. The bill instructs the buyer to pay the agreed price into a specified bank account within a certain number of days after receiving the bill. Fig. 14.9 illustrates the process.

(iv) **Documentary letters of credit.** Fig. 14.10 shows how these provide further assurances to the exporter and his bank, as the documents proving the ownership of the goods remain in their possession until a formal promise of payment

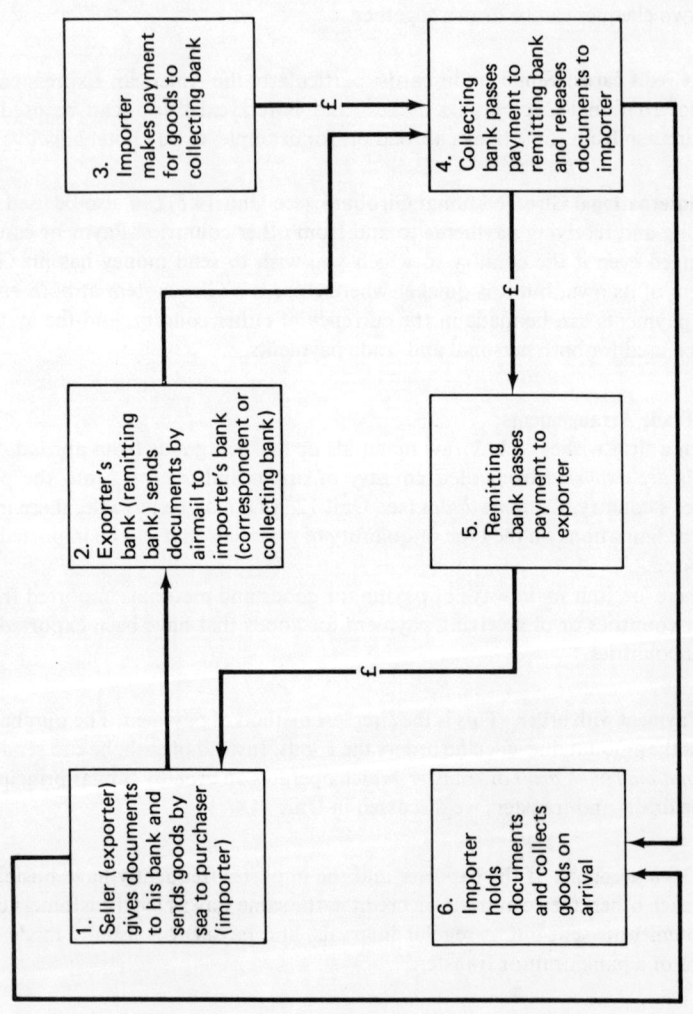

Fig. 14.9 Procedure for acceptance of a bill of exchange

1. Seller (exporter) gives documents to his bank and sends goods by sea to purchaser (importer)

2. Exporter's bank (remitting bank) sends documents by airmail to importer's bank (correspondent or collecting bank)

3. Importer makes payment for goods to collecting bank

4. Collecting bank passes payment to remitting bank and releases documents to importer

5. Remitting bank passes payment to exporter

6. Importer holds documents and collects goods on arrival

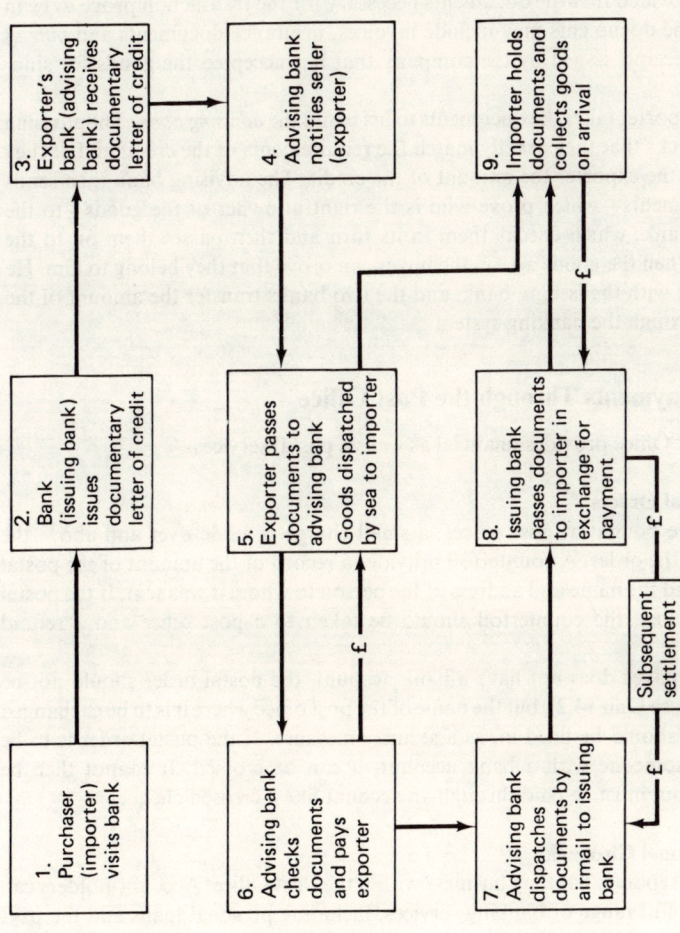

Fig. 14.10 Procedure for use of documentary letters of credit

1. Purchaser (importer) visits bank

2. Bank (issuing bank) issues documentary letter of credit

3. Exporter's bank (advising bank) receives documentary letter of credit

4. Advising bank notifies seller (exporter)

5. Exporter passes documents to advising bank

   Goods dispatched by sea to importer

6. Advising bank checks documents and pays exporter

7. Advising bank dispatches documents by airmail to issuing bank

8. Issuing bank passes documents to importer in exchange for payment

9. Importer holds documents and collects goods on arrival

Subsequent settlement

is received from the buyer. The system involves two banks. One, the *issuing bank*, acts on behalf of the purchaser of the goods, who is called the *applicant*. If the applicant is creditworthy—that is, he has some means of repaying the debt—the issuing bank issues a credit, not necessarily by letter, in favour of the seller of the goods (that is, the exporter, who is known as the *beneficiary* during the transaction). The credit is a promise that the exporter will be paid for the goods provided that the documents necessary for the transaction prove to be in order. The documents may include invoices, insurance documents and *bills of lading* (receipts issued by the company that has accepted the goods for shipment).

The exporter takes the documents to his bank, the *advising bank*. The advising bank checks that they exactly match the requirements of the credit and, if they do, pays the exporter the amount of the credit. The advising bank then sends the documents—which prove who is the rightful owner of the goods—to the issuing bank, which checks them in its turn and then passes them on to the buyer. When the goods arrive, the buyer can prove that they belong to him. He settles up with the issuing bank, and the two banks transfer the amount of the credit through the banking system.

14.8 Payments Through the Post Office

The Post Office provides financial as well as postal services.

(a) Postal Orders

These are bought at post offices; a small charge is made over and above the value of the order. A counterfoil provides a record of the amount of the postal order, and the name and address of the person to whom it was sent. If the postal order is lost, the counterfoil should be taken to a post office and a refund claimed.

If the payee does not have a bank account, the postal order should not be crossed (see Unit 14.2), but the name of the post office where it is to be exchanged for cash should be filled in, as a security measure. If the postal order is to be sent to someone with a bank account, it can be crossed. It cannot then be cashed, but must be paid through an account like a crossed cheque.

(b) National Girobank

This is a separate banking business within the Post Office. Account-holders can obtain a full range of banking services, including personal loans and the payment of standing orders. You may encounter the system at work in various circumstances.

(i) **If your organization has a National Girobank account.** Customers who have a Girobank account can make their payments for goods and services through the transfer service. The customer fills in a transfer/deposit form (Fig. 14.11(*a*)) with details of the payment, deletes the word 'Deposit' on the form and puts it in an envelope (supplied and postage paid by National Girobank) and posts it.

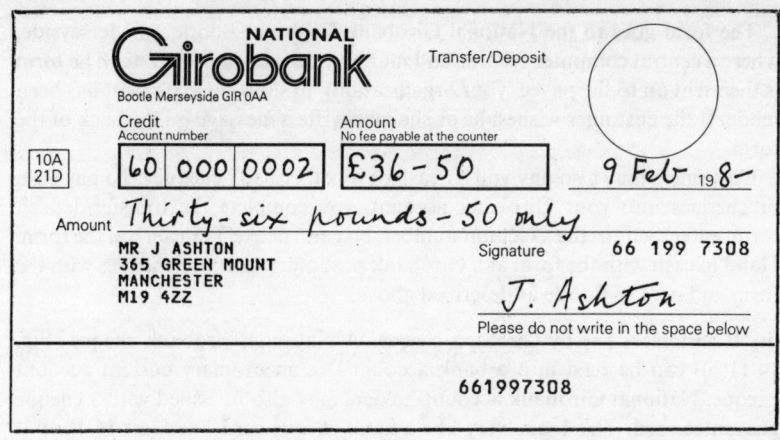

(a)

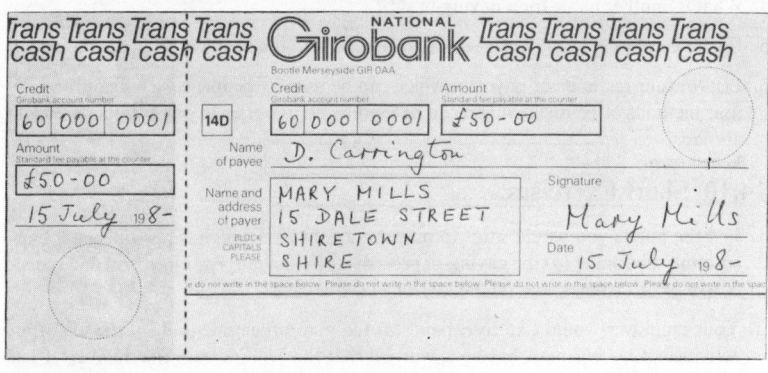

(b)

(c)

Fig. 14.11   National Girobank documents: (a) transfer/deposit form, (b) cheque,
(c) Transcash form

The form goes to the National Girobank Centre at Bootle on Merseyside, where a central computer records and monitors all such transactions. The form is then sent on to the payee (your organization), to show that payment has been made. If the customer wishes, he or she may write a message on the back of the form.

Customers may also pay you by cash or by other bank cheques. To pay cash or cheques into your Girobank account, you complete the transfer/deposit form, enter 'Self' in the 'Account number' box and delete'Transfer' on the form. Hand in cash with the form at a Girobank post office. Enclose cheques with the form and post to Bootle as described above.

(ii) **If customers pay by Girobank cheque.** A National Girobank cheque (Fig. 14.11(b)) can be paid into a bank account like an ordinary current account cheque. National Girobank account-holders may also be issued with a cheque guarantee card. This looks very like a bank cheque card (see Unit 14.4(a)); it operates in a similar way and, in addition, enables the card-holder to cash Girobank cheques of up to £50 at any Girobank post office or £100 at a nominated post office.

(iii) **If your organization makes payments to individual Girobank account-holders.** To make a payment from one Girobank account into another, the transfer/deposit form system should be used (see (i) above). If your organization has no Girobank account, money can still be credited to other people's Giro-bank accounts. A *Transcash form* (Fig. 14.11(c)) should be completed at the post office and handed in together with the cash to be credited. A small charge is made for this service.

14.9 Quick Questions

1. What is meant by the three groups of numbers at the bottom of a cheque?

2. What is the main difference between crossed and open cheques? Which is safer?

3. What is an authorized signatory?

4. What is another name for a paying-in slip?

5. List three ways in which a payee can make certain that a payment will be honoured.

6. List (a) four methods of payment which can be used by people travelling abroad, (b) four methods of payment which can be used by an importer to pay for goods bought abroad.

14.10 Short Exercises

1. List the points you would want to make to a colleague who has just opened a bank account, explaining (a) the paying-in procedure, (b) the purpose of general and special crossings on cheques, and (c) the uses of a cheque card.

2. Your employer would like to expand (a) the mail order side and (b) the exporting activities of his business, but he is worried that this will increase the number of bad debts and payment problems. Make brief notes of the points you could make in explaining to him how these dangers could be reduced.

Unit Fifteen

Towards the Paperless Office

15.1 Introduction to Computers

Much of the information which is stored and communicated in an office can be held in a form that you can neither see nor touch. Computerized information or *data* is not kept on paper, card or film, but is stored in coded form in the computer's 'memory' or on magnetic tape or disc.

The computer itself is a machine, a piece of *hardware*. It has to be told what to do with the data it is given, that is, it has to be *programmed*. These operating instructions or *programs* are the *software*.

(a) Hardware

Fig. 15.1 shows in chart form how the main parts of a computer interact. At the heart of the machine is the *central processing unit* (CPU). Part of this is used to store programs and information in the *memory*, the *main core* or *immediate access store*. Here, too, instructions given to the computer are decoded, in the *control unit*, and passed on to other parts of the computer. The remaining part of the CPU is the *arithmetic unit*, where calculation and other processing functions are carried out, and alterations to the program are made.

Computers do not have to store everything in the CPU. Additional data can be kept in a *backing store* until needed. This backing store usually takes the form of magnetic discs or tape.

There are three main types of computer.

(i) **Mainframe computers.** This is the name given to the biggest computer installations (Fig. 15.2). The CPU can occupy several large cabinets and may have to be installed in an air-conditioned room. It is linked to a number of *terminals*, which can be sited in offices some distance away from it. Each terminal has a keyboard, similar to a typewriter keyboard, and a screen or *visual display unit* (VDU), rather like a television set, which displays data that has been input via the keyboard or that is stored on a *file* on a tape or disc.

(ii) **Minicomputers.** As their name implies, these are much smaller than the mainframes; a minicomputer's CPU is small enough to be sited at a desk or *workstation* in the office, alongside the VDU and keyboard. Because of this they are sometimes referred to as *stand-alone* or *autonomous* machines. They can also be linked to a central mainframe if required.

(iii) **Microcomputers.** Modern manufacturing methods enable all the major components of a CPU to be packed on to a single silicon slice or *chip* approximately 6mm square, called a *microprocessor*. The same methods are also used in the production of memory microchips. The result is that a microcomputer

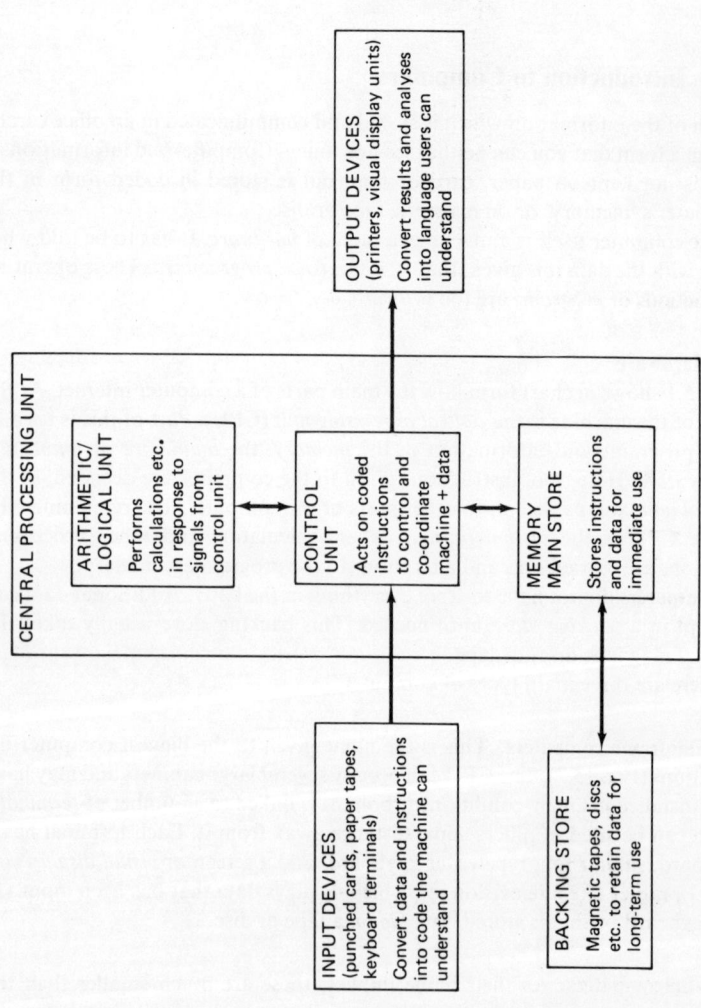

Fig. 15.1 *Basic parts of a computer*

CENTRAL PROCESSING UNIT

ARITHMETIC/ LOGICAL UNIT

Performs calculations etc. in response to signals from control unit

CONTROL UNIT

Acts on coded instructions to control and co-ordinate machine + data

MEMORY MAIN STORE

Stores instructions and data for immediate use

OUTPUT DEVICES (printers, visual display units)

Convert results and analyses into language users can understand

INPUT DEVICES (punched cards, paper tapes, keyboard terminals)

Convert data and instructions into code the machine can understand

BACKING STORE

Magnetic tapes, discs etc. to retain data for long-term use

Fig. 15.2 *Mainframe computer installation. 1. Printer. 2. Terminal. 3. Visual display unit. 4. Keyboard. The cabinets in the rear contain the central processing unit and its associated power supply and cooling equipment*

(Fig. 15.3), controlled by such a chip located under the keyboard, now possesses the computing power that was once only available on a mainframe computer, with the added advantages of great compactness, low power consumption and cheapness. Microcomputers can be connected to ordinary television sets instead of to a VDU, and range in scope from games and hobby machines for the home enthusiast to business systems capable of a wide range of tasks.

(b) Computer Software
If a business computer is to operate effectively, it must be set to work in the right way, and on the right problems. The operating systems and programs used for this are the *software*. Two groups of people are involved in the design of computer software.

(i) **Systems analysts/designers.** These are the people who identify how the computer might be able to speed up or enhance the efficiency of particular operations, and who work out what information is required and what procedures need to be followed to enable the computer to be used to best effect. They look at how information is processed at present, discuss possible improvements with those concerned, and draw up a specification.

(ii) **Computer programmers.** The programmer uses the analyst's specification

Fig. 15.3   Microcomputer. 1. Monitor for visual display. 2. Disc drives for floppy discs. 3. Keyboard. 4. Printer. 5. Hard copy

to work out, step by step, what the computer must be told to do in order to achieve the desired savings in time and cost. Every instruction must be given to the computer in the special *language* the computer understands—the statements, verbs and names that tell it what to do with information when it gets it. The most widely used of these languages is *COBOL* (Common Business-Oriented Language).

15.2 Input Devices

All the data which the computer is to store or process must be fed into the CPU in some way. The machines used for this are called *input devices*. Input devices for mainframe computers take four main forms.

(a) Punched Cards or Paper Tapes

These translate information from original invoices, orders and other documents into a series of holes punched in columns on pieces of card or paper. A machine with a keyboard is used to type in the required information, and this is then re-entered by another operator. The computer compares the two entries and indicates any differences between them; errors can then be corrected. A *card reader* is used to transfer data from the cards on to magnetic tape for input into the CPU.

This input method requires a team of punch operators as well as specialist computer staff to get information into the mainframe computer. For this reason it is sometimes referred to as *remote job entry* (RJE).

Neither punched cards nor paper tapes are now widely employed, but you may still encounter office systems that use them.

(b) Key-to-disc Systems

Key-to-disc systems accept data keyed directly on to a keyboard by an operator. Each operator works at a *keystation*, consisting of a keyboard together with a visual display unit which shows the operator the data that has just been entered or *keyed in*. The data can thus be checked easily, just as a copy typist can check the paper copy of a letter as it comes up through the carriage of the typewriter. It is then recorded electronically on a disc (these are discussed in Unit 15.4(*a*)).

The data is transferred from the disc to the mainframe computer's magnetic tape or disc automatically, and much faster than with any system using punched cards.

Both (*a*) and (*b*) require information to be input in batches, when enough data has built up to make an input session worth while or when a deadline has been reached.

(c) Optical Mark Recognition (OMR) and Optical Character Recognition (OCR)

Using a black ink ballpoint pen, a typewriter and a code-system of small horizontal marks (for OMR) or actual letters and numbers (for OCR) on specially prepared forms, data can be prepared for input into a computer without using punching or keyboard devices. Optical character readers are designed to recognize characters in certain type faces, printed or typed on plain paper. The reader scans the typed page, converting each character to a code that the computer can store in its memory.

(d) On-line Input

On-line input can be done directly by the members of staff of the department using the computer (the user department). This direct access input is achieved by means of *interactive terminals*. These again normally comprise a visual display unit and a keyboard, but the keyboard is capable of transmitting data directly to the mainframe computer. Codes and passwords can be used to make sure that a user does not gain access to confidential information held by the computer unless authorized to do so. Checking systems are incorporated to help to ensure the accuracy of input data.

Input to mini- and micro-computers is achieved directly via the keyboard and screen, the keyed-in data being stored in the computer's memory.

15.3 Output Devices

Information is retrieved from the computer by means of *output devices*.

(a) Visual Display Units

These can be used to call up information from the computer's memory. The required information appears on the screen when the user keys in the appropriate instructions (see Fig. 15.2).

(b) Printers

Where a permanent record of information ('hard copy') is needed, an electronic printer may be linked to the computer to produce *printout*. Printers, of which there are many different makes, are of three main types:

  (i) *high-speed printers*, printing a whole line at a time;

  (ii) *dot-matrix printers*, forming letters and characters from a series of tiny dots, at speeds of up to 300 characters per second;

  (iii) *daisy-wheel printers*, which print one character after another using a mechanism similar to the daisy-wheel typewriter (see Unit 5.7); their operation is slower than that of other printers but the quality of printing is higher.

Dot-matrix and daisy-wheel printers are those most often used in offices. High-speed and dot-matrix printers generally use continuous stationery, that is, a single long paper strip that will fold up concertina-style into collection trays and that can be torn off into manageable sections as required (Fig. 15.4). Daisy-wheel printers are best suited for high-quality business letters printed on single sheets of plain or letter-headed paper.

Fig. 15.4   Computer printout

(c) Computer Output Microfilm

Computerized data can be microfilmed and stored in an appropriate microform (see Unit 6.5). This can be done either by photographing the information on the VDU screen or paper printout, or by devices linked directly to the computer.

15.4 Computerized Information Storage

The computer's memory and backing store can be used as a substitute for a conventional paper or microform filing system. When someone wants to consult the 'file' it can be retrieved with the aid of one of the output devices discussed in Unit 15.3.

(a) Data-storage Devices
Besides the computer's internal working memory, various devices are used to store data in a computer.

(i) **Magnetic tape.** Data is recorded along the length of the tape, rather as sound is recorded on an ordinary tape-recorder. This was the medium for data storage for many years, especially for mainframe computers. It is still extensively used, especially for storing infrequently used reference data, for an unlimited amount of data can be stored on tapes that can be easily changed, and the tape itself is cheap. It tends to deteriorate in storage, however, and must be protected from stray magnetic fields while it is stored, because these can damage the records it contains. Its most serious disadvantage is that it can take a long time to search several thousand feet of tape in order to find a particular piece of information, and these delays are now largely unacceptable.

(ii) **Hard discs.** Data is recorded on concentric tracks on the disc surface, in much the same manner as on magnetic tape. The disc to be searched for a given record is put into a *disc drive*, where it rotates at high speed while a read/write mechanism moves across it. This allows any record held on the disc to be read or amended within a fraction of a second. Interchangeable disc packs may be used, with multiple disc 'platters' to each.

The advantages of this system include the high speed of data retrieval and the very large capacity of each disc; the discs must, however, be carefully stored in a very clean environment (dust or even smoke on the disc surface can cause the flying read/write head to damage the disc) and they are also sensitive to shock and vibration.

(iii) **Floppy discs (or diskettes).** These take the form of a flexible disc within a protective cover. They come in 8-inch and 5¼-inch (204- and 139-mm) sizes, and also as 3-inch (77-mm) 'minidiscs'; discs of the same size may be interchangeable. They are operated in much the same way as are hard discs, but their storage capacity is much less.

Floppy discs and the appropriate disc drives are cheap to buy, but the discs must be carefully handled and stored and the drives require regular maintenance.

(b) Advantages and Disadvantages of Computers

(i) **Advantages.** Computers have a wide range of advantages as a means of storing information.

1. Computerized filing systems take up far less space than paper filing systems of equivalent capacity.

2. Information can be stored and retrieved very quickly, so that real savings of time and staff costs can be made and office efficiency can be improved.

3. If necessary, two or more people may be able to examine the same 'file' on separate VDU screens, perhaps many miles apart, at the same time.

4. If data is to be processed or analysed by the computer at a later stage, it makes sense to use the computer's memory as an alternative to a conventional filing system in the meantime.

5. Computers are versatile, and can organize data in different ways. A printout or VDU screen can show you the same basic data presented either as a graph, or as tables of numbers, or in words. A very wide range of business software is now available, and a manager can choose a system matched to his or her department's particular needs.

6. Business software has become more 'user friendly', and users may need only a few hours of preliminary instruction, rather than detailed specific training in computer applications, in order to follow the programmed input directions or questions as displayed on the VDU. Several software manufacturers now make their products resemble 'paper' office procedures as far as possible, to make it easier for staff to make the change to computer use.

(ii) **Disadvantages.** Computers also have their drawbacks.

1. They can create large piles of printout, which may then produce its own storage problems.

2. If users do not have direct access to the computer, and other people have to prepare data for remote job entry, delays can arise and the confidentiality of information can be endangered.

3. Large computers are expensive to buy and operate.

15.5 Data-processing

Once the appropriate data has been fed in, providing a *data base*, the right computer, properly programmed, can help the management of an organization to make all sorts of business decisions.

Although all the questions the computer can answer could be dealt with by individuals working with pen and paper, this would take much longer. And the sooner that accurate information is available, the sooner effective decisions can be taken.

Computers are used to process many different kinds of information.

(a) Financial Information

The organization's accounts can be computerized and every transaction which takes place can be entered. The computer will work out how much is owed, and print out invoices and statements to be sent to customers (see Unit 19). The accountant can thus get an up-to-the-minute picture of the company's financial position.

The computer can also carry out calculations to tell management whether the business is making as much profit as planned, and whether any division or department is spending more than has been budgeted, while there is still time to put things right.

(b) Sales Information

Every time a customer places an order, information about the type and quantity of goods sold can be entered. The sales manager can therefore identify which items are selling well, and can compare the information with last year's figures, noting any patterns or trends that might help to predict future sales.

(c) Stock Control

The sales data can also help with stock control. The computer can record all the items available for sale, and then deduct every one that is sold from the total stock. Management can thus obtain a quick and accurate picture of available stock, and of how much it is worth, whenever it is needed.

(d) Production Information

The progress of each job that is carried out, or of each item that is made, can be monitored by the computer. Delays can be spotted, and the value of the work in progress ascertained.

(e) Personnel Planning

Every member of staff employed by the organization can have his or her personal details entered into the computer. The computer can then provide information about the numbers of staff with certain skills or experience, for instance, or the number approaching retirement age, as well as carrying out more complex calculations about employment costs, wages and so on.

In order to achieve all this, accurate information must be fed into the computer in the first place. Inaccurate input leads to inaccurate output—'garbage in, garbage out', as the Americans say.

This input data is usually taken from original documents of some kind— orders, invoices, correspondence and so forth. But there are ways in which information can be passed from one computer to another, between or within organizations, without the need for any paper documents at all. Groups of users can be linked together in an electronic *network*, comprising a series of terminals or mini- or micro-computers, a telephone system and other equipment. An important component of some network systems is the word-processor.

15.6 Text- and Word-processing

Computer technology is not just about numbers. Words, too, can be processed. Mini- and micro-computers can be programmed to do this, and many machines are *dedicated* to (used exclusively for) word-processing (Fig. 15.5).

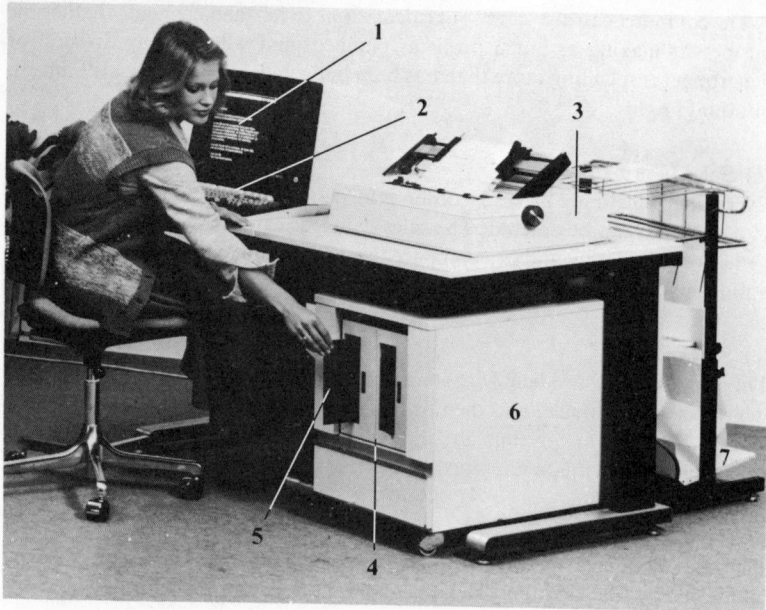

Fig. 15.5   Word-processor. 1. Visual display monitor. 2. Keyboard. 3. Printer. 4. Memory store. 5. Disc. 6. Central processing unit. 7. Continuous stationery

(a) Equipment

A word-processor installation consists of a modified typewriter keyboard, a VDU, a printer and a tape or disc store. There are two broad categories.

(i) **Stand-alone systems.** The operator works at a self-contained workstation which holds all the equipment needed to process any kind of text.

(ii) **Communicating and shared-logic systems.** Several operators, working at different keyboards, share access to the same computerized data base, that is, each is able to work on files stored on a central hard-disc storage unit.

(b) Uses

Word-processors can be used in several ways.

(i) **Standard letters.** Sentences, paragraphs and indeed whole letters can be stored on floppy discs. Suppose that the office manager decides that letters are to be sent to 300 people, all saying pretty much the same thing. The word-processor's software allows the operator to input the standard letter on to one file on a work disc, while all the addressees' names and addresses are input to another file. The machine then controls all the printing, putting each name, address and the appropriate salutation on as many copies of the letter as there are addressees, with little or no intervention by the operator.

(ii) **Text editing.** A document that has been keyed in and stored can be summoned to the VDU screen and altered. New passages can be added, and old information can be removed. The layout of the document can also be altered— to centre the headings, change the length of paragraphs, or justify the margins (see Unit 5.7(*d*)). The final version can then be printed automatically.

(iii) **Processing.** Data stored in the word-processor's memory (or taken into the memory from discs) can be combined with text. A report can thus be revised to include up-to-date information about, for instance, sales figures or staff numbers, and can then be printed out in a standard format. The machine itself will then perform the necessary calculations and fill in the results at the appropriate points in the text of the report.

(iv) **Electronic mail.** Shared-logic word-processors can be used to 'send' letters and other documents, without the need for paper, envelopes or stamps. A letter keyed into one word-processor in the system can be called up on the VDU screen of another. It can be read, and answered in the same way.

Letters sent electronically can be printed out by the printer at either end if necessary. Or they can be stored in the memory, or destroyed.

(*c*) **Advantages of Word-processors**

(i) **Easy editing.** The VDU screen of most word-processors allows you to see a full page of type, before it is printed. You can thus check the layout at a glance, and picture the effect of alterations or, if necessary, try them out. If the revised layout isn't an improvement after all, you can change it back again without retyping.

(ii) **Speed.** A trained word-processor operator can produce letters and reports in a fraction of the time a typist would take. This is partly because standard letters can be dealt with automatically, and partly because typing speeds tend to increase when an operator knows that errors are easy to correct. Checking, too, is quicker. Once a document has been checked for accuracy, it does not need rechecking the next time it is 'typed'. Only those parts that have been altered need be examined: if the rest was right before, it will be right now.

(iii) **Direct dictation.** A highly skilled word-processor operator can work fast enough to key-in a letter as someone dictates it. This speeds things up still further, and cuts out the need for shorthand dictation.

(iv) **High-quality output.** Even standard letters look as though they have been individually typed. Letters daubed with correcting fluid are a thing of the past. Mistakes are corrected on the screen, not on the paper.

(v) **Job satisfaction.** Word-processors can take away some of the repetitive element found in some typing jobs, and leave staff free for more interesting work.

(vi) **Cost-effectiveness.** Although word-processors are expensive, management can save money by making sure that all the parts of the system are fully used all the time. A printer, for instance, can be shared between several keyboards, and can be printing copies of one document while the operators are working on others.

(*d*) **Learning to Use a Word-processor**
If you are to use a word-processor effectively, you will need some special training. This can be provided by the supplier of the equipment; alternatively, your organization may arrange for you to take a recognized training course. The basic qualities you need in order to make a success of your training are listed below.

(i) **Fast, accurate typing.** A two-finger typist can use a word-processor, but not to best effect.

(ii) **An interest in the system,** to enable you to explore and exploit the equipment to the full.

(iii) **A high degree of concentration,** especially if you will be working in a large word-processing installation where there can be noise or distraction (although this may well be less than you might meet with in a typing pool).

(iv) **Transcribing ability and language skills,** to transfer information from short-hand, audio or longhand, with correct spelling, punctuation and grammar.

(v) **Communication skills,** to explain to the originators of the work you are processing the scope and limitations of the equipment and to help them to help you to use the equipment fully and effectively.

15.7 Viewdata and Teletext

If your own organization's computer systems cannot provide the information you require, you may find that you can obtain it through a national *viewdata* or *teletext* system.

(*a*) **Viewdata**
British Telecom's viewdata system, Prestel (a registered trademark), was the first public viewdata system in the world. By linking a television set—basically an ordinary set with certain modifications—to the ordinary telephone system and thence to a central computer store of information, British Telecom have brought the answers to innumerable questions out of the library and on to the television screen (Fig. 15.6). To use the system, you dial the Prestel telephone number and then use the special keypad to tell the computer which 'page' of information you wish to consult. This then appears on the screen.

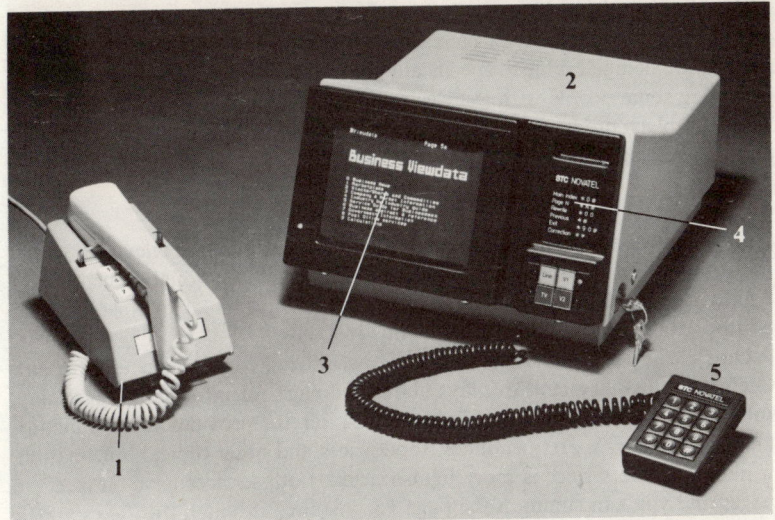

Fig. 15.6   Prestel system. 1. Telephone. 2. Receiver. 3. Television screen showing 'Business index' page. 4. Guide to Prestel symbols. 5. Keypad

The information contained in Prestel's 'pages' is provided by companies, Government departments, newspapers and institutions. The topics covered include, among many others, business courses, business and export information, commodity prices, exchange rates, government and industrial statistics, industrial relations advice, office equipment and services, pensions advice, shipping news and services, stock market reports, travel information and weather. All are updated frequently.

All these are listed in *The Prestel Directory* (published by Directel Ltd, Edgbaston House, 3 Duchess Place, Edgbaston, Birmingham B16 8NW). This provides alphabetical lists of subjects and of information-providers. Alternatively you can use the index which is built into the Prestel system. Users pay both a telephone call charge for the use of the telephone line and a time-based charge (cheap rates apply after 6.00 p.m. and at weekends). In addition, some of the information provided is charged on a page-by-page basis.

But viewdata is not just a one-way source of information. Through a system known as *Closed User Groups* (CUG), members of a group of subscribers can communicate with each other privately through viewdata, by keying in a special pass code known only to them. The Gateway system, for instance, uses the public viewdata system as a way into the computers of other businesses, banks, airlines, insurance companies and so on. The travel industry has quickly taken advantage of this kind of two-way exchange of information. The travel agent can summon information about fares, routes, departure times and ticket availability to the screen. When you have decided on your booking, the agent can make a reservation for you directly through the system.

Viewdata is still in its early days at the time of writing, and the range of information it can supply is increasing all the time. New types of viewdata receiver are being developed specifically for business users. Viewdata is already providing some people with the electronic equivalent of mail order shopping. They can place orders through the system, keying in a credit card number to authorize payment.

(b) Teletext Services

Unlike the two-way viewdata system, teletext services use the television screen for one-way information only. Ceefax and Oracle (Optional Reception of Announcement by Coded Line Electronics) are available to those with an appropriate television decoder and control set.

Oracle, the ITV service, covers news, weather, leisure and entertainment. Ceefax, the BBC system, displays about 500 pages of information each day, split between BBC1 and BBC2: the BBC1 service provides news bulletins, financial reports, sports headlines, food prices and other topical information, while the BBC2 service is more light-hearted. Both services have an index to pages and you can summon the page you require, although this takes a little longer than with Prestel.

15.8 Looking Ahead

Computers are finding their way into more and more parts of business life and this trend is likely to continue as hardware prices fall, the power of even small machines increases dramatically and the choice and versatility of software widens too. For managers thinking of buying computer systems, *communication between computers* is likely to become an important consideration and will play a large part in business management in the future.

For example, if many microcomputers within an office block are interconnected via a common network, each operator within the block can share the expensive resources of, say, hard disc storage, printers and external communications equipment. This last may be used to communicate via the telephone network to a central office computer and, indeed, to any compatible computer installation worldwide. The physical interchange of information on paper begins to become unnecessary. Electronic transmission is instantaneous, and is less prone to human error. Copies of documents can be stored on discs, and need only be printed if specifically required. Central data banks like Prestel can provide information on many subjects for little more than the cost of a telephone call.

Taking this trend to its logical conclusion, it might be imagined that computer communications could one day render the office obsolete, with all its staff working from computers installed in their homes. Although this is technically possible, most people need the social contact they get through working with their colleagues. The office may be changing fast, but it is unlikely to disappear altogether.

15.9 Quick Questions

1. State what the following sets of initials stand for: (*a*) CPU, (*b*) VDU, (*c*) COBOL, (*d*) OCR.

2. Write down what you understand by the terms (*a*) computer hardware, (*b*) computer software.

3. Name three functions carried out by the central processing unit of a computer.

4. What is (*a*) a stand-alone word-processing system, (*b*) a shared-logic word-processing system?

5. List four uses of a word-processor.

6. List three uses each of (*a*) viewdata, and (*b*) teletext.

15.10 Short Exercises

1. Make brief notes about the ways in which the introduction of a computer would change the work of *either* the sales office *or* the buying office (these are discussed in Units 17 and 18).

2. Your office manager is considering recruiting an additional typist, to help cope with the increasing burden of routine correspondence and reports, but is wondering whether a word-processor might be a better solution. Prepare some notes to help him in coming to his decision.

Unit Sixteen

Production/Operations

16.1 Introduction

Every organization exists for a purpose. The rest of its activities revolve around this central purpose, which may be the production of goods or the provision of services.

(a) Production

Manufacturing organizations exist to produce goods. Some small manufacturers make only one product—a specialist component for a machine, perhaps. Larger firms make a range of products—several different models of car or washing machine, for instance. Yet other companies have a series of different ranges of, say, refrigerators, freezers, ovens, extractor fans or washing machines.

For all these organizations, production of the right number of goods, of the right kind, at the right price, and at the right time, is vital. Once produced, the finished products must be stored until needed, and then distributed to the firm's customers. There should always be a large enough quantity of the product available to meet the regular demands of customers—delay in supplying the customer may mean lost business. But there should not be such large stocks that the firm has all its money tied up in products which it has no hope of selling for a long time.

The people who are primarily concerned with this 'making' activity are the *production* team of the business.

(b) Operations

Insurance companies work out the cost of insuring your life or your property, and agree to pay out a sum of money if you die or if your possessions are lost, stolen or destroyed. Shops buy and sell merchandise. Hotels and restaurants provide accommodation and food. Travel companies put together package holidays and sell air tickets.

The people primarily concerned with providing these services are the 'doing' or *operational* part of the organization.

All the other activities which we will consider in later Units are vital to an organization's success. But without production or operations, there would be no point in carrying on the business.

The procedures and documents used in service organizations depend very much on the type of services provided. Although manufacturing concerns vary, there are some features you will meet wherever you go.

16.2 Production Documentation

There are many different phases in the production of a product, and information is needed at every stage.

(a) Specifications
The design office draws up plans for new products or improvements to existing ones. These designs are converted into specifications, showing exactly how the item will be made.

(b) Progress Records
Once a product is ready to go into production (that is, a new 'job' is to be started), relevant details from the specification are entered on a progress record. This shows the order in which work on the job is to be done, and by whom and when it should be carried out.

(c) Job 'Cards'
The cost of each job must be carefully monitored so that management, and sometimes also the customer, can be kept informed. The amount of time spent by each craftsman, apprentice, labourer or machine on each part of the work, and the amount of raw materials used, are recorded on the supervisor's job 'card'.

(d) Stock Records
Completed products are added to stock, unless they have been made on a special order for a customer. The stock of each product is recorded on a stock record card. As each new item is completed, it is added to the list of stocks held in the stores or warehouse (Fig. 16.1). Stocks of raw materials or other items bought from a supplier (purchasing is discussed in Unit 18) are also held in store and stocks of these items must be recorded as well.

Item: *size 2 widgets*				Maximum stock	2 000		
				Reorder point	500		
		Receipts		Issues			
Date	No. received	Invoice	Supplier	No. issued	Requisition	Department	Balance in stock
15/6	2 000	K 2184	*Wills*				2 000
16/6				500	TP 1212	*Wheels*	1 500
22/6				1 000	TP 1294	*Spares*	500
25/6	1 500	K 6841	*Wills*				2 000

Fig. 16.1   Stock record card

(*e*) **Invoices and Requisitions**
When an item is sold, it is transferred from the warehouse or store to the *goods outwards* section of the dispatch department. A copy of the invoice on which the details of the sale are recorded (see Unit 17.2(*f*)) authorizes the warehouse staff to release the item. Other items which are needed for internal use may be released against a requisition (see Unit 5.5).

(*f*) **Delivery Notes**
Dispatch staff, drivers and packers use another document, the delivery note, to find out where and when the goods are to be delivered.

(*g*) **Delivery Schedules**
The dispatch office staff work out a delivery schedule, for regular journeys, and a daily delivery programme for each of the firm's vehicles.

(*h*) **Vehicle Maintenance Records**
For each of the firm's lorries and vans, records must be kept of insurance and road tax payments and of servicing and repairs.

(*i*) **Orders**
The dispatch department and stores also handle goods coming into the organization. Items bought from suppliers are delivered to the *goods inwards* section of dispatch and are checked against a copy of the order and against the delivery note which accompanies them.

If everything is in order, a copy of the delivery note is signed by the supervisor, and the driver who delivered the goods takes this back to his employer as proof that the goods were delivered.

(*j*) **Goods Received Notes**
Once the incoming goods have been checked and put in store, a goods received note is sent to the buyer and to the accounts department.

The records needed at each stage of production and distribution can be kept in any of the ways discussed in Unit 6. Alternatively, the whole production process from the design stage onwards can be recorded by a computer. So traditional records, like job record 'cards', may not actually be cards at all, but a computer printout or words on a VDU screen.

16.3 Production Office Procedures

We have space to deal only with some of the many different kinds of activity in which you may take part if you work in a factory or works office.

(*a*) **Work in Progress Queries**
Customers for whom jobs are in progress may call in to see when the goods will

be ready. You can find the answer by checking the progress record for that particular item.

(b) Costing

To find out how much each job has cost, you need to know:

(i) how many man- and/or machine-hours have been used (you will find the answer to this on the supervisor's job 'card');

(ii) what quantities of materials or components have been used (this, too, should be recorded on the job 'card');

(iii) the cost per metre (or per kilogramme) of raw materials;

(iv) the cost of each man-hour and each machine-hour. You probably won't need to know the exact hourly rate of pay of each worker who devoted time to the job: a standard formula is often used. So if the standard figure per man-hour is, say, £5, that should be multiplied by the number of man-hours. (One man-hour could be made up of one person working for a whole hour, or four people working for a quarter of an hour each.)

(c) Calculating Piece Rates

When the operators making a product are paid extra for working more quickly and producing more in a given time, they may earn extra money—a *piece rate bonus*. This calls for careful records of the number of items produced by each operator. Often quite complex formulae are used to work out how much extra the operator gets for each item produced.

(d) Stock Control

The purpose of stock control is to make sure that the right number of each type of product is always available. This is important, as otherwise the firm might find itself out of stock, and lose sales as a result. Too high a stock level means money tied up unproductively, and valuable space wasted.

Several steps must be followed to ensure that an accurate picture of the current stock position is always to hand.

(i) **Recording incoming stock.** This may be done either centrally, through the use of a *stock record card* index, punched card or computer system, or locally. A local system implies that a card (sometimes called a *bin card*) is attached to the rack where the product is stored; the quantity of incoming stock is written on the card.

(ii) **Recording outgoing stock.** Whenever stock is issued, the date, quantity and requisition number must be recorded—again on the stock record card (Fig. 16.1).

(iii) **Keeping a running balance,** so that you know how much stock is held. The final column of the stock record card shows this. A minimum stock level for each item is fixed at a level which allows time for the item to be re-ordered before it runs out (see Unit 5.5). When the balance in stock reaches the re-order point, an order must be placed immediately.

(iv) **Re-ordering when stocks run low.** Usually the stores notify the purchasing department, which in turn places the order with the supplier.

(v) **Stocktaking.** The running balance may not always be accurate, especially if a number of people have access to the stores, so from time to time a physical count will be necessary to check that there really are, say, 1 500 widgets in the bin. Spot checks may be made by the firm's auditors, to make sure that widgets are not unaccountably disappearing. Once a year at stocktaking an accurate count must be made so that the accountants preparing the final accounts can check the *book stock* (what the records say there should be) against the *physical stock* (what there actually is).

(vi) **Liaising with dispatch.** If the goods in the store or warehouse are sent to people outside the building, delivery notes or copies of requisitions must be passed on to the drivers who are to deliver the items.

16.4 Quick Questions

1. What is the main purpose of the production/operations department of an organization?
2. What is a specification?
3. List the main items of information required in order to cost a job.
4. What are piece rates?
5. Why is stock control important?
6. What is meant by (a) book stock, (b) physical stock?

16.5 Short Exercises

1. Read carefully the procedure for handling production documentation or, if you can, find out what the procedure is in your organization. Prepare a flow chart showing the main items of paperwork raised from the time when a job is started to its dispatch.

2. Prepare a list showing the home and business address of each member of your study group. With the help of a local map:

   (a) Plan the route that you would give to a driver who was to leave your study centre with a parcel to be delivered to each address.
   (b) Calculate the approximate journey time.
   (c) Calculate the approximate cost of the journey, assuming that vehicle costs (including petrol) are 14p per km and the driver is paid at the rate of £2.50 per hour. (The driver works from 8.30 a.m. to 5.00 p.m. and is entitled to a total of $1\frac{1}{2}$ hours break during the day. Any overtime is payable at time and a half.)
   (d) List the documentation that you will give to the driver, who is to be paid cash on delivery.

Unit Seventeen

Sales and Marketing

17.1 Introduction

However good the products and services supplied by the operational parts of the organization, people have to be persuaded to buy them.

(a) Marketing

Market research tries to identify how much public interest there will be in a new product or service. If management decides that a market exists, the goods will be produced or a service will be provided. The existence of the product or service must then be brought to the public attention.

(i) **Advertising.** Commercial television and radio, newspapers and magazines— the *media*—will, on payment of a fee, carry an advertisement for the product or service. Advertisements can also be placed on hoardings and billboards, or carried on buses or trains. For all except the simplest advertisements, professional copywriters and design staff are used. Many organizations advertise through a professional agency whose specialist staff design the advertisement and buy advertising space in the appropriate media.

(ii) **Special promotions.** People can be encouraged to buy a product by offering it at a very low price, or with a free gift or competition entry form.

(iii) **Mail shots.** Sometimes a leaflet or brochure is designed, explaining the product or service and its particular attractions. The leaflet can be distributed to the homes of potential customers (see Unit 12.6(c)) or handed out to shoppers in the high street.

(iv) **Presentations.** Existing or potential customers can be invited to attend a presentation, on the firm's own premises or elsewhere—a hotel or conference centre perhaps. Films, tape/slide presentations, leaflets and oral presentations can be used to explain the merits of the product or service and to convince customers that it is worth buying. More general information about the company and its other products can also be included.

(v) **Sponsorship.** Sporting events, such as a horse race or a golf tournament, can be sponsored by the organization, thus keeping its name, rather than any particular product, in the public eye. It is supposed that this increased public awareness helps to sell all the firm's products.

(vi) **Package design.** Some products will 'sell themselves' if they look attractive enough. The design of appealing packaging is also often a marketing activity; it is particularly important for processed foods, where the shopper is choosing from a row of apparently similar products on the supermarket shelf.

(b) Sales

(i) **Sales representatives.** The 'reps' deal directly with the firm's customers, persuading them to buy both existing and new products. They travel round a region or 'territory', visiting either homes or business premises depending on the nature of the products they are selling.

(ii) **Telephone sales.** Instead of travelling to see customers, some firms encourage the sales staff to contact customers by telephone, to discuss requirements, to bring new products to the customers' notice and to take orders.

(iii) **Sales office.** Customers who decide to place an order will contact the sales office, either direct or through the sales representative. The sales office staff check the details of the order and the availability of the stock (see also Unit 17.2(e)). They notify the warehouse that goods are required, and tell the accounts department the details for payment.

17.2 Sales Documentation

(a) Catalogues and Price Lists

All the products or services offered by the firm are listed in a *catalogue* or *inventory*. Each item in the catalogue has its own reference number. This is used by the sales staff and the customer, to avoid confusion when several similar products are available.

The price of each item is also listed, either in the catalogue itself or on a separate price list, if prices change frequently. The list should give both the basic price and any tax, such as value added tax (see Unit 19.5), which will be paid by the customer.

The catalogue and price list must be updated regularly, to make sure that the information they contain is accurate.

(b) Enquiries

Requests for information about the firm's products may be made orally to the sales representative or the sales office. Often, though, a potential customer writes a *letter of enquiry* (Fig. 17.1) to ask about the price or availability of a particular item.

(c) Tenders

When a potential customer wants several firms to compete for his business, he may ask the sales staff of each firm to submit a tender, giving details of what they could do to meet his needs, their delivery dates and their prices. Building contracts are often awarded using this method.

Power Point Products p.l.c.

55 Queen Street   Coventry   CO6 5QX
Telephone Coventry (0203) 46891
Telex 337677   P POINT G

Our Ref: M/PO/419/JG   16 February 19..
Your Ref:

Sales Manager
Live Wire Electrics Ltd
54 King Street
Gloucester
GL8 4VE

Dear Sir

<u>13 Amp Cartridge Fuses</u>

We are currently seeking a new source of supply for 13A ASTA

certified BS 1362 cartridge fuses for our 3 pin, 13 amp range

of plugs. Initially we require twenty thousand fuses with the

prospect of a regular monthly order.

Please send me your quotation, including your most favourable

terms and delivery arrangements.

Yours faithfully

B.R. Hickson

B.R.Hickson
Buyer

Power Point Products p.l.c.
Manufacturers of electrical power points
Registered Office: 55 Queen Street Coventry CO6 5QX
Registered No: 1073847 England
Directors: J. K. Brown, R. V. Wilson, M. Sherman, P. Sherman

Fig. 17.1   Letter of enquiry

(*d*) **Quotations**

Except where tenders have been invited, the initial letter of enquiry is answered with a quotation (see Fig. 17.2), which tells the customer how much the goods or services will cost, and the terms on which payment may be made. Some firms offer *bulk discounts*, meaning that a customer who buys a large enough quantity of goods will get each item at a reduced price. *Trade discounts* are offered to fellow-traders, who will need to *mark the goods up* (add more to the price at which they bought them) before passing them on to their own customers.

| 54 King Street
Gloucester
GL8 4VE
(Registered Office)
Registered No:
342921 (England) | *LIVE WIRE*
ELECTRICS
LTD | Telephone Gloucester (0452)
69413
Telex 794381 LIWIRE G
VAT No 421 1871 69
Bankers Midland Bank
173 High Street
Gloucester
Account No 51427159 |

QUOTATION

Ref SO/H 572/E   21 February 19..

To: Power Point Products p.l.c.
      55 Queen Street
      Coventry CO6 5QX

For the attention of B. R. Hickson Esq

In reply to your enquiry dated 16 February 19.., we have pleasure
in quoting as follows:

20 000 13A ASTA cert. BS 1362 cartridge fuses @ £3.50 per box
of 100 (as illustrated in enclosed catalogue, product no H619)

Delivery: 5 days from receipt of order: our transport

Terms: Trade discount 40%
       Cash discount 2½% for settlement within one month
                     5% for settlement within one week
       VAT standard rate

We look forward to receiving your further instructions.

Fig. 17.2   Quotation

(*e*) **Orders**

If the customer decides that the quotation is satisfactory, he sends his order (see Fig. 17.3) into the sales office. The sales office staff check the details of the order and make sure that the goods are available.

Power Point Products p.l.c.

55 Queen Street   Coventry   CO6 5QX
Telephone Coventry (0203) 46891
Telex 337677 P POINT G

ORDER: No. F5871

Date: 10 March 19..

To: Live Wire Electrics Ltd
54 King Street
Gloucester GL8 4VE

Please supply

Quantity	Description	Product No.	Price
	13A ASTA CERT		
20 000	BS 1362	H619	£3.50
			per 100
	cartridge fuses		

Deliver to our Goods Inwards Section, entrance at 46 Prince Street, Coventry.

B.R. Hickson

B. R. Hickson
Buyer

Fig. 17.3   Order

(f) Invoices

The sales office prepares an invoice (Fig. 17.4). There are usually five copies of this, and sometimes as many as eight. The document is laid out in a way that allows the price of the goods to be left off some copies, where the information is not needed. Price may be shown on the top three copies only. Copies of the invoice are distributed as follows:

(i) The top copy is sent to the customer. It is usually addressed to the accounts department if the customer is another business organization. Where regular orders are to be placed, the invoice is used as a means of notifying the

54 King Street
Gloucester
GL8 4VE
(Registered Office)
Registered No:
342921 (England)

LIVE WIRE
ELECTRICS
LTD

Telephone Gloucester (0452)
69413
Telex 794381 LIWIRE G
VAT No 421 1871 69
Bankers Midland Bank
173 High Street
Gloucester
Account No 51427159

INVOICE: No 018649/I

To: POWER POINT PRODUCTS p.l.c.
55 QUEEN STREET
COVENTRY CO6 5QX
Reference SO/H 572/E

DELIVER TO: PPP GOODS INWARDS
46 PRINCE ST. COVENTRY

YOUR ORDER NO: F5871

Product no: H619

Invoice date: 14 March 19..

Tax point: 14/3/..

To sale of electrical components

Quantity	Description	Unit price	Goods value £ p	Deduct discount @ 40%	VAT rate	VAT amount	Gross value (including VAT) £ p
20 000	13A ASTA cert, BS 1362 cartridge fuses	£3.50 per box of 100	700.00	£420.00	15%	£63.00	£ 483.00

Invoice value £ 483.00

Carriage: By our driver

Note: Our standard terms of business and conditions
of sale apply to this transaction

Cash discount: 2½ % for settlement within one month
5% for settlement within one week

Our statement will follow within one month

Fig. 17.4 Invoice

customer of the number and cost of the goods being sent on this occasion, rather than as a request for payment.

(ii) The seller's own accounts section gets a copy so that the details of the transaction can be entered in the accounts and the accounts staff know when to expect payment.

(iii) One copy is kept on the sales office file, in case any query arises and to provide sales information to management.

(iv) The sales office sends one copy to the firm's own stores or warehouse.

This authorizes them to release the goods, and may be kept for stock control purposes.

(v) The dispatch department gets a copy which serves as a delivery note, authorizing them to deliver the goods to the purchaser.

Where additional copies are *raised* (made), these may serve as:

(vi) duplicate delivery notes, to be kept by the customer after the goods have been delivered; or

(vii) advice notes, which are sent to the customer's purchasing department to advise that the goods are on their way.

(g) Credit Notes

If the goods which have been sold are not after all required by the customer and he returns them, undamaged, to the supplier, he is entitled to credit. The same applies if he is returning goods because they arrived in poor condition. Equally, if a customer has been overcharged on the invoice, he is entitled to credit (though the invoice itself must never be altered).

A credit note (Fig. 17.5) must be issued, showing the details, and copies sent to the accounts departments of both organizations.

CREDIT NOTE

Live Wire Electrics Ltd   No 1216/C
54 King Street
Gloucester   5 April 19..
GL8 4VE

Dr to:

       Power Point Products p.l.c.
Reference: SO/H 572/E   55 Queen Street
       Coventry
       CO6 5QX

Invoice No: 018649/I   Order No: F5871   VAT No: 421 1871 69

Date	Description	Product number	Amount
19.. 14 March	2 crates 13A fuses	H619	£120.00

Fig. 17.5   Credit note (usually printed in red)

(h) Debit Notes

If the customer has been undercharged for the goods—either in error or because of a price change—a debit note (Fig 17.6) must be sent. Again, the accounts departments of both organizations must get copies.

```
                     DEBIT NOTE

Live Wire Electrics Ltd              No 451
54 King Street                         13 December 19..
Gloucester
GL8 4VE                        Dr to:
                               Power Point Products p.l.c.
Reference:  SO/H 572/E         55 Queen Street
                               Coventry
                               C06 5QX

Invoice No: 32146     Order No: 516     VAT No: 421 1871 69
```

Date	Description	Amount
19.. 1 December	Undercharge	£ 21.09

*Fig. 17.6   Debit note (**usually printed in black**)*

(i) Day-books

Each order received may be entered in a day-book. This day-by-day record shows the name of the customer, the order number, the invoice number and the value of the order. It serves as a quick means of checking whether an order has actually been received and an invoice issued.

17.3 Sales Office Procedures

If you work in sales, you must understand your own organization's sales systems thoroughly. You will also need to develop a friendly and efficient manner when dealing with customers and other departments.

The activities in which you may become involved include:

(a) **Telephone enquiries.** Customers may telephone to ask for a catalogue or a quotation, or to check the progress of their orders. You need to be familiar with the layout and contents of the catalogue, and listen carefully to what the customer wants.

(b) **Work in progress.** If a customer wants to know when to expect delivery, you can trace how far the goods have got, partly from the sales office's own paperwork and partly by liaising with the production and warehouse staff.

(*c*) **Checking orders.** You must make sure that the details tie in with those in the quotation.

(*d*) **Preparing advice notes and invoices.** All details, especially sizes and prices, must be checked against the order and the quotation.

(*e*) **Updating catalogues and price lists.**

(*f*) **Liaising with sales representatives and dispatch.**

(*g*) **Analysis of sales figures.** This may be particularly important immediately after an advertising campaign: management will need to know whether the advertising has increased sales of a product, and who is buying it.

(*h*) **Liaising with the accounts section,** and providing them with accurate information on all transactions. This is very important if customers are to be charged the right amount for the goods they have bought.

(*i*) **Filing.** All orders and copy invoices must be filed in the right place, so that they can be found when wanted. Once an order has been dealt with, its records may be transferred from a 'live' file to a 'completed orders' file.

17.4 Quick Questions

1. What is the main purpose of the sales department of an organization?
2. List six ways in which the marketing department of an organization can bring its products to the attention of potential customers.
3. What are the 'media'?
4. List six important documents used in the sales office.
5. To whom are the copies of an invoice usually sent?
6. What is (*a*) a credit note, (*b*) a debit note?

17.5 Short Exercises

1. Read carefully the procedure for handling sales office documentation or, if you can, find out what the procedure is in your organization. Prepare a flow chart showing the main items of paperwork raised from the initial enquiry to the dispatch of the goods or the supply of the services.
2. Your study group has decided to organize a disco for 500 people. How will you set about marketing this event, and what systems will you need to set up the sale and recording of the tickets?

Unit Eighteen

Purchasing

18.1 Introduction

The purchasing manager, or *buyer*, of an organization is responsible for buying the things the organization needs in order to make and sell its products. There are four main kinds of purchase.

(a) Raw Materials
In a manufacturing business, the components and materials from which its products are made must usually be bought from other firms.

(b) Capital Equipment
The machines (*plant*) needed to produce the goods, together with other types of equipment—computers, copiers, typewriters, food- and drink-vending machines—must also be purchased. These are some of the firm's *assets*.

(c) General Supplies
Office stationery and food for the canteen come into this category. They are used or consumed during the process of keeping the business running, and are sometimes referred to as *consumable items*.

(d) Services
Cleaners, caterers, office removers, shop-fitters, painters and decorators may be hired on either a regular or an occasional basis. The buyer may be responsible for arranging the appropriate contracts for such services and for negotiating the best price for the supply of essential services like electricity.

If you work in the buying or purchasing office, you will meet much of the documentation we discussed in Unit 17, but you will be looking at it all from the other side.

18.2 Purchasing Documentation

(a) Requisitions
These are internal documents, used when a department requires new supplies or equipment (see Fig. 5.4 on page 68). The requisition is signed by someone in authority in the user department, and must contain precise information about make, type, quantity, size and so on, so that the buyer can see what is required. For complex components and equipment, a very exact specification is needed; this is generally put together after detailed discussions between the buyer and the manager of the user department.

(b) Trade Guides and Directories
Purchasing staff can track down possible sources of supply by looking up the item needed in the classified section of a directory such as *Kelly's Directory of Manufacturers and Merchants*. This is available in most public libraries, or direct from Kelly's Directories Ltd, East Grinstead, Sussex.

(c) Letters of Enquiry
When a possible supplier has been identified, a letter is sent, or a telephone call is made, to enquire about prices, delivery and suitability. A letter of enquiry (see Fig. 17.1 on page 199) usually includes details of size and quantity, taken from the requisition or specification.

(d) Catalogues, Price Lists and Quotations
Sometimes the letter of enquiry prompts the supplier to send back a catalogue and a price list. For more complex items, or where the buyer has asked for a special price, a precise quotation (Fig. 17.2) is sent.

(e) Orders
When the buyer and/or user department have decided which of the suppliers can best meet their needs, they will place an order. This is normally done by means of a preprinted form (Fig. 17.3). Sometimes the supplier sends a blank order form with the quotation; sometimes the buying department uses its own standard form.

Information for writing the order is taken from the quotation or catalogue on the one hand, and the requisition or specification on the other. It must be checked carefully, to make sure that it is right in every detail. Several copies of the order are needed. They are sent to:

(i) the supplier, to tell him what is required where and when;

(ii) the buyer's own dispatch department (goods inwards section), so they know what deliveries to expect;

(iii) the warehouse or stores, to tell them to expect new stock and give them time to prepare storage space;

(iv) the accounts department, so that they can check the details against the supplier's invoice and statement when they arrive, before making the appropriate payment;

(v) the buyer's own file, in case of future queries. The orders are usually kept in date order (chronologically). From time to time the buyer will check to see which orders remain outstanding, and will 'chase' those suppliers whose deliveries are overdue.

(f) Invoices
When the invoice (Fig. 17.4) arrives from the supplier, the details must be checked against the order. Sometimes this is the responsibility of the buying office, sometimes that of the accounts department. Any difference between the two documents must be queried. The invoice is passed to accounts for payment, or to await the supplier's statement at the end of the month.

(g) Day-books
As in other parts of the organization, a day-by-day record may also be kept as a quick means of checking the date and details of orders placed.

18.3 Purchasing Office Procedures

Liaison with other people, inside and outside the organization, calls for good communication skills and a clear understanding of your own company's systems. In addition, you may be asked:

(a) to check quotations against requisitions or specifications;

(b) to prepare order forms, which will be signed by the buyer or purchasing manager;

(c) to check advice notes and/or invoices received from suppliers;

(d) to file orders, advice notes and invoices;

(e) to query overdue orders.

18.4 Quick Questions

1. What is the main purpose of the purchasing or buying department of an organization?

2. List four kinds of purchase made by the buying department.

3. What is the name given to the document which a department sends to a buyer when goods are to be purchased on its behalf?

4. List six important documents used in the purchasing office.

5. Where does the information for writing an order come from?

6. To whom are the copies of an order usually sent?

18.5 Short Exercises

1. Read carefully the procedure for handling purchasing office documentation or, if you can, find out what the procedure is in your organization. Prepare a flow chart showing the main items of paperwork raised from the receipt of a requisition or specification to the delivery of the goods.

2. When invoices arrive from suppliers, should they be checked by the buying department or by the accounts department? Review the arguments for and against your decision, and make brief notes.

Unit Nineteen

Accounts

19.1 Introduction

When goods and services pass from seller to buyer, money (or some other form of payment) passes from buyer to seller. But when dealing with other businesses firms do not usually send cash with their order (cwo). Nor do they pay immediately they receive the goods (cash on delivery, COD). Instead they trade on *credit*. At regular intervals, or on an agreed date, the buyer *settles his account*, that is, he pays the seller for all the goods or services received during that payment period.

Both the buyer and the seller must record the payments they have made and received: this is what the accounts section of a business is for. The information kept in the accounts department has various purposes:

(*a*) to identify who owes money to the organization—overdue payments must be collected, or the organization will run out of money;

(*b*) to identify who the organization owes money to—overdue debts must be settled or the organization will end up in court;

(*c*) to identify whether the amount of money coming into and held by the organization is greater than the amount going out—that is, whether the firm is *solvent* (it is illegal for a business to carry on trading when it has no money to pay its debts);

(*d*) to enable the performance of the business to be monitored by its owners and managers, so that they can make sensible business decisions;

(*e*) to enable the tax authorities to assess the tax which the business must pay to the state;

(*f*) to comply, in the United Kingdom, with the requirements of the Companies Acts (see Unit 1.8(*c*)), and with the corresponding legislation in other countries.

The first two of these purposes are those with which you are most likely to be concerned. The others are normally the job of qualified accountants.

19.2 Sales Ledger

Dealings with customers are recorded in the *sales ledger*. Strictly speaking, a ledger is a large book, usually leather-bound, but in fact very few organizations keep their accounts in books like this nowadays. Mechanized accounting (see Unit 19.6) has largely taken over from the heavy volumes of earlier years. But old names take a long time to die out.

In the sales ledger, each customer has a separate numbered page or card or computer identification code. This is the customer's *account* with the supplier. The procedure for keeping the sales ledger is as follows.

(a) Invoices

When the sales office has agreed a sale, a copy of the invoice is passed to the accounts section.

(b) Credit Notes

If a customer has been overcharged, or charged for goods he has not had, a credit note is raised (Fig. 17.5, page 203).

(c) Debit Notes

If a customer has been undercharged or not charged at all, a debit note is raised (Fig. 17.6).

(d) Sales Day-book

Details of invoices and of credit and debit notes are recorded in the sales day-book. This is a book of *original entry*, so called because it is the first place where information from many different original documents—invoices to all organizations that have purchased goods—is brought together and entered in one place.

The day-book provides a permanent record of each day's transactions. Each entry contains:

  (i)   the customer's name and account number;
 (ii)   a brief description of the items sold;
(iii)   the price of each item;
(iv)   the total value of the order.

(e) Posting to the Ledger

Information from the sales day-book is *posted* to the appropriate account. This means that it is entered on the customer's own page or card—this is his or her *personal account* and bears an account number. Most of the entries in the sales ledger are *debit entries*, that is, they indicate that the customer, who has *received* goods or services from the selling organization, owes it money. A few are *credit entries*, where a credit note has been raised or payment received—that is, the customer has *given* money to the seller (see (*l*) below).

(f) Balancing

The difference between the total of the debit entries in the customer's account and the total of the credit entries is the *balance*. If the debit entries add up to more than the credit entries, this is a *debit balance*—that is, the customer owes money.

If the credit entries in the customer's account add up to more than the debit entries, this is a *credit balance*—that is, money is owed to the customer.

Mechanized accounting systems (see Unit 19.6) keep a running balance, so you can see at a glance the state of the customer's account. Where accounts are kept by hand, the debit and credit entries must each be totalled and the balance calculated regularly.

(g) Statements

At regular intervals, usually monthly, the customer is asked to pay off the outstanding debit balance—that is, to pay the amount he owes. A statement is issued as a request for payment. The statement is, in effect, a copy of the relevant part of the sales ledger account. It lists all the invoices, debit and credit notes issued during the month, and shows any payments received. The balance is the amount which the customer must pay (Fig. 19.1). A perforated remittance advice is often attached to this statement.

---

54 King Street
Gloucester
GL8 4VE
(Registered Office)
Registered No:
342921 (England)

LIVE WIRE ELECTRICS LTD

Telephone Gloucester (0452) 69413
Telex 794381 LIWIRE G
VAT No 421 1871 69
Bankers Midland Bank
173 High Street
Gloucester
Account No 51427159

STATEMENT

10 April 19..

TO: POWER POINT PRODUCTS p.l.c.
55 QUEEN STREET
COVENTRY CO6 5QX
Reference SO/H 572/E

Terms 2½% for settlement within one month
5% for settlement within one week

Date	Reference no (invoices debit notes, credit notes)	Details	Debits £ p	Credits £ p	Balance £ p
14.3...	018649/I	to goods	483.00		483.00
28.3...	018922/I	to goods	483.00		966.00
5.4...	1216/C	by returns		120.00	846.00
					The last amount in this column is now due

Please make cheques payable to Live Wire Electrics Ltd

Live Wire Electrics Ltd

Remittance Advice

National Girobank
Account No

301 6029

0419830084600

Power Point Products p.l.c.
55 Queen Street
Coventry CO6 5QX

Reference SO/H 572/E

AMOUNT
£ 846.00

Please detach this portion and enclose with remittance or use
Bank Giro Credit on reverse

Fig. 19.1 Customer's statement

(*h*) **Remittances**
The customer usually sends a cheque in settlement of the account, although other forms of payment may be used (see Unit 14.6). The remittance will be accompanied either by the customer's own remittance advice slip, or by the remittance advice portion torn off the supplier's statement; these tell the supplier just what the payment is for.

(*i*) **Banking**
Remittances inwards are paid into the organization's bank account. The counterfoil or duplicate copy of the bank giro credit slip (see Unit 14.3) is retained.

(*j*) **Cash Book**
The amount of the remittance received (whether paid by cash or by cheque) is entered in the cash book. Because this money is coming into the organization it is entered in the left-hand or debit columns (Fig. 19.2). The rule in accounting is that you debit the account that *receives*. And remittances in payment for goods are received by the seller.
   Like the sales day-book, the cash book is a book of original entry. The information it contains helps to keep a running check on payments into and out of the organization. But for accounting purposes, the details of that information must also be recorded in the appropriate accounts. For remittances inwards, two entries must be made—one to update the seller's sales account, the other to update the customer's personal account in the sales ledger.

(*k*) **Sales Account**
Because the remittance inwards is in payment for goods sold, it is recorded in the sales account. Because the sales account is *receiving* payment, the entry is recorded as a debit entry, in the left-hand columns of the ledger or card.

(*l*) **Personal Account**
Just as information from the sales day-book has to be recorded in the customer's personal account, to show the value of the goods he or she has bought (see (*d*) and (*e*) above), so the remittances sent in settlement must be recorded. Whereas the information transferred from the sales day-book is recorded as a debit entry, information transferred from the cash book is recorded as a credit entry in the personal account. This is because, in accounting, you must credit the account which *gives*, and the customer has now given payment to the seller. This credit entry is deducted from the outstanding balance, so that the customer will not be asked to pay again.

(*m*) **Receipts and Acknowledgements**
These tell the customer that his payment has been received and his account credited. They are not always sent in response to cheque payments, because the customer can see from his bank statement whether or not his cheque has been cleared.

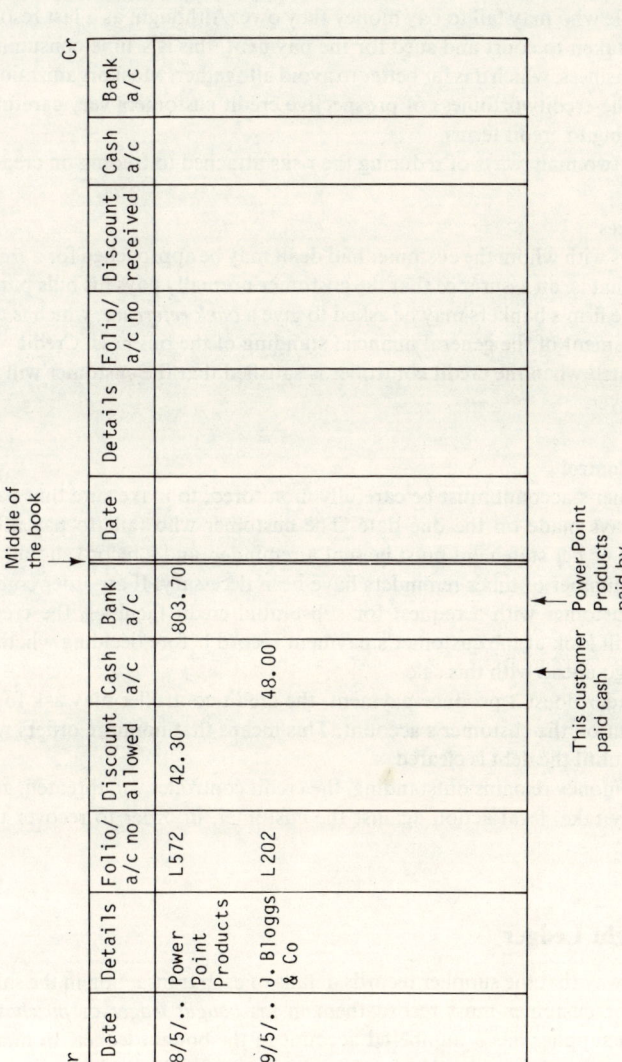

Fig. 19.2 Supplier's cash book

19.3 Credit Sales

Because business customers seldom like to pay for goods and services as soon as the supplier has delivered them, most organizations need to make sure that they don't sell goods on credit to people who are likely to become *bad debtors*, that is, people who may fail to pay money they owe. Although, as a last resort, they can be taken to court and sued for the payment, this is a time-consuming and costly business, which it is far better to avoid altogether. Most organizations investigate the creditworthiness of prospective credit customers very carefully before agreeing to credit terms.

There are two main ways of reducing the risks attached to trading on credit.

(*a*) References

Other traders with whom the customer had dealt may be approached for a *trade reference*—that is, an assurance that the customer normally pays his bills punctually. Or the firm's bankers may be asked to give a *bank reference*, which is the bank's assessment of the general financial standing of the business. Credit will only be granted when the credit controller is satisfied that the customer will be a prompt payer.

(*b*) Credit Control

Each customer's account must be carefully monitored, to make sure that payment is always made on the due date. The customer who fails to pay after receiving his or her statement must be sent a reminder, and a record should be kept of the number of times reminders have been necessary. If an order comes in from a customer with a request for substantial credit facilities, the credit controller will look at the customer's payment record before deciding whether it is wise to go ahead with this sale.

If a reminder doesn't produce payment, the credit controller may ask for a *stop* to be put on the customer's account. This means that no more orders will be accepted until the debt is cleared.

If a lot of money remains outstanding, the credit controller will threaten, and then actually take, legal action against the customer, in order to recover the payment.

19.4 Bought Ledger

In the same way that the supplier records details of each transaction in the sales ledger, so the customer must record them in his *bought ledger* or *purchases ledger*. Each supplier has a numbered account in the bought ledger. In many ways the procedure resembles that for the sales ledger (see Unit 19.2).

(*a*) Orders

Whenever the buyer places an order, a copy is sent to his or her own organization's accounts section.

(b) Invoices, Credit and Debit Notes

When an invoice arrives from a supplier, its details must be checked against the order. (In some organizations this is done in the buying office.) Credit and debit notes are also checked. This process is easy because all the documents are numbered, and each shows the relevant cross-references.

(c) Purchases Day-book

Invoice and credit and debit note details are entered in a day-book. Like the sales day-book, this is a book of original entry, providing a permanent record of each day's transactions. It contains:

(i) the name and account number of each supplier;
(ii) a brief description of the item;
(iii) the price of each item;
(iv) the total value of the order.

(d) Posting to the Ledger

Information from the day-book is posted to the ledger—that is, it is entered on the supplier's own page or card. Most of the entries in the bought ledger are credit entries, indicating that the supplier has provided goods or services and is owed money. Debit entries are made where the supplier has overcharged and sent a credit note to indicate that he owes the buyer money.

(e) Balancing

Like the sales ledger, the bought ledger must be balanced regularly, so that the organization can check the state of its account with each of its suppliers. The procedure is the same as for the sales ledger.

(f) Statements

When the supplier's statement is received, it is checked against the invoices, credit and debit notes held in the accounts section, to make sure that the seller is asking for the right amount.

(g) Remittances

When the payment has been approved, the cashier usually draws a cheque on the firm's bank account to settle with the supplier. This is sent to the supplier, with a remittance advice showing for which statement the payment is in settlement.

(h) Cash Book

Details of the remittances outwards are entered in the right-hand (credit) columns of the buyer's cash book (Fig. 19.3) This is because the buyer has *given* money to the seller, and in accounting you must credit the account that gives. If the remittance was made in cash, the amount is credited to 'cash'. If the remittance was by cheque, the amount is credited to 'bank'.

Fig. 19.3 Buyer's cash book

Because the cash book is a book of original entry, the information entered here must also be recorded both in the purchases account and in the supplier's personal account in the bought ledger.

(*i*) Purchases Account
Because the remittance outwards is in payment for goods bought, it is recorded in the purchases account. Because the purchases account is *giving* money to the supplier, the entry is recorded as a credit entry, in the right-hand columns of the ledger or card.

(*j*) Personal Account
Just as information from the purchases day-book was recorded as credit on the supplier's page or card in the purchases ledger (see (*c*) and (*d*) above), so the money paid in settlement to the supplier must be entered. Because the supplier has *received* payment, this entry is a debit entry.

19.5 Value Added Tax (VAT)
In certain countries, the prices at which goods are bought and sold are not just a matter for the organizations directly concerned. The state may impose a tax on the 'value added' while goods are in the hands of the business—that is, the difference between the cost of the materials and components bought by the business and the price at which the goods are sold (that is, the price actually paid by the customer after any discounts have been applied).

(*a*) Registration
In the United Kingdom, all businesses with annual sales above a certain figure are required to register with the Customs and Excise authorities. Each is given a *registration number* which should appear on all invoices and statements issued by the organization. These registered firms must collect VAT payments from their customers and hand the payments over to the Customs and Excise.

A firm that is registered for VAT does not have to pay VAT on its own purchases. If VAT is charged by its suppliers, the registered firm can deduct the amount it has paid from the sum handed over to the Customs and Excise when the goods are finally finished and sold.

(*b*) VAT Rates
The rate at which VAT is charged is fixed by the Government and varies from time to time: Fig. 17.4 shows an invoice which includes VAT at 15 per cent.

Some goods are *zero-rated*. This means that the rate of VAT charged on them is nil, so that no VAT is payable, but the firm can reclaim VAT that it has paid to the suppliers of materials used in making the goods. Other goods are *exempt* from VAT and again no VAT is payable, but in these cases tax paid to suppliers cannot be reclaimed.

(c) Tax Points

This is the date at which VAT is chargeable. It is either the date when the goods were delivered, or the date when the invoice was sent.

19.6 Accounting Aids

(a) Ready Reckoners

A ready reckoner is a small book which contains the answers to all sorts of calculations, already worked out to save time and trouble. The multiplication tables will help you to work out how much to charge a customer for, say, 121 items at £4.59 each. The percentage tables will help you to work out a bulk discount of 22 per cent on a price of £1350.44.

(b) Adding Machines

Adding machines take the drudgery out of adding and subtracting long columns of figures when totalling invoices or statements. To record a figure on the manual adding machine (Fig. 19.4) you press the keys for the appropriate digits. To add another figure to the first, turn the handle and then key in the numbers.

Each entry is printed out on a slip of paper called a *tally roll*.

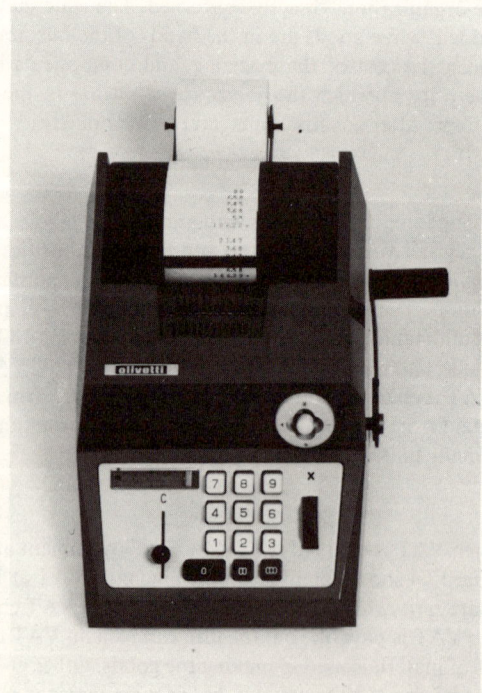

(c) Electronic Calculators

For office work it is useful to have a calculator that provides a permanent record of calculations, so that you can trace errors more readily. So, unlike most pocket calculators, many desk-top machines have a printing facility as well as a display panel (Fig. 19.5).

Fig. 19.5   Electronic desk-top calculator

The operating procedures vary from one calculator to another, and a user's handbook is normally supplied with the equipment. The handbook should be kept in a safe place, close to the machine, perhaps even tied in position to stop it disappearing.

The calculations which you can carry out on an electronic calculator include:

(i) *addition*, for invoice and many other kinds of work;

(ii) *subtraction*, for deducting credits and discounts;

(iii) *division*, for working out the cost per unit;

(iv) *multiplication*, for working out the total cost of a number of units at the same price;

(v) *percentages*, to calculate percentage discounts and mark-ups;

(vi) *constant operation*, to multiply a series of items by the same number, as in VAT calculations.

These basic functions are common to most calculators; some carry many more. For example, a *percentage difference key* will calculate the difference between the base number and any other number, and display the answer as a percentage of the base. Many machines also have a *memory* facility, which is particularly useful for invoice work. The answer to one calculation is stored in the memory while the next calculation is carried out, and then the results of two or more such calculations can be added together.

(d) Accounting Machines

(i) **Mechanized accounting machines** have both a typewriter keyboard and a numerical keyboard. Invoices and statements can be totalled and discounts calculated as they are typed, the machine automatically checking for errors. Information is recorded on ledger cards and statements simultaneously.

Some offices still use this kind of machine, but they are by no means as common as they once were.

(ii) **Computerized accounting machines** (Fig. 19.6) are pre-programmed to process several documents at once, printing them out at high speed. Like the traditional accounting machine, the computerized version has both a typewriter and a numerical keyboard. It can calculate wages and prepare statistical reports, in addition to carrying out all the basic accounting procedures.

Fig. 19.6 Computerized accounting machine. 1. Typewriter keyboard. 2. Numerical keyboard for calculations. 3. Function and programming keys, to tell the machine what to do. 4. Split platen, allowing more than one document to be fed through at once. 5. VDU, for checking entries and calculations before they are printed out by the machine

Computerized accounting machines are sometimes referred to as *visible-record computers* (VRCs), because the data is stored visibly, rather than on discs or tapes. Ledger cards must be presorted before being fed in, in the same order as the information about new transactions is to be recorded, otherwise transactions will be recorded on the wrong cards. *Magnetic ledger cards* (MLCs) have a magnetic strip down one or more sides. These strips hold a copy of the printing on the card in magnetic form, including the name and address of the account-holder, so that such basic information does not have to be keyed into the machine before each transaction is recorded.

(e) Computers

Where the accounts are totally computerized, details for the order or the invoice are input to the computer using one of the input devices discussed in Unit 15.2.

In the accounts field, the computer can be programmed to:

   (i) print out an order or invoice, with the required number of copies;
  (ii) update the information currently held on stock levels;
 (iii) make appropriate ledger entries in the firm's accounts;
 (iv) print out statements at regular intervals;
  (v) print out bank giro credit transfers to notify the bank of payments to be made.

Usually all these pieces of output are printed out, and then sent if necessary by post. But it is possible, as we saw in Unit 15.8, for one computer to 'speak' direct to another, so that a credit entered in the supplier's accounts automatically results in a debit in the customer's accounts. If the bank's computer is also part of this network, the bank accounts of both supplier and customer can be updated at the same time, without the need for cheques or credit transfers.

19.7 Quick Questions

1. What is the main purpose of the accounts department of an organization?

2. List three reasons why all organizations must produce an annual set of final accounts.

3. List six important documents used in dealing with the sales ledger.

4. What is (a) credit control, (b) a bad debtor?

5. What do the letters VAT stand for? What is VAT?

6. How do you know whether an entry in the accounts should be a debit or a credit? On which side of the ledger do the debit entries go?

19.8 Short Exercises

1. Read carefully the procedure for handling sales ledger documentation or, if you can, find out what the procedure is in your organization. Prepare a flow chart showing the main items of paperwork involved, from the arrival of the invoice to the issue of a receipt on acknowledgement of payment.

2. Choose two books of original entry, and for each of them explain (a) what source documents are needed, (b) what information it contains, (c) what it is used for, and (d) why it is necessary.

Unit Twenty

Personnel and Payroll

20.1 Introduction

Businesses need *people*, to make their products, offer their services, persuade customers to buy and keep the accounts. Staffing the organization and paying the staff are tasks that are carried out, in most larger organizations, by specialist personnel and payroll sections.

(a) Staffing/Personnel

Getting the right people in the right place at the right time, to do the things that the organization needs them to do, is a complex activity.

(i) **Manpower planning.** The personnel department's staff must work out how many people are (and will be) needed in each section of the organization, this year, next year, and in the future. To do this, they need to monitor the number of people employed, the work they do, and the proportion who leave or retire each year or who are absent through sickness.

(ii) **Organization.** The personnel department helps managers to design jobs that will increase the organization's efficiency and prove reasonably satisfying for the people doing them. In some organizations, job descriptions (see Unit 20.2(*a*)) are written for each job.

(iii) **Recruitment and selection.** Extra and replacement staff must be brought into the organization. The department manager decides what sort of skills and qualifications are needed for the job; the personnel department then places an advertisement or contacts a recruitment agency, sends out application forms and calls people in for interviews and, possibly, tests (see Unit 23.6). The department manager decides who best fits the job, and an offer of employment is made, again through the personnel department.

(iv) **Contracts of employment.** Each new employee must be given a *contract* (see Unit 20.2(*f*)) within thirteen weeks of joining the organization.

(v) **Training and development.** New employees must become familiar with the organization, and learn how to do their jobs. Much of this training can be carried out in the section in which they work. But if several new recruits or trainees arrive at once, it may be helpful to co-ordinate their training to save time.

Some organizations run a system of *performance appraisal*, which helps managers to identify ways in which their employees would benefit from further training.

(vi) **Remuneration.** All employees expect to be paid for the work they do. The payroll section looks after the issue of weekly or monthly cash payments and credit transfers. The personnel department sets up a *payment structure*, so that people doing similar jobs are paid at similar rates, and people whose work is more demanding are paid more highly. Sometimes specific *payment systems* are introduced; payment by results or piece rates (see Unit 16.3(*c*)) are intended to ensure that people who produce more are paid more. (The actual payment of wages and salaries to staff is the responsibility of the payroll section, however— see (*b*) below.)

(vii) **Employee relations.** In many countries, employees may if they wish join a *trade union*—that is, an organization which exists to work for the improvement of its members' pay and conditions of employment through negotiation with employers. Sometimes the employer negotiates directly with union members at the workplace or at the union's offices. In some industries the employers belong to an employers' federation which negotiates with the union's national officers on behalf of all its members. Negotiation over pay rates and the agreement of procedures for dealing with disputes and disciplinary problems are often coordinated by the personnel department.

(viii) **Welfare.** Some organizations feel a responsibility for the general wellbeing of their employees, and are willing to help them out in times of trouble. So personnel staff may visit sick employees, attend funerals, provide advice on family problems and, occasionally, lend money to help an employee over a bad patch.

(*b*) **Payroll/Wages**

(i) **Wages.** The payroll section calculates the wages due each week to those who are paid weekly—in the United Kingdom, these are mainly the production workers.

(ii) **Salaries.** These are calculated monthly, and are usually paid by bank giro credit. In the United Kingdom, most office workers, managers and professional employees are paid monthly.

(iii) **Deductions.** The payroll section must calculate the amount which each employee has to pay in National Insurance contributions and PAYE (Pay As You Earn) income tax. These amounts must be paid over, at intervals, to the Inland Revenue. Other deductions to be calculated include contributions to the organization's own occupational pension or superannuation scheme. These are normally calculated as a percentage of the employee's pay, and are supplemented by contributions from the employer. The money is invested in a pension fund and when the employee retires he or she will receive a regular pension from the fund.

(iv) **Payment.** The cash payroll must be made up so that there is a pay packet for each of the weekly-paid employees, and a credit transfer for each of the salaried staff.

(v) **Itemized pay statements.** These must be prepared for all employees (see Unit 20.3(j)).

20.2 Personnel Documentation

The information kept in the personnel department relates to people who also work for the organization, and much of it is highly confidential. If you have access to any of the information listed in this Unit, respect that confidentiality. Maybe you do know what your colleagues are being paid or how long they kept their previous jobs; but you certainly need not make it public.

In the personnel section, rather more than in some other departments, the amount and type of documentation varies quite widely from one organization to another. We will look at a pattern typical of a medium-sized organization with a specialist personnel department.

(*a*) **Job Descriptions**
These help employees and their managers to understand what their jobs involve. Some are very specific, listing each task in detail (compare Fig. 1.1). Others are more general.

(*b*) **Personnel Specifications**
These describe the skills, knowledge and personal qualities needed to succeed in any particular job.

(*c*) **Advertisements**
Vacant posts are advertised in the local or national papers, or in magazines. The advertisement should make it clear what the job demands, and what it offers.

(*d*) **Application Forms**
People replying to the personnel department's advertisements may be asked to fill in a standard application form (see Unit 23.4). This provides enough basic information to indicate whether the applicant has the right educational and work background to meet the personnel specification.

(*e*) **Correspondence**
Letters are sent inviting people for interview, offering positions, rejecting applications or requesting references. Standard letters for all these purposes are used by all but the smallest personnel sections, to save time.

(*f*) **Contracts of Employment**
These set out the name of the employer and employee, the job title, the date

employment began, and details regarding payment, holidays, sick pay, pensions and the company rules.

(g) Personal Files
The application form of a successful candidate for employment forms the basis of his or her personal file, which also includes copies of all relevant correspondence, references, contract of employment and so on.

(h) Personal Record Cards/Computer File
The employee's name, address, department, job title, salary and grade, together with other basic particulars, may be recorded on a visible-edge index card or by computer code. This record is updated whenever the employee's rate of pay, or any other detail, is changed. It thus provides a running record of the employee's career with the organization. This can be consulted far more quickly than the file. Absence due to sickness may be recorded on the back of the card.

(i) Change of Conditions Forms
These are action documents and must be signed by someone in authority. They are used to authorize:

   (i)   the addition of a new recruit to the payroll;
  (ii)   a change in rate of pay;
 (iii)   a change in hours of work;
 (iv)   a change in job title;
  (v)   a change in department;
 (vi)   the removal from the payroll of someone who has left.

Copies may be sent to payroll and the training section, as well as to the department where the employee is (or was, or will be) working.

(j) Collective Records
Running analyses of numbers leaving and joining the organization, or of sickness absence and accidents, may be kept in a day-book or worked out from a computer printout. This may help management to detect areas where employees are dissatisfied or where there are staff shortages.

(k) Training Records
If the organization takes people off the job to train them, either in its own training department or at an outside college, a record should be kept of what training has been given, and where and when it took place. While the trainee's own personal file should include this information, and possibly his or her record card as well, a central record helps management to assess the amount and type of training given to a particular group of employees, like supervisors or accounts clerks.

(l) Performance Appraisal Records
Some organizations encourage their managers to make regular reports on the

progress of members of their staff. Copies of these *appraisal forms* may be sent through to the personnel department. Overall performance gradings may be extracted from this report and added to the record card/computer file. The form itself is usually added to the employee's personal file.

20.3 Payroll Documentation

The exact nature of the work of a payroll section depends on whether or not it uses a computer: usually this is one of the first areas of a firm's work to be computerized. This is because payroll procedures must be repeated at regular intervals—weekly or monthly—and require some quite complex calculations. The basic information required is the same for both manual and computerized systems, however.

(a) Personal Records
Each employee has a personal record, showing his or her hourly, weekly or annual rate of pay, as authorized by the personnel department on the most recent change of conditions form received (see Unit 20.2(*i*)). It should also show any specific allowances—for clothing, shifts, or working in a city like London, where travel and accommodation costs are the highest in the country—together with the employee's tax code (see Unit 20.4(*d*)(i)).

All payments and deductions made are recorded on the personal record.

(b) Authorization of a General Award
When a general increase in pay is granted across several grades of employee— a 10 per cent increase for clerical grades, for instance—it would be tedious for a fresh change of conditions form to be produced for each employee. Instead, the personnel manager may pass through a list of names and the rates of pay to be applied. Provided that this is duly signed and authorized, the personal record of each employee can be updated accordingly.

(c) Clock Cards/Time Sheets
In some companies, employees are required to clock or sign in, to show their time of arrival at work.

(i) **Clock systems.** These are used for hourly-paid employees. Each person has a card, which is kept in a rack near the entrance to the works. On arrival, the employee takes his or her own card from the rack and inserts it in a slot in the clock or time machine. The machine stamps the time on the card, which is then replaced in another rack. The procedure is repeated when the employee leaves the works.

(ii) **Signing-in.** Weekly- or monthly-paid staff may sign in on a time sheet, instead of 'punching the clock'.

(iii) **Flexible working hours/flexitime.** A growing number of companies allow their employees to decide for themselves what time they arrive for work in the morning, and what time they leave in the evening, provided they are at work during *core time*—say between 11 a.m. and 4 p.m.—and provided they work a specified number of hours each month. Special time-recording equipment is used to monitor this flexitime system; each employee uses a personal coded key to record the number of time units he or she has worked.

(d) Pass-outs

If people leave the workplace during the course of the working day, they may have to get permission from their supervisor or manager. A pass will be issued, showing whether the missing time is to be paid or unpaid.

(e) Sickness Records

A form is issued, either by the personnel department or by the employee's own manager, which records days and part-days lost through sickness. The form should show whether or not the employee is entitled to payment while absent sick. This payment is likely to be in two parts. Unless the employee has been absent for eight weeks already in the tax year, or falls into a category which is specifically excluded, he or she will be entitled to statutory sick pay from the fourth day of a period of absence from work; the rates for this are laid down by the government. In addition, some employees may be entitled to payments from the organization's own occupational sick pay scheme.

Careful records must be kept of payments made under both the statutory sick pay and the occupational sick pay schemes. Statutory sick pay can be reclaimed from the state by deducting the amounts paid to employees from the amount of National Insurance paid over to the Inland Revenue by the employer. These records will be inspected from time to time to make sure that statutory sick pay has only been paid to employees who were entitled to receive it. Payments under an occupational sick pay scheme cannot be reclaimed.

The Department of Health and Social Security issues special forms that must be given to employees who are excluded from the statutory sick pay scheme or who have exhausted their entitlement and must transfer to state sickness benefit.

(f) Tax Tables and Codes

These are issued by the tax authorities, and tell the employer how much tax each employee must pay (see Unit 20.4(d)(ii)). A separate notification of coding is sent to the employer for each employee, and this coding is entered on his or her personal record.

(g) Certificate P45

When an employee leaves an organization, the payroll department prepares a record of his or her pay and tax position for the year to date—a 'certificate P45'. Part 1 is sent to the tax office, and Parts 2 and 3 are given to the employee. When he or she starts a new job, the new employer will ask for Parts 2 and 3. Part 3 goes to the tax office, and the employer keeps Part 2 for reference.

(h) Certificate P60

The tax *(fiscal)* year ends on 5 April. After that date, each employee must be given an *annual certificate of pay and tax deduction*. This shows how much he or she has been paid, and how much tax has been deducted; it is usually issued on the Inland Revenue form P60. The employee should keep this document carefully, as it may need to be produced when claiming certain state benefits.

(i) Employers' Guide to National Insurance Contributions

This is issued by the Department of Health and Social Security. It tells the employer how much to deduct from each employee's pay to cover National Insurance contributions.

(j) Itemized Pay Statements

Every pay-day, each employee receives a statement explaining all payments made to him or her, and setting out what deductions have been made.

(k) The Payroll

The payroll itself is the master record of all payments made each week or month.

(l) Credit Transfers

Staff who are paid by bank giro credit (see Unit 14.5) must be listed on a credit transfer, which is in effect a copy of the salaries payroll.

20.4 Payroll Procedures

In order to calculate how much pay an employee should receive each month or week, you must have certain information.

(a) Rate of Pay

You need to know at what rate of pay each employee is entitled to be paid—per hour, per week or per month. This information can be found on the employee's personal record.

(b) Hours of Work

If basic pay is related to time spent at work, you need to know how many hours have been spent there this week/month. This information comes from the clock card or time sheet. These may have been processed and summarized for you before they reach the payroll department, or you may have the task of working out, from each person's card, how many hours pay he or she is entitled to.

(c) Add-ons/Allowances

These take several forms:

(i) **Piece rate bonuses** (see Unit 16.3(c)). Each person's entitlement must be worked out and added to his or her pay.

(ii) **Commission.** Sales staff often get commission on the value of the products they sell, on top of their wages or salaries. The sales office provides information for the calculation of commission payments.

(iii) **Overtime.** Some employees are entitled to be paid extra for hours worked in addition to their normal hours. One common pattern is time and a half (that is, $1\frac{1}{2}$ hours' pay for each extra hour worked) on weekdays and double time (two hours' pay for each hour worked) on Sundays. To work out a man's entitlement, you need to know his basic hourly rate, how many extra hours he has worked and at what rate payment is due. So if a man is paid £4.00 per hour and works 38 hours per week, his basic pay is £152 per week. If he works 8 hours overtime during the week and 3 hours on Sunday, he should also receive $1\frac{1}{2} \times £4.00 \times 8 = £48$ plus $2 \times £4.00 \times 3 = £24$, that is, £72 overtime. His total gross pay will thus be £224 for that week.

(d) Statutory Deductions
In the United Kingdom, certain deductions from pay must be made by law.

(i) **Tax codes.** The Inland Revenue requires each citizen to complete an income tax return, usually once a year, on the basis of which the tax office calculates how much of his or her pay is not subject to tax, that is, the *tax-free allowances*. These vary according to marital status, the amount of any interest being paid on a mortgage or home loan and other factors, and are expressed as a three-digit code for each individual. The Inland Revenue notifies both the employee and the employer of the code which is to apply during the tax year. If circumstances change, the taxpayer should notify the Inland Revenue, and the tax code will be altered.

(ii) **Tax tables.** The tax office also provide two tables, A and B, for each week in the year (Figs. 20.1 and 20.2).

Table A shows how much people on each code number can earn before they start paying tax, that is, how much *free pay* they are entitled to. The figures refer to the employee's total earnings in the tax year to date, that is, from the previous 6 April. The employee's entitlement to tax-free pay in the year to date is deducted from the amount he has actually earned, including the amount he is due to be paid this week. The balance is his *taxable pay*.

Table B shows how much tax should have been paid in the year to date, including this week, for each pound of taxable pay, from which you can work out the total tax that should have been paid. If you then subtract the tax that has already been paid this year, the remainder is the amount that should be deducted this week.

An example will make this clear.

Suppose Clive Cruise's tax code is 199, and that you have to calculate how much tax you should deduct from his pay for month 3 (6 June to 5 July) of the income tax year. The procedure is as follows:

MONTH 3
June 6 to July 5

TABLE A–FREE PAY

Code	Total free pay to date	Code	Total free pay to date	Code	Total free pay to date	Code	Total free pay to date	Code	Total free pay to date	Code	Total free pay to date	Code	Total free pay to date	Code	Total free pay to date
	£		£		£		£		£		£		£		£
0	NIL	51	129·75	101	254·85	151	379·80	201	504·75	251	629·85	301	754·80	351	879·75
1	4·80	52	132·30	102	257·25	152	382·35	202	507·30	252	632·25	302	757·35	352	882·30
2	7·35	53	134·85	103	259·80	153	384·75	203	509·85	253	634·80	303	759·75	353	884·85
3	9·75	54	137·25	104	262·35	154	387·30	204	512·25	254	637·35	304	762·30	354	887·25
4	12·30	55	139·80	105	264·75	155	389·85	205	514·80	255	639·75	305	764·85	355	889·80
5	14·85	56	142·35	106	267·30	156	392·25	206	517·35	256	642·30	306	767·25	356	892·35
6	17·25	57	144·75	107	269·85	157	394·80	207	519·75	257	644·85	307	769·80	357	894·75
7	19·80	58	147·30	108	272·25	158	397·35	208	522·30	258	647·25	308	772·35	358	897·30
8	22·35	59	149·85	109	274·80	159	399·75	209	524·85	259	649·80	309	774·75	359	899·85
9	24·75	60	152·25	110	277·35	160	402·30	210	527·25	260	652·35	310	777·30	360	902·25
10	27·30														
11	29·85	61	154·80	111	279·75	161	404·85	211	529·80	261	654·75	311	779·85		
12	32·25	62	157·35	112	282·30	162	407·25	212	532·35	262	657·30	312	782·25		
13	34·80	63	159·75	113	284·85	163	409·80	213	534·75	263	659·85	313	784·80		
14	37·35	64	162·30	114	287·25	164	412·35	214	537·30	264	662·25	314	787·35		
15	39·75	65	164·85	115	289·80	165	414·75	215	539·85	265	664·80	315	789·75		
16	42·30	66	167·25	116	292·35	166	417·30	216	542·25	266	667·35	316	792·30		
17	44·85	67	169·80	117	294·75	167	419·85	217	544·80	267	669·75	317	794·85		
18	47·25	68	172·35	118	297·30	168	422·25	218	547·35	268	672·30	318	797·25		
19	49·80	69	174·75	119	299·85	169	424·80	219	549·75	269	674·85	319	799·80		
20	52·35	70	177·30	120	302·25	170	427·35	220	552·30	270	677·25	320	802·35		
21	54·75	71	179·85	121	304·80	171	429·75	221	554·85	271	679·80	321	804·75		
22	57·30	72	182·25	122	307·35	172	432·30	222	557·25	272	682·35	322	807·30		
23	59·85	73	184·80	123	309·75	173	434·85	223	559·80	273	684·75	323	809·85		
24	62·25	74	187·35	124	312·30	174	437·25	224	562·35	274	687·30	324	812·25		
25	64·80	75	189·75	125	314·85	175	439·80	225	564·75	275	689·85	325	814·80		
26	67·35	76	192·30	126	317·25	176	442·35	226	567·30	276	692·25	326	817·35		
27	69·75	77	194·85	127	319·80	177	444·75	227	569·85	277	694·80	327	819·75		
28	72·30	78	197·25	128	322·35	178	447·30	228	572·25	278	697·35	328	822·30		
29	74·85	79	199·80	129	324·75	179	449·85	229	574·80	279	699·75	329	824·85		
30	77·25	80	202·35	130	327·30	180	452·25	230	577·35	280	702·30	330	827·25		
31	79·80	81	204·75	131	329·85	181	454·80	231	579·75	281	704·85	331	829·80		
32	82·35	82	207·30	132	332·25	182	457·35	232	582·30	282	707·25	332	832·35		
33	84·75	83	209·85	133	334·80	183	459·75	233	584·85	283	709·80	333	834·75		
34	87·30	84	212·25	134	337·35	184	462·30	234	587·25	284	712·35	334	837·30		
35	89·85	85	214·80	135	339·75	185	464·85	235	589·80	285	714·75	335	839·85		
36	92·25	86	217·35	136	342·30	186	467·25	236	592·35	286	717·30	336	842·25		
37	94·80	87	219·75	137	344·85	187	469·80	237	594·75	287	719·85	337	844·80		
38	97·35	88	222·30	138	347·25	188	472·35	238	597·30	288	722·25	338	847·35		
39	99·75	89	224·85	139	349·80	189	474·75	239	599·85	289	724·80	339	849·75		
40	102·30	90	227·25	140	352·35	190	477·30	240	602·25	290	727·35	340	852·30		
41	104·85	91	229·80	141	354·75	191	479·85	241	604·80	291	729·75	341	854·85		
42	107·25	92	232·35	142	357·30	192	482·25	242	607·35	292	732·30	342	857·25		
43	109·80	93	234·75	143	359·85	193	484·80	243	609·75	293	734·85	343	859·80		
44	112·35	94	237·30	144	362·25	194	487·35	244	612·30	294	737·25	344	862·35		
45	114·75	95	239·85	145	364·80	195	489·75	245	614·85	295	739·80	345	864·75		
46	117·30	96	242·25	146	367·35	196	492·30	246	617·25	296	742·35	346	867·30		
47	119·85	97	244·80	147	369·75	197	494·80	247	619·80	297	744·75	347	869·85		
48	122·25	98	247·35	148	372·30	198	497·25	248	622·35	298	747·30	348	872·25		
49	124·80	99	249·75	149	374·85	199	499·80	249	624·75	299	749·85	349	874·80		
50	127·35	100	252·30	150	377·25	200	502·35	250	627·30	300	752·25	350	877·35		

Fig. 20.1   Extract from Inland Revenue PAYE Tax Tables A—Free Pay

Table A, the free pay table, is arranged in date order, with both weekly and monthly tables. Turn to the page which shows the table for the month you want, month 3.

Check through the figures in bold type to find 199, Clive's tax code.

Read off, from the adjoining column, the amount of tax-free pay to which he is entitled, up to and including month 3. The figure shown is £499.80.

TABLE B

TAX DUE ON TAXABLE PAY FROM £361 TO £720

Total TAXABLE PAY to date	Total TAX DUE to date	Total TAXABLE PAY to date	Total TAX DUE to date	Total TAXABLE PAY to date	Total TAX DUE to date	Total TAXABLE PAY to date	Total TAX DUE to date	Total TAXABLE PAY to date	Total TAX DUE to date	Total TAXABLE PAY to date	Total TAX DUE to date
£	£	£	£	£	£	£	£	£	£	£	£
361	108·30	421	126·30	481	144·30	541	162·30	601	180·30	661	198·30
362	108·60	422	126·60	482	144·60	542	162·60	602	180·60	662	198·60
363	108·90	423	126·90	483	144·90	543	162·90	603	180·90	663	198·90
364	109·20	424	127·20	484	145·20	544	163·20	604	181·20	664	199·20
365	109·50	425	127·50	485	145·50	545	163·50	605	181·50	665	199·50
366	109·80	426	127·80	486	145·80	546	163·80	606	181·80	666	199·80
367	110·10	427	128·10	487	146·10	547	164·10	607	182·10	667	200·10
368	110·40	428	128·40	488	146·40	548	164·40	608	182·40	668	200·40
369	110·70	429	128·70	489	146·70	549	164·70	609	182·70	669	200·70
370	111·00	430	129·00	490	147·00	550	165·00	610	183·00	670	201·00
371	111·30	431	129·30	491	147·30	551	165·30	611	183·30	671	201·30
372	111·60	432	129·60	492	147·60	552	165·60	612	183·60	672	201·60
373	111·90	433	129·90	493	147·90	553	165·90	613	183·90	673	201·90
374	112·20	434	130·20	494	148·20	554	166·20	614	184·20	674	202·20
375	112·50	435	130·50	495	148·50	555	166·50	615	184·50	675	202·50
376	112·80	436	130·80	496	148·80	556	166·80	616	184·80	676	202·80
377	113·10	437	131·10	497	149·10	557	167·10	617	185·10	677	203·10
378	113·40	438	131·40	498	149·40	558	167·40	618	185·40	678	203·40
379	113·70	439	131·70	499	149·70	559	167·70	619	185·70	679	203·70
380	114·00	440	132·00	500	150·00	560	168·00	620	186·00	680	204·00
381	114·30	441	132·30	501	150·30	561	168·30	621	186·30	681	204·30
382	114·60	442	132·60	502	150·60	562	168·60	622	186·60	682	204·60
383	114·90	443	132·90	503	150·90	563	168·90	623	186·90	683	204·90
384	115·20	444	133·20	504	151·20	564	169·20	624	187·20	684	205·20
385	115·50	445	133·50	505	151·50	565	169·50	625	187·50	685	205·50
386	115·80	446	133·80	506	151·80	566	169·80	626	187·80	686	205·80
387	116·10	447	134·10	507	152·10	567	170·10	627	188·10	687	206·10
388	116·40	448	134·40	508	152·40	568	170·40	628	188·40	688	206·40
389	116·70	449	134·70	509	152·70	569	170·70	629	188·70	689	206·70
390	117·00	450	135·00	510	153·00	570	171·00	630	189·00	690	207·00
391	117·30	451	135·30	511	153·30	571	171·30	631	189·30	691	207·30
392	117·60	452	135·60	512	153·60	572	171·60	632	189·60	692	207·60
393	117·90	453	135·90	513	153·90	573	171·90	633	189·90	693	207·90
394	118·20	454	136·20	514	154·20	574	172·20	634	190·20	694	208·20
395	118·50	455	136·50	515	154·50	575	172·50	635	190·50	695	208·50
396	118·80	456	136·80	516	154·80	576	172·80	636	190·80	696	208·80
397	119·10	457	137·10	517	155·10	577	173·10	637	191·10	697	209·10
398	119·40	458	137·40	518	155·40	578	173·40	638	191·40	698	209·40
399	119·70	459	137·70	519	155·70	579	173·70	639	191·70	699	209·70
400	120·00	460	138·00	520	156·00	580	174·00	640	192·00	700	210·00
401	120·30	461	138·30	521	156·30	581	174·30	641	192·30	701	210·30
402	120·60	462	138·60	522	156·60	582	174·60	642	192·60	702	210·60
403	120·90	463	138·90	523	156·90	583	174·90	643	192·90	703	210·90
404	121·20	464	139·20	524	157·20	584	175·20	644	193·20	704	211·20
405	121·50	465	139·50	525	157·50	585	175·50	645	193·50	705	211·50
406	121·80	466	139·80	526	157·80	586	175·80	646	193·80	706	211·80
407	122·10	467	140·10	527	158·10	587	176·10	647	194·10	707	212·10
408	122·40	468	140·40	528	158·40	588	176·40	648	194·40	708	212·40
409	122·70	469	140·70	529	158·70	589	176·70	649	194·70	709	212·70
410	123·00	470	141·00	530	159·00	590	177·00	650	195·00	710	213·00
411	123·30	471	141·30	531	159·30	591	177·30	651	195·30	711	213·30
412	123·60	472	141·60	532	159·60	592	177·60	652	195·60	712	213·60
413	123·90	473	141·90	533	159·90	593	177·90	653	195·90	713	213·90
414	124·20	474	142·20	534	160·20	594	178·20	654	196·20	714	214·20
415	124·50	475	142·50	535	160·50	595	178·50	655	196·50	715	214·50
416	124·80	476	142·80	536	160·80	596	178·80	656	196·80	716	214·80
417	125·10	477	143·10	537	161·10	597	179·10	657	197·10	717	215·10
418	125·40	478	143·40	538	161·40	598	179·40	658	197·40	718	215·40
419	125·70	479	143·70	539	161·70	599	179·70	659	197·70	719	215·70
420	126·00	480	144·00	540	162·00	600	180·00	660	198·00	720	216·00

Fig. 20.2   Extract from Inland Revenue PAYE Tax Tables B

Check Clive's pay record to see how much he has actually been paid in the tax year to date. (The figure you want is his gross pay minus any contributions to the company pensions fund, as these are not taxable.) Suppose that this figure is £1128.00.

Deduct Clive's free pay, £499.80, from his actual pay, £1128.00. This leaves £628.20 of taxable pay in the year so far.

Now turn to Table B, which is arranged in numerical order. Find the page which shows tax due on taxable pay from £361 to £720.

Check through the figures in heavy type to find £628, Clive's taxable pay to date.

Read off, from the adjoining column, the amount of tax Clive should have paid to date. The figure shown is £188.40.

Check Clive's pay record to see how much tax has actually been deducted so far this tax year, up to and including month 2. Suppose this figure is £125.70.

Deduct the tax Clive has actually paid, £125.70, from the amount he should have paid after month 3's tax has been deducted, £188.40. This leaves £62.70 tax to be deducted this month.

(iii) **National Insurance/Social Security contributions.** These are used by government to pay for such things as state sickness benefits, unemployment benefits and pensions. Unlike income tax, the contribution rate is linked directly to the rate of pay, regardless of the individual's personal circumstances, so no special personal codes are necessary. But the amount deducted from each employee's pay does depend upon whether he or she is a member of an occupational pension scheme which is contracted out of the British state scheme.

(e) Other Deductions

Apart from tax and National Insurance, no deductions can be made without the written authority of the employee concerned or, in some cases, a court order. Trade union membership subscriptions ('union dues'), pension and savings schemes and sports and social club subscriptions are among the more usual authorized or *voluntary deductions*. Code letters are generally used to identify the reasons why such deductions have been made.

(f) Other Circumstances

Other circumstances relating to the individual's pay entitlement must be taken into account. Where he or she is absent due to genuine sickness, entitlement to both statutory and occupational sick pay may have to be considered (see Unit 20.3(e)).

(g) Updating the Records

Each employee's pay entitlement must be recorded, usually in three separate places. All three require the same basic information: gross pay, additional pay, National Insurance, tax and other deductions, and net pay. Each of these is recorded on a year-to-date basis as well as for the current week or month. The three records required are:

   (i) the itemized salary or pay statement or salary or pay advice (Fig. 20.3);

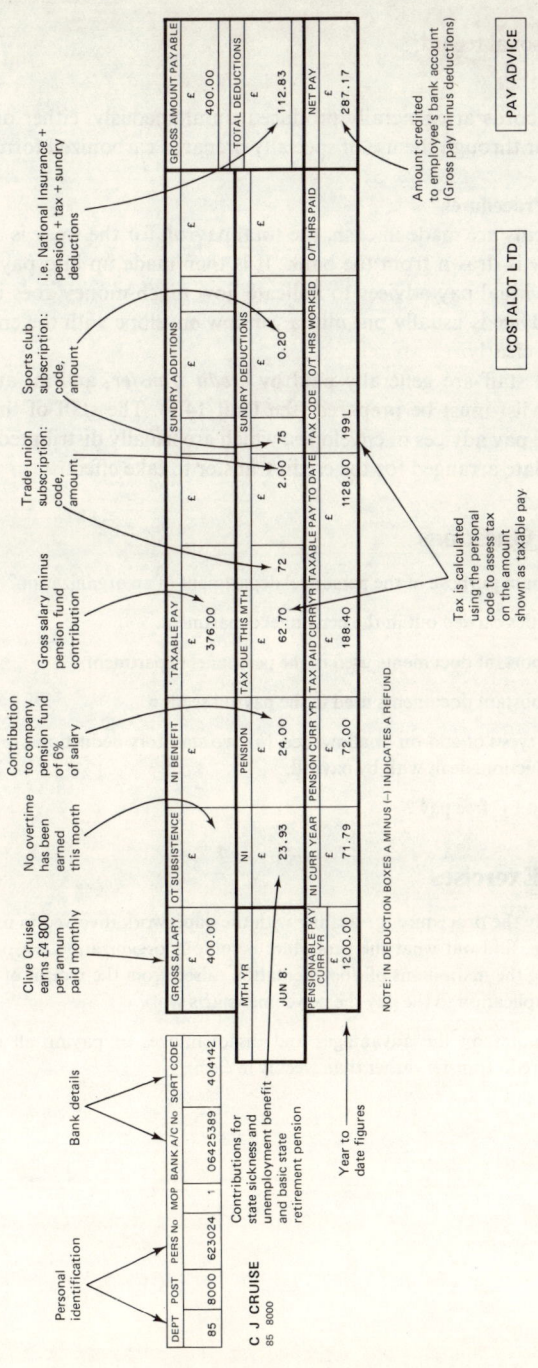

Fig. 20.3 Salary or pay advice

Personal identification

Bank details

DEPT	POST	PERS No	MOP	BANK A/c No	SORT CODE
85	8000	623024	1	06425389	404142

C J CRUISE
85 8000

Contributions for state sickness and unemployment benefit and basic state retirement pension

Year to date figures

Clive Cruise earns £4 800 per annum paid monthly

GROSS SALARY	OT SUBSISTENCE
£	£
400.00	

No overtime has been earned this month

Contribution to company pension fund of 6% of salary

NI BENEFIT	NI
£	£
	23.93

MTH YR		PENSION
JUN 8.		£
		24.00

NI CURR YEAR	PENSION CURR YR
£	£
71.79	72.00

PENSIONABLE PAY CURR YR
£
1200.00

Gross salary minus pension fund contribution

*TAXABLE PAY
376.00

TAX DUE THIS MTH
£
62.70

TAXABLE PAY TO DATE
£
1128.00

Tax is calculated using the personal code to assess tax on the amount shown as taxable pay

Trade union subscription: code, amount

Sports club subscription: code, amount

SUNDRY ADDITIONS		
£		£

SUNDRY DEDUCTIONS		
72	2.00	75	0.20

TAX PAID CURR YR	TAX CODE	O/T HRS WORKED	O/T HRS PAID
£	199L		
188.40			

GROSS AMOUNT PAYABLE
£
400.00

i.e. National Insurance + pension + tax + sundry deductions

TOTAL DEDUCTIONS
£
112.83

NET PAY
£
287.17

Amount credited to employee's bank account (Gross pay minus deductions)

COSTALOT LTD   PAY ADVICE

NOTE: IN DEDUCTION BOXES A MINUS (–) INDICATES A REFUND

(ii) the personal record;

(iii) the payroll.

These three records are generally produced simultaneously, either on a computer printer or through the use of specially prepared carbonized forms.

(*h*) Payment Procedures

(i) If payments are made in cash, the total payroll for the week is added up and the money is drawn from the bank. It is then made up into pay packets, using the individual pay advices to indicate how much money goes into each packet. The advice is usually put into a window envelope with the employee's name showing clearly.

(ii) Salaried staff are generally paid by *credit transfer*, and an authorized credit transfer list must be prepared (see Unit 14.5). The staff of the payroll section put the pay advices in envelopes, which are usually distributed a day or two after the date arranged for the credit transfer to take effect.

20.5 Quick Questions

1. What is the main purpose of the personnel department of an organization?

2. List six activities carried out in the personnel department.

3. List eight important documents used in the personnel department.

4. List eight important documents used in the payroll section.

5. List (*a*) three types of add-on or allowance, (*b*) two statutory deductions, (*c*) one non-statutory deduction, dealt with by payroll.

6. What is meant by 'free pay'?

20.6 Short Exercises

1. Read carefully the procedure for dealing with the paperwork involved in recruitment or, if you can, find out what the procedure is in your organization. Prepare a flow chart showing the main items of documentation raised from the receipt of the initial enquiry or application to the day the newcomer starts work.

2. Make brief notes on the advantages and disadvantages of paying all employees monthly by credit transfer rather than weekly in cash.

Unit Twenty-one

Management Services

21.1 Introduction

Some of the activities which are carried on in larger organizations are not directly concerned with products, money or people—the main focus of our discussion so far; their purpose is rather to service the organization itself, providing information and expertise to ensure that the company operates as efficiently as possible.

Because their work is so specialized, we can give only a brief overview of it here.

21.2 Organization and Methods Investigation (O and M)

Specialists in this field systematically examine the way in which work is done, with a view to developing the best methods and systems.

(a) Work Measurement

The time each task or part of a job should take can be worked out by timing the work of someone who is experienced in the task. This can be taken as the standard time for the task, and used to calculate piece rates and bonus payments for production workers, rewarding those who work more quickly.

(b) Method Study

Method study experts watch staff at work and suggest improvements in the way their work is done. For example, they may use charts and diagrams to plot the movements made by people, paper and materials, and aim to speed up the work by eliminating unnecessary or duplicated movements.

(c) Systems Design

O and M specialists examine the systems used to deal with matters like stock control, accounts, sales and personnel, to see if any better way of handling these tasks can be found. For instance, in an office they might look at:

    (i) the number of copies of each document that are made, and what each is used for;
    (ii) the layout of each document—its clarity and brevity;
    (iii) the number and purpose of contacts with other departments.

After detailed analysis, the specialists might find unnecessary duplication of effort—such as the entering of the same information three times over on different documents, requiring three separate operations. The O and M specialist might suggest using carbonized forms with overlays, or photocopying, to avoid the need for repetitive work.

If you work in an O and M department, you will be trained to understand the techniques used there.

21.3 Data-processing

While mini- and micro-computers are becoming steadily more common in user departments (see Unit 15), most organizations still regard the design of systems and programs to meet their specific needs as a job for specialists. Systems analysts and programmers undertake this work for management; where a system of remote job entry is used, other specialists such as punched card machine operators may also be used to prepare batches of data for input (see Unit 15.2).

A most important function of the data-processing staff is liaison with user departments. It is their job to help users to understand what the computer can and can't do. The computer is there to serve the needs of the business, not to dictate them.

21.4 Legal Services

In small companies, the company secretary and his or her staff advise the directors on legal matters. Larger organizations usually have a specialist legal department, to advise on everything from employment law to the patenting of products, and from consumer credit regulations to the requirements of the Clean Air Act. Unit 1.8 lists a few of the matters with which it will be concerned.

21.5 Premises

Some organizations operate from a number of different sites—like chains of retail shops, banks and building societies. These chains need specialists to negotiate the purchase or leasing of suitable premises.

Once obtained, the premises must be fitted out to meet the organization's needs; often, the new shop or office must be made to look like all the others. Large organizations employ surveyors, builders and interior designers for this purpose, together with painters, carpenters and plumbers to maintain the buildings.

Smaller organizations employ specialist consultants for the legal and professional aspects of the work. Office- and shop-fitting is usually contracted out— that is, another firm is paid to take over the responsibility for decorating the interior in accordance with an agreed design.

21.6 Insurance

In the United Kingdom it is illegal to drive a car unless you are insured against the risk of injury to another person—a *third party*—or to operate a business if you are not insured against injury to employees and other visitors. Besides the risk of personal injury, most companies insure against (*a*) the risk of damage to property by fire or other accident;

(*b*) the risk of loss of property—theft of goods, equipment or money.

Most large firms take out insurance policies with specialist insurance companies, by which the insurance company agrees, in return for a payment (the *premium*), to compensate the firm for loss arising from one of the risks covered by the policy.

Because there are many different insurance companies, each offering slightly different cover and terms, some organizations use a *broker*, who helps them to get the best terms. Larger firms may have their own insurance section, to deal with the various types of insurance.

21.7 Quick Questions

1. Name two types of activity carried out by the management services department of an organization.

2. What do the letters 'O and M' stand for? What is 'O and M'?

3. Name three elements of 'O and M' work.

4. Name three types of staff employed by the premises section.

5. List three risks against which a company should insure.

6. What is a premium? What does a person paying a premium get in return for his or her money?

21.8 Short Exercises

1. Find out the job titles of staff employed in the management services department of your organization. Compare these with the job titles produced by other members of your study group.

2. A colleague feels that taking out insurance and paying expensive premiums is a waste of money. Prepare brief notes of the points you would make to try to persuade him to change his mind.

Office Services

22.1 Introduction

Another way in which business efficiency can be increased is by centralizing a number of essential office activities. So instead of each department maintaining its own filing system, for instance, all the files for the organization as a whole are kept together in a central *registry*. General typing services, too, can be more streamlined and be used more effectively if they are centralized in a *secretariat*.

Filing and typing centres can be classified as *ancillary* (subservient) to the main purposes of the business. Among the other ancillary services you may find are the stationery stores, the post room and the reception office.

22.2 Reception

A receptionist may have up to five main duties.

To receive visitors and make them feel welcome. Most organizations like to enjoy good public relations. And the way in which visitors are received when they call on the firm can make or mar their impressions of the organization.

To direct strangers to the building and help them to find the person they have come to visit.

To act as a security screen. Although most organizations welcome visitors, not everyone is free to come and go as he or she chooses. The receptionist can check whether or not visitors have appointments or have genuine business. If they have just walked in out of the rain, they must be sent on their way.

To act as a telephonist. Not all receptionists are required to operate switchboards, but in smaller companies the jobs of receptionist and telephonist are often combined in order to make full use of the receptionist's time.

To help out with general office duties. The receptionist may be asked to do some typing, filing or other clerical tasks, during quiet periods.

In order to carry out these duties you need:

(i) a pleasant, helpful and resourceful nature, to cope with the many different situations you will meet;

(ii) a good memory for names and faces, so you can greet people personally;

(iii) a good knowledge of the people in your organization, and some idea of the work they do, so that you can offer an alternative contact for a person who is not available;

(iv) the ability to direct people clearly and without confusing them, so they don't get lost on their way through the building;

(v) a clear, pleasant speaking voice—audible but not too loud—and a tidy and pleasant appearance;

(vi) patience, to deal with people who don't know what they want;

(vii) tact, to deal with unwelcome visitors;

(viii) a methodical approach to office routine (see Unit 22.3);

(ix) additional office skills, if your job includes general clerical duties;

(x) telephonist skills, if your job includes the operation of the switchboard.

You will meet many different kinds of people if you work in reception. Apart from regular deliveries from the postman and the milkman, these will include:

(i) **Customers and clients** to whom the organization sells its goods and services may call in, to enquire about prices or delivery dates, for example, or to find out about new products or to collect samples.

(ii) **Suppliers and sales representatives** who sell goods to the organization also visit from time to time, to negotiate prices or delivery dates or to tell the buyer about new products.

(iii) **Job applicants** who are interested in working for the organization also call. Some are there by appointment, having been invited for interview by the personnel department or a department manager. Others have called in 'on the off-chance', to ask if there are any jobs going.

(iv) **Officials.** An inspector from the local authority department of environmental health may call, to inspect the premises and see if there are any health or safety hazards.

A policeman may call to talk to the personnel manager about a past employee who is in trouble.

The disablement resettlement officer may come to talk to the personnel manager about a grant for employing a disabled worker.

These and other official visitors will not always have appointments, but they will expect to be able to see the person they have come to visit.

(v) **Other business contacts,** such as the organization's advertising agents, insurance agents, shop-fitters, window-cleaners, bank manager or indeed any other organization or individual whose services are used, may visit from time to time.

(vi) **Canvassers** collecting money for charity, or votes for a political party, may come into reception—perhaps rattling a money box.

(vii) **The general public.** Schoolchildren doing projects, people complaining about factory noise, dust or smell or about the quality of the firm's products, even the homeless or the drunk and disorderly—all may march or stumble into your reception area, sooner or later.

So how will you deal with them when they do?

22.3 Reception Procedures and Documentation

(a) Preparation
The first rule of the efficient receptionist is to 'be prepared'.

(i) **Appointments lists.** Make sure you know whom to expect, and when to expect them. Secretaries should provide you with a list of names and appointment times of the visitors their managers have arranged to see. Enter these, in order of their appointment times, in an appointments book (see Fig. 22.1, where times are given according to the 24-hour clock, which some firms prefer—13.00 means 1 p.m., 15.30 means 3.30 p.m., and so on).

Date	Time	Name	Company	To see
5. 4. 8-	09·30	J. Miles	Live Wire	M. Squires
"	10·15	F. Slin	Power Point Products	L. Kidd
"	13·00	M. Wall	Costalot	Y. Gates

Fig. 22.1   Part of a page from an appointments book

(ii) **Callers' card index.** Whenever a caller gives you his or her business card (see Fig. 22.2), keep it. Stick it to an index card and file it in a card index, alphabetically under the name of the caller's organization. Then when someone asks 'who do we usually deal with at Costalot?', you can retrieve the Costalot card from your index, and tell them.

(iii) **Telephone numbers/contact points.** Make sure you know whom to contact when each visitor arrives, and have a note of the telephone number ready to hand. A telephone index, kept up to date, is a great time-saver, especially if your duties in reception also include operating the switchboard.

Make sure, too, that you know the name and job title of all the managers who may receive visitors. Then if a visitor asks for Mrs Wakefield, who you know is the buyer and who is on holiday, you can ask if Mr Brompton, the deputy buyer, could help.

Fig. 22.2   Callers' card index

(iv) **Stationery.** Keep a message pad and a sharpened pencil close to the reception counter. The names and messages from unexpected visitors can be passed on to the people they had hoped to see.

(v) **Staff log books.** These can help you to keep track of staff movements, so you know whether or not the person a visitor wishes to see is actually in the building. You won't then waste valuable time trying to contact people who are out at lunch. The log may be a book or a visual control board with 'in' and 'out' signs for each person.

(vi) **Change.** If there are pay telephones or vending machines in the reception area, keep a stock of the appropriate coins handy so that you can give change to visitors who want to use these facilities.

(vii) **Emergencies.** Make sure you know where the nearest first aid box is kept, and the extension numbers of first aiders and of the nurse or doctor if there is one. Visitors, staff and even passers-by may all look to you for help if they are suddenly taken ill. For any emergency that looks serious, call an ambulance by telephoning the emergency operator (999 in the United Kingdom).

(b) Receiving Visitors

Try to remember the names and faces of regular visitors and to greet them by name. Even if you don't know them, all visitors should be greeted with a smile. Remember that many of them are nervous and unsure of themselves. They are on unfamiliar ground, so they may feel at a disadvantage. And for some, like

job applicants and suppliers hoping to negotiate a new contract, much depends
on the outcome of their visit. So look up from whatever you are doing and say
'Good morning—how can I help you?', as if you are pleased to see them and
really do want to help.

A stranger will then usually either tell you his name—'Harrow of Eden
Brothers, to see Miss Griffiths'—or give you his business card (see Fig. 22.2).
Sometimes he will do both.

You may recognize the name from your appointments list; otherwise you can
ask 'Is Miss Griffiths expecting you?' or 'Have you an appointment?', in a
friendly and positive way.

(i) **Visitors with appointments.** If the visitor does have an appointment, ask him
or her to sign the visitors' book alongside the entry you have already made, or
a separate callers' register. Meanwhile you can telephone through to the department where he or she is expected. Remember that the visitor can hear what
you say. 'Hello, this is reception. Mr Harrow has arrived for his 11 o'clock
appointment with Miss Griffiths' sounds better than 'Hi there; it's Sally. That
bloke from Eden Brothers is here again'.

Then you can direct the visitor to Miss Griffiths' office, or ask him to take a
seat until her secretary arrives to collect him.

(ii) **Visitors without appointments.** People who visit regularly do not always
need a specific appointment. They may just call in and ask if—say—Mr Sayles
can see them. If you recognize the visitor and know of no reason why Mr Sayles
would not wish to see him, you should telephone Mr Sayles' secretary and say
something like 'Hello, this is reception. I have Mr Soper at the desk. He
wondered if Mr Sayles could spare him a few minutes?' If the answer is 'yes',
you can deal with the visitor as though he had an appointment; if not, ask if you
can make an appointment for Mr Soper, or whether they would prefer him to
write or telephone for one. Pass the reply on to Mr Soper, with an apology and
a smile.

Occasionally a complete stranger will walk into reception and ask to see
perhaps the sales manager or the managing director. If there is a chance that the
manager concerned might be prepared to see the visitor without an appointment, you must find out the reason for the visit. 'Could you tell me what it's in
connection with?' is more polite than 'What's it about then?' or 'What do you
want him for?' Then you can telephone Mr Wilson's secretary and say 'Hello,
this is reception. I have a Mr Mortimer here from the local residents' association.
He wondered if Mr Wilson could spare him a few minutes to discuss the summer
fete the association is planning'.

As before, be guided by Mr Wilson or his secretary. If the visitor cannot be
seen without an appointment, you must tell him so, politely but firmly, and
suggest that he writes to Mr Wilson with an outline of his proposals and/or to
ask for an appointment.

(c) **At the End of the Visit**
As each visitor leaves the building, you may be required to note the fact, or to ask him or her to sign out. As you do so, say something like 'Thank you for calling, Mr Harrow. Goodbye.'

(d) **Unwelcome Visitors**
If a visitor who has no appointment appears unwilling to leave, you must be firm but polite. Repeat that Mr Sayles is not available, and explain again that the visitor should write or telephone for an appointment. Allow time for this to sink in—most people will accept it, once they have thought about it for a few minutes.

If the intruder becomes aggressive, you may have to call a security officer, if there is one, or even a police officer. Avoid this if you can, though. The sight of visitors being bundled into police vans on your doorstep probably won't do much for your organization's public image.

22.4 The Registry

In many organizations, each department or part of the business has its own filing section, with one or more filing clerks to operate it: this is *decentralized* filing. But in others it has been found to be more efficient or less expensive to set up a *centralized* filing system in a central *registry*.

(a) **Advantages of Centralized Filing**
   (i) Specialist staff can be used more effectively. The filing work from a group of six departments may keep four registry clerks occupied: this is a more efficient use of staff than having one clerk in each of six departments.
   (ii) Equipment can be more fully used and economies may be possible. Suppose that six departments each require four and a half filing cabinets; that means that there will be five cabinets in each department, making a total of thirty. If their files were all stored together, they could manage with only twenty-seven cabinets, a saving of three. Other filing-room equipment—staplers, staple-removers, absent folders, guide cards, the files themselves—are similarly less likely to be duplicated unnecessarily in different parts of the building.
   (iii) All the information on a particular subject can be stored together, so anyone consulting, say, the Sweep-it-Up Ltd file or file 50.67 will find all the correspondence exchanged with the company by all departments, and therefore have a complete picture.
   (iv) A standardized system of filing can be used throughout the organization. This avoids problems when staff transfer from one department to another.
   (v) A supervisor can be put in charge of the whole system, to make sure that all the filing clerks know their work and can do it effectively. Strict procedures for the requisitioning and return of files can be set up, and these may reduce the number of files mislaid, as well as deterring people from asking for files unnecessarily.

(vi) Centralization allows all records to be kept in one place, which can be securely locked at night and supervised during the day. This means that no unauthorized person can remove or damage files.

(b) Disadvantages of Centralized Filing

(i) Centralized filing staff spend all their working day filing. Many would prefer the variety that can be introduced by helping with other tasks in a department when its filing is up to date. This can also help the department, particularly at busy times.

(ii) Sending material to and from the central filing room gives rise to delays which office staff may find inconvenient.

(iii) A department dealing with an individual or an organization in one context may find it distracting to be confronted with piles of irrelevant paper relating to the work of other departments.

(iv) Whichever standardized system is used, it will not meet the needs of all departments. For instance, if a subject classification suits most departments, those for whom alphabetical, geographical or chronological classification would be better (like personnel, export and dispatch) will have to conform.

(v) Centralized filing requires formal requisitioning procedures to make it work. Registry staff may find it hard to learn about, or feel involved with, the work of any particular department. Some see this as a disadvantage.

(vi) Although all files are secure against outsiders, more people have access to them than where they are kept on a departmental basis. Confidential matters can thus become common knowledge in the organization unless great care is taken to restrict access to particular files.

The choice between the centralized and the non-centralized systems is a management decision. If you are to operate either effectively, you should be aware of the pitfalls of both.

22.5 Secretariat

Like filing, shorthand, audio and copy typing and word-processing can be handled on either a departmental or a centralized (*pool*) basis.

(a) Advantages of Centralization

(i) Staff are fully used—they are not dependent on the uneven flow of work from just one department.

(ii) Staff develop their typing skills to the utmost, through constant practice. In the typing pool there are fewer distractions, like ringing telephones and visitors, than in most other departments.

(iii) Equipment, especially expensive electronic typewriters and word-processors, is more intensively used.

(iv) The house style, or preferred layout of business correspondence, is more uniformly used, and the secretariat supervisor can keep a close eye on points of layout and style.

(v) The overall standard of work should be higher as it is checked not only by the originator of the work but often also by the secretariat supervisor or another senior staff member.

(b) Disadvantages of Centralization

(i) Secretariat typing staff spend all their time typing, and cannot enjoy the variety of tasks dealt with by a department typist.

(ii) Some departments produce work with a technical content. This takes time to master. It would be wasteful to train all the secretariat staff in this specialism—so the workload from that department tends to fall on one or two people anyway.

(iii) The secretariat staff are isolated from the rest of the work of the department or section whose work they are doing, and this can make it difficult for them to apply the common sense and knowledge of departmental procedures that is sometimes necessary to make sense of a piece of dictation or copy typing.

(iv) Delays can occur at busy periods, and this will cause frustration if the originators of the work had not expected them.

(v) Confidentiality is reduced, as more people have access to information.

22.6 The Post Room

In larger organizations, another area of office services may be centralized: the handling of the mail, with a central post room processing all the letters and parcels coming into and leaving the firm.

Again, there are advantages and disadvantages from management's point of view. The advantages generally relate to the degree of specialization post room staff can develop, and the more intensive use of expensive equipment. The disadvantages stem from the uneven flow of work and the lack of staff involvement in other departmental duties.

(a) Incoming Mail

(i) Each morning mail is either collected in a locked *private box* rented at the local Post Office sorting office, or delivered by Post Office staff in a *private bag*.

(ii) If the head postmaster operates a *Selectapost* system for your organization, incoming mail addressed to particular departments or sections will already have been put into separate batches, one for each department, at the Post Office.

(iii) When the mail arrives in the post room, the 'Private and Confidential' and 'Personal' letters are put directly into pigeon-holes or folders for the departments concerned.

(iv) The rest of the mail is *faced*, or put into piles with the address facing upwards. Each envelope should be checked to make sure that it is indeed addressed to your organization. Mail that has been wrongly delivered must be returned to the Post Office.

(v) After facing, the envelopes are *tapped*—stood upright on a flat surface and tapped to make sure the contents fall to the bottom.

(vi) The top edge of the envelope is inserted into a letter-opening machine (see Fig. 22.3) and a thin strip is cut off the top so that the contents can be removed. Some machines are automatic, and envelopes are fed through them on a conveyor belt.

(vii) The contents are date-stamped using an automatic time- and date-stamping machine.

(viii) Enclosures and used envelopes are dealt with as described in Unit 11.2.

(ix) Remittances are dealt with as explained in Unit 13.3.

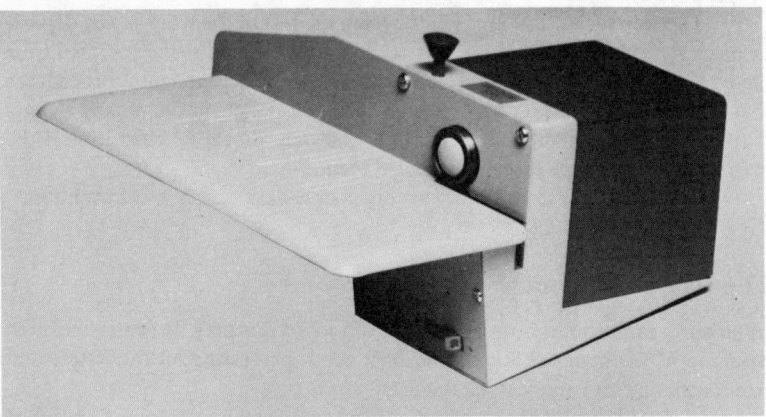

Fig. 22.3   Letter-opening machine: the letter to be opened is placed on the tray, with the side to be opened against the cutter

(b) Distribution

The letters and enclosures are sorted into folders or pigeon-holes, perhaps on a mobile trolley. The mail is then either delivered to each department by messenger, or collected by members of staff.

Letters which are to be seen by more than one person can be treated in one of three ways.

(i) *A distribution stamp* can be impressed on the letter, or (ii) a preprinted *circulation slip* (Fig. 22.4) can be stapled to it. The initials of those who are to see the letter are ticked; alternatively, they can be marked 1, 2, 3 and so on, in the order in which it is to be sent to them.

(iii) The words '*Copy sent to A and B*' can be written on the letter, which is then copied and a copy sent to each person. This method should be used if the letter is urgent.

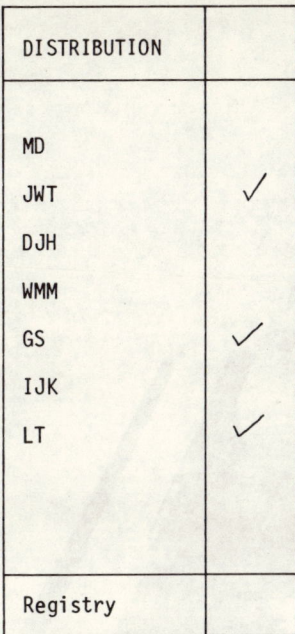

Fig. 22.4   Circulation slip

(c) Outgoing Mail

Towards the end of each working day, outgoing mail is either collected or brought to the post room, which provides a complete service for the handling of outgoing mail.

(i) **Addressing.** This can be speeded up, particularly for a bulk mailing of a lot of identical letters or brochures, by the use of an addressing machine. The post room staff prepare address plates with the names and addresses of all the people on the mailing list. The plates are kept in alphabetical order and, when wanted, are stacked in the addressing machine. As each envelope passes through the machine, one plate descends on to it, printing a name and address. Envelopes and plates are then automatically stacked in separate trays.

Addressing machines can also be used to impress the inside name and address on statements and invoices, to print staff names and numbers on clock cards, and to produce lists of customers or potential customers.

(ii) **Collating and inserting.** Where a series of documents, brochures or other items is to be sent to a large number of people, these have to be sorted into sets and put into envelopes. The post room staff can do this either by hand or using a collating machine (see Unit 10.2).

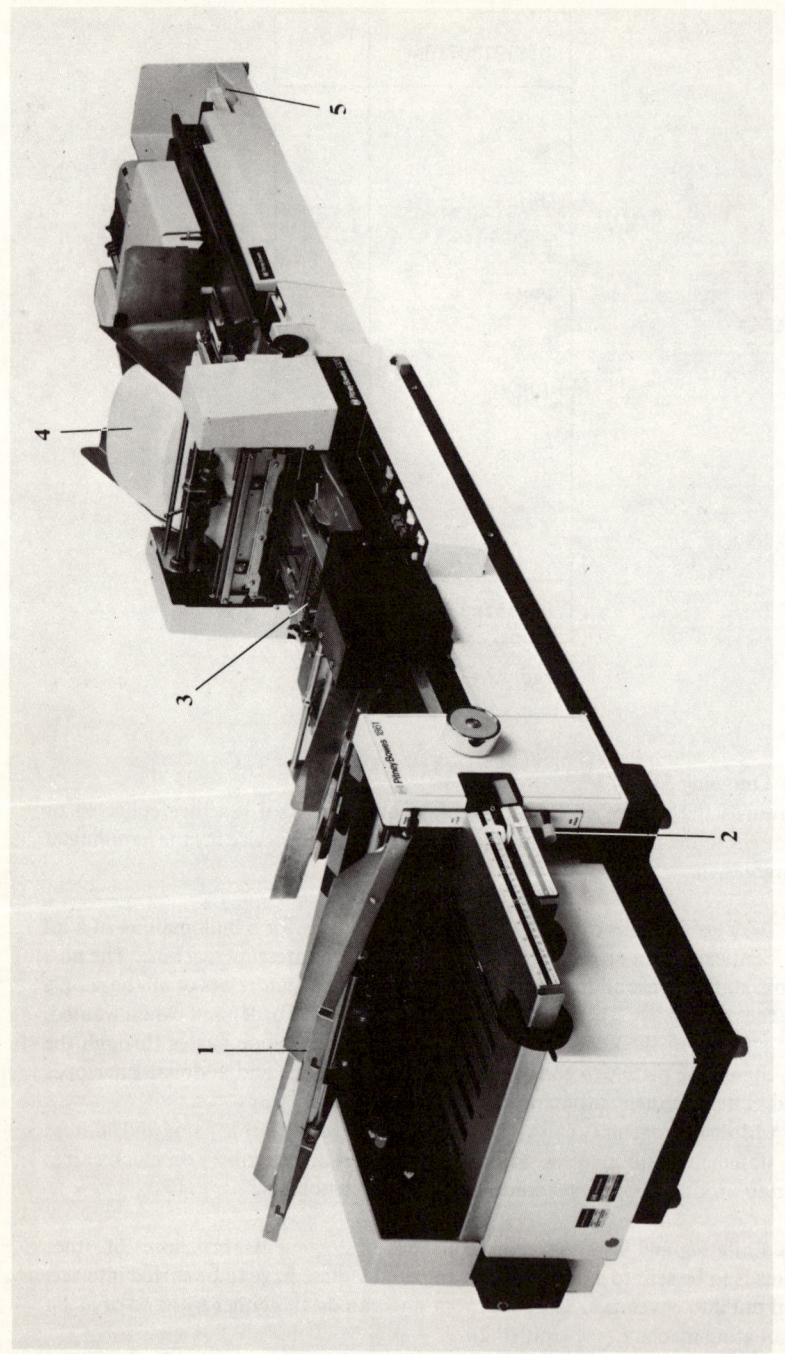

Fig. 22.5 Machine which addresses, collates, folds and stuffs. 1. Feeder tray for enclosures. 2. Fold settings. 3. Operator check-list. 4. Open envelopes. 5. Stacking tray for stuffed envelopes

Some collating machines can be linked to other post room equipment to provide a completely automated system for handling the mail. The machine shown in Fig. 22.5 prints the addresses on envelopes, collates the items to be sent out, folds and inserts them (*stuffs* them) in the envelopes. Finally the envelopes are sealed and franked to the correct postal value.

(iii) **Weighing and franking.** This follows the procedures outlined in Unit 11.5.

(iv) **Posting.** After franking, mail that has been processed in the post room, together with mail that has come down from departments ready for posting, is either collected by Post Office van or put into a lockable private bag, rented from the Post Office, which is taken to the Post Office by post room staff.

22.7 Quick Questions

1. What do you understand by the term 'ancillary services'? Name three types of clerical work which fall into this category.

2. List five functions of the receptionist.

3. An unexpected caller has presented you, the receptionist, with a business card. What would you do with it, (a) immediately, (b) after the caller had gone?

4. List five advantages and five disadvantages of a centralized audio typing pool.

5. List three ways of dealing with incoming mail which is to be circulated to several people.

6. What, in the context of the post room, is 'stuffing'?

22.8 Short Exercises

1. List the advantages and disadvantages of a centralized filing department or registry.

2. You are operating the firm's switchboard in reception when a caller comes through demanding to speak to the managing director. The caller's voice is loud and his speech is slightly slurred. What would you say to him?

Unit Twenty-three

Getting and Keeping an Office Job

23.1 Introduction

What will employers look for in you when you apply for a job? What will they expect of you once you have started work?

These are not easy questions to answer. Much will depend on the kind of office job you are applying for, and the size and type of organization you hope to join.

But for any job, you do need to show that you have the right basic *skills*, the right *knowledge* and the right *attitude*.

(a) Skills

(i) **Skill with words.** You must be able to read reasonably quickly and accurately. Filing, for instance, quickly falls into chaos if the filing clerk doesn't know the alphabet. And in any office job there are documents to be examined, instructions to be read, maybe letters to be typed.

(ii) **Skill with figures.** Especially if you are expected to handle money or deal with accounts, you must be able to add up, subtract and work out percentages. Even where adding machines and calculators are available, many employers still look for people with 'a head for figures'.

(iii) **Skill with people.** Jobs in reception or involving face-to-face or telephone contact call for the ability to listen, understand and communicate. Many office jobs mean working in a team. Social misfits or people who clearly dislike their fellow-men are not likely to succeed in jobs like these.

(iv) **Skills in office practice.** The ability to type or to operate a word-processor, experience in duplicating or copying or in handling mail room equipment— these are among the practical skills which you can acquire by following a course in office practice.

(b) Knowledge

(i) **General business knowledge.** Employers will expect you to have some understanding of what business is for, and what work in a particular department might involve.

(ii) **Knowledge of the employer's business.** Employers are impressed by the candidate who not only knows in general terms what the organization does, but who also has some idea of how big it is, how many sites it occupies and what its main products are.

(iii) **Knowledge of office practice.** An understanding of ordering and invoicing procedures, and of basic accounts work and petty cash, is useful in sales, purchasing and accounts.

(c) **Attitudes**
Although knowledge and skill are very important, your attitude to work is often the deciding factor. Employers expect:

(i) **Willingness to work.** Most employers are unimpressed by people who appear more interested in what they will get out of a job—money, holidays, sick pay—than in what they can put into it.

(ii) **Reliability.** Employers need to know that you will turn up for work on time, every day. So be sure not to arrive late for your interview or on your first morning.

(iii) **Honesty and integrity.** Many office jobs include responsibility for money or confidential information. Your employer must be sure that you won't be tempted to put your fingers in the till, or to gossip about company secrets.

(iv) **Conformity.** People are usually most at ease with people they feel they can understand. But many employers do not understand the attractions of passing fashion trends, even though they may be important to you and your friends. They expect people to dress fairly conventionally for interview and for work, and to avoid way-out hair-styles and make-up.

If you feel that you can persuade an employer that you have most of these qualities—to some degree at least—you are ready to start looking for an office job. In *Job Finding: a Step by Step Guide* (Penny Hackett, published by John Murray) the whole process is discussed in detail. Here we shall outline the main elements only.

23.2 Learning about Opportunities

There are four main sources of information about office jobs in the United Kingdom.

(a) **Government Employment Services**
Many employers notify the local authority Careers Office if they are looking for people under the age of 18, and the Jobcentre or Employment Office if they need someone older. The employer provides basic information about the job—its title, the hours and the rate of pay—and about the sort of person required, such as the amount and kind of previous experience, educational qualifications, special abilities. In a Jobcentre, this information is displayed on cards in the front office, so that you can browse through them. When you find one that

interests you, you can ask the staff to arrange an interview for you, or to get you an application form.

(b) Commercial Agencies
You will recognize these by the notices in their windows proclaiming slogans like:

$$£4\,000\text{ per annum}\qquad\text{Invoice clerk—local}$$

You can use these agencies to find either a temporary or a permanent job. If you are under 18, however, the law forbids an agency to introduce you to an employer unless you have already had advice from your careers officer about what sort of job to look for.

(c) The Media
Your local paper and your local radio station are good sources of information. If the employer has worded his advertisement clearly, you should be able to assess what the job requires and what it would be like to work for the organization.

Office jobs appear in two basic forms in the local newspaper. *Classified advertisements* are usually fairly brief, giving the name of the firm, the job title, a brief indication of duties and benefits and a name and address or telephone number to contact for more information.

Some firms try to attract attention by using *display advertising*, extending over two or more columns of the newspaper and often framed in a 'box'. Although some organizations only use this more expensive style of advertising for senior and highly paid positions, others use a single large advertisement to recruit for several different jobs, giving brief details of each. It is certainly worth reading quickly through these *composite* advertisements, to make sure that you are not missing a good office opportunity just because the top line says something about welders.

Some local radio stations have special services allowing employers to advertise the vacancies they are trying to fill; listeners can ring the radio station for more information.

(d) The Grapevine and Direct Approaches
Friends and relatives may tell you about vacancies at their own places of work, and you can then apply.

If there is a company for which you would particularly like to work, there is nothing to stop you writing or telephoning to ask if they have any suitable openings, even if none have been advertised. It is usually best to address your enquiry to the personnel officer, making it clear what sort of work you are looking for and what relevant experience you have. This method can be successful but it can cost a lot in time, waiting for replies, and postage. Also it is disheartening if you keep drawing a blank. But if you really want a job, every long-shot effort is worth making.

23.3 Making Contact with Employers

Once you have found a position for which you would like to apply, you should:

(a) Read the advertisement again carefully or consult the agency, to find out exactly what form your application should take.

(b) Before telephoning in response to an advertisement, make a note of the name of the person you wish to speak to, where the advertisement appeared, what the job title is, and what qualifications you have that fit you for the job. Be ready for a telephone interview, and bear in mind the points on spoken communication made in Units 2 and 3.

(c) When writing for a position, refer to the advertisement and make it clear why you are interested in this particular post and what relevant qualifications, experience and qualities you possess. Write (or, if you can, type) a formal business letter, following the guidance given in Unit 4.

23.4 Completing an Application Form

The application form provides a chance for you to think through and put before the recruiter everything that helps to make you suitable for the position for which you are applying. Answer all the questions honestly and as fully as space permits. If you are about to sit school or college examinations, or are awaiting the results, say so. Never pretend to have passed an examination if you haven't; and make sure that you can talk reasonably knowledgeably and enthusiastically about any hobbies or interests you claim to have.

Try to avoid errors while filling in the form. Fig. 23.1 shows some of the basic mistakes that make personnel managers shake their heads and mutter: 'How can he possibly do a job like that if he can't even fill in an application form properly?' Go through the form and see how many mistakes you can find. Seventeen are listed in the Appendix.

When completing an application form you should:

(a) use a dictionary if you are uncertain about spelling;

(b) fill in the form faintly in pencil first or make notes on a spare piece of paper;

(c) ask someone else to read it through;

(d) copy it out neatly in ink, without spelling mistakes and without crossing out, and erase the pencil marks fully.

Most employers see so many untidy forms that yours will then stand out and will give them a favourable first impression of you.

When you have completed the form, return it without delay, with any other requested documents, such as copies of educational certificates. Most recruiters work to a fairly tight time schedule and do not consider application forms that are not received until after interviewing has started.

Section 1: Personal details
Surname: *John Richard*   Forenames: *Doe*
Address: *43 Halifax Road*   Telephone: *9261*
Date of birth: *20th February 198_*
Place of birth   *at home*
Nationality: *English*
Marital status   *?*
Position applied for: *the one you advertised*

Section 2: Educational details
(Please start with the most recent.)

School/college (Name and address)	Date started	Date left	Examinations passed (with grades)
Church Road Juniors	*1969*	*1975*	*None*
Mill Lane Secondary	*1975*	*1980*	*O level art, woodwork, biology, CSE English, maths, geography.*

Section 3 : Previous employment

(Please list all employment for the last twelve years, starting with the most recent, and giving month and year.)

Company (name and address)	Date started	Date left	Job title	Reason for leaving
Costalot Limited	*1980*		*General Clerk*	*Haven't decided*

Signature: *JOHN DOE* ....

Fig. 23.1   *Job application form*

23.5 Attending for an Interview

In broad terms, a job interview enables the employer to assess whether or not you will be an asset to the organization, and whether you have the knowledge, skills and attitudes needed for the post. You can do a good deal to convince him or her that you have.

(a) **Before the Interview**

(i) Confirm that you will attend for interview at the time and place specified. You can do this by letter or telephone, depending on how much time is available.

(ii) Do some homework. Find out as much as you can about the organization and what it does, and about what the job might involve. Some of the sources of company information listed in Unit 4.6 will help you.

(iii) Allow plenty of time to get to the interview. Aim to enter the building about ten minutes before the time of the appointment.

(iv) Wear clothes that are neat, tidy and not too extreme.

(v) Be polite to everyone you meet, from the moment you enter the organization's premises. Tell the receptionist your name, the name of the person you have come to see, and the time of the appointment.

(vi) Interviewers often shake hands with applicants at the first meeting. Try to give a firm but friendly handshake, so they will think you are a firm but friendly person.

(b) **During the Interview**

During the interview, behave as naturally as you can: be yourself, but try to present yourself in a positive light. Remember, this is your chance to explain what you can do, how well you can do it, and why you want to do it for this particular organization.

(i) Answer all the interviewer's questions clearly, directly and honestly. Provide extra detail and examples where you can, rather than just 'yes' or 'no'.

(ii) Try to judge how much information the interviewer wants from you. Don't clam up after a few words, but don't rattle on for minutes on end unless the interviewer is clearly encouraging you to do so.

(iii) Smile occasionally, but not all the time.

(iv) Listen carefully to everything the interviewer says. This will help you to form an impression of the firm and reduce the risk that you will ask a question about something you have already been told.

(v) Look at the interviewer—but don't stare.

(vi) Don't fidget.

(vii) Don't allow yourself to be put on the defensive, even if the interviewer seems to be implying that he doesn't think much of your qualifications or experience.

(viii) Never run down your present employer (if you have one), or you may be thought disloyal. Instead put forward the positive reasons why you want to join the new organization.

(ix) Have your certificates, work samples and a testimonial (letter of recommendation from a previous employer) with you if you have any, but do not produce them until the interviewer asks for them.

(x) Be prepared to ask one or two questions, if you are invited to do so. It's better to ask something related to the content of the job, the training or the promotion prospects than to dive straight in demanding to know the pay and the hours of work. You want to give the employer the impression that you are interested in what you will put into the job, as well as what you can expect to get out of it.

(xi) At the end of the interview, thank the interviewer for his or her time and shake hands again if you are invited to do so.

23.6 Completing a Test

In addition to interviews, some organizations also use tests to help them assess your ability. These are designed to test your *performance*, *aptitude* and *knowledge*.

(a) Performance Tests
If you are applying for a job as an audio typist, the typing supervisor may well ask you to type back the contents of part of an audio cassette. Before you start, he or she should explain any particular layout or other requirements of the organization, and let you know what the time limit is. If the machine is strange to you, don't be afraid to ask for a few moments to familiarize yourself with the margins, tabs, and so forth before timing begins. If you are taking shorthand dictation and find it inaudible or too fast, it is sometimes useful to lean forward saying 'I'm sorry, I didn't quite catch that'. In trying to repeat the word more clearly, the dictator will unconsciously slow down. It is better if you can produce your own shorthand notebook, with a rubber band round the used portion, than if you have to start borrowing pads and pencils.

Other jobs for which performance tests are likely to be encountered are those of copy typist and telephonist. You may also find yourself required to complete a similar sort of work sample for other office jobs—completing part of a record card or ledger, for instance, or filing documents or operating an accounting machine.

(b) Aptitude Tests
If you are applying for a job of which you have no previous experience, you could be given a test designed to measure how easily you may be able to develop the skills and knowledge needed. Clerical aptitude tests, for instance, may require you to copy words or numbers, or to note mistakes in lists of words or numbers, such as

Wigan Lancs	Wigan Lincs
026894	062894

(c) Knowledge Tests
At some interviews you may be asked to complete a written test to see whether or not you have the foundation of knowledge the job requires. The travel company Costalot Ltd might, for example, ask applicants to name the capital cities of major countries, to say where large rivers are, and to indicate what currencies are in use in particular areas of the world.

If you find yourself faced with a test of any kind, listen carefully to the instructions given to you, keep an eye on the time and try to work steadily. The tests are not imposed on you to make you feel inadequate. They are designed to help the organization, and you, to find out if you are really suited to the job for which you are applying. If the tests show that you are not, you could be saved a lot of unhappiness and frustration in trying to struggle with the wrong job.

23.7 Providing Additional Information

(a) References
You may be asked to give the names of one or two *referees*, who might be able to provide accurate information about your character and your approach to work. There may be a question to this effect on the application form, or you may be asked at your interview. Referees should not be related to you in any way; if you have been employed before, you should normally include your last employer. Permission should always be obtained before giving anyone's name as a referee.

(b) Medical Information
Some organizations attach a medical questionnaire to their application forms, to find out whether you have any illness or disability that might prove a problem if they were to employ you. Or you may be asked to undergo a medical examination.

Most organizations respect the confidential nature of any medical information they obtain about you, and generally it is to your benefit as well as theirs that you should not be placed in a job that is beyond your physical or mental capabilities.

23.8 Getting the Job

If the organization decide to offer you the job, they will either write or telephone to let you know when and where to report for work and what, if anything, to bring with you. If the offer comes in writing, you should write back without delay, thanking them, and accepting or declining. This is an exciting moment and if you accept the job let them know how pleased you are and say you look forward to joining them on the appointed date.

Make sure you collect Parts 2 and 3 of your Certificate P45 (see Unit 20.3(g)) from your present employer if you have one. If you haven't worked before, your new employer will give you a form to fill in. These matters must be sorted out early on, so your new employer can deduct the right amount of tax and National Insurance contributions from your pay.

Report for work *on time* on your first day, and every day.

23.9 Finding Your Way Around

During your first few days in your new job, you will be absorbing five kinds of information.

(a) Geography of the Building

You may already have some idea of the layout of the building from your interview visit. If the premises are quite small, you will soon find your way around and by the end of your first day you will know where the lavatories are, where to leave your coat, where to go for lunch and other domestic details. In a larger establishment with several different offices, production departments and other activities, it may take rather longer before you can walk along a corridor knowing precisely which way to turn when you get to the other end.

Many employers will arrange a guided tour of the building on your first day. You probably won't be able to memorize every detail at once, but try at least to get an idea of the general shape of the place. If there is no guided tour, someone in the department will probably be introduced as your *sponsor* or *guide*. This person may be a team leader, or one of the other clerks in the department. Either way, don't be frightened to ask your sponsor whenever you are unsure of your way.

(b) Who's Who

When you applied for the job you were probably interviewed by your department manager, or at least had a chat with him or her; if not, the personnel officer or an assistant should introduce you at this stage.

Your department manager is concerned with all the activities discussed in Unit 1.4, and on your first day will probably spend time with you to explain the work of the department and your place in it.

Your manager will introduce you to other people in the department. If it is a small one, you may meet everybody on your first day. In a larger department, you may meet just your supervisor, team leader, sponsor and one or two other people—perhaps those nearest your own age or doing the same job. Meeting a lot of new people all at once can be confusing and nobody will expect you to remember everyone. One way of trying to fix some of their names in your memory is to repeat them aloud. So when your manager says 'And this is Mrs Green, your section leader', say 'Hello, Mrs Green', rather than just 'Hello'.

To introduce you to the rest of the organization, your manager may give you an organization chart (Fig. 1.2).

(c) The Organization

When you join an organization, particularly if it is a large one, you may find that people are very eager to tell you all about it. You may be shown a film or given a booklet, explaining the history of the company since its foundation. You may be given lists of the products it makes and the services it provides. You may be told how many people are employed, on how many different jobs and in how many different places, what is the firm's annual *turnover* (how much it sells in a year), and what plans it has for the future.

Although the information may sound irrelevant to your immediate concerns as a new recruit, it can be very useful to you. Knowing about what the company does can help you deal with queries and solve problems later on, and knowing about its size and the volume of business handled can help you to recognize the achievements of the organization and perhaps even make you feel proud to be a part of it.

Again, you may find it difficult to absorb all this information in your first few days. Keep the booklets or make notes of what you are told, however, and go back through them occasionally after you have been at work for a few weeks.

(d) Terms and Conditions of Employment

Within thirteen weeks of starting work, you should be given a written statement of your terms and conditions of employment, or an actual contract to sign (see Unit 1.8(d)). The manager will probably draw your attention to your hours of working, whether you must sign in or use a time clock to record your attendance, and when, where and for how long you can take your lunch and other breaks. He may also talk about holiday arrangements, what you should do if you are ill, and who you should see if you need time off for any reason. He should also explain specific rules, such as whether or not you may smoke in the office, and any particular requirements there may be about what you should wear.

Listen carefully to all this, and read your contract through before you sign it. And remember—once you have signed you must keep your side of the bargain.

(e) Your Job

Last, but by no means least, you will need to absorb information about your job. The amount and complexity of this will depend on the nature of the job and on the amount of similar previous experience you have had. Your manager, supervisor or team leader may explain the tasks to you and you can ask questions about any points that are not clear. Make sure you understand what to do with each of the pieces of work assigned to you, what procedures you should follow and what manuals you should consult, and whom you should ask if you have any problems. You also need to know what you should do when you have finished a piece of work: where it should be put or to whom it should be given, and where the next piece of work comes from.

There may be machines for you to operate in this job that you have not encountered before. Different makes of duplicating and copying equipment, for instance, have different operating instructions, even though the basic principles are the same. Even if you think you know what to do, it is often wisest to ask the person training you to watch you the first time you operate the machine, to make sure nothing goes wrong.

Clearly, all the details of your new office job are not likely to be covered on your first day and it may be several weeks or even months before you are fully trained. Usually you will find that your manager, supervisor and colleagues are ready and willing to offer help when you get stuck. Don't be frightened to ask for their help—but do keep in mind that they have got their own jobs to do too. So thank them for any help they give, and remember their advice.

When things go wrong—as they do for everyone at times—don't panic or walk out. Think the problem through! You know you can cope. So keep calm, keep trying—and keep working.

Unless matters are really desperate, never leave a permanent job within a year of starting it, and never give in your notice until you have another job to go to. If you do decide to move on, give your employer the amount of written notice specified in your contract of employment, explain briefly why you are leaving if you feel it would be courteous to do so, and thank him or her for the experience you have gained while working with them. And make sure you collect your Certificate P45 to give to your new employer.

If you wish, you can also ask your old firm for a testimonial, although many larger companies prefer to supply a reference direct to your new employer.

Throughout your office career, try to conduct yourself in such a way that when your employer is asked to write a reference for you, there are no doubts at all about your success in office practice.

23.10 Quick Questions

1. List three main sources of information about office employment.

2. List three things to remember when completing an application form.

3. What is the purpose of the employment interview, from the employer's point of view?

4. List three kinds of pre-employment test, and indicate what each is used to assess.

5. What, in the employment context, is a referee?

6. List three things you will need to learn about during your induction (that is, your introduction to the new job and the organization).

23.11 Short Exercises

1. Copy out the headings on the application form (Fig. 23.1) and fill in the form using your own details instead of those of John Doe. Ask another member of your study group, or a friend or colleague, to go through it with you (a) to see if it contains any errors, and (b) to discuss your suitability for an office job.

2. What are the things you expect to find most difficult about starting work in a new job? Make brief notes, and indicate how your difficulties could be lessened.

Appendix

The following mistakes were made by John Doe when he completed the form in Fig. 23.1:

1. The surname and forenames are mixed up.
2. The name of the town is omitted from the address.
3. The exchange or code is omitted from the telephone number.
4. The date of birth is obviously wrong.
5. 'February' is wrongly spelt.
6. The place of birth should be given as the town or country—employers aren't interested in whether you were born at home or in hospital.
7. If John and his parents were born in England he probably has British (not English) nationality.
8. The question mark against 'marital status' seems to indicate that John does not understand the question. He should have said whether he is married, single, divorced or separated from his wife.
9. The organization may have advertised several positions recently. The particular job title should be given.
10. The school addresses are not given.
11. Church Road Junior School should have been listed second, as the form asks for the most recent school to be given first.
12. John's O-level and CSE grades are not given.
13. The address for Costalot is not given.
14. 'Date started' is incomplete - the month as well as the year is required on this form.
15. The gap under 'date left' is confusing. Is it an oversight? Can't he remember? Is he still there? The words 'to date' should be inserted if he is still employed.
16. 'Haven't decided' also creates confusion—he probably means he is still employed and has not yet decided to leave, but he should have said so more clearly.
17. A signature should not be written in block capitals; it is supposed to be distinctive and a means of identifying the person concerned. Except for signatures, however, all forms should be completed in block capitals unless they specifically direct otherwise.

Assignments

Unit One

Talk to someone you know who works in an office. Draw up a description of his or her job, using the headings that appear in the job description in Fig. 1.1.

Unit Two

Imagine that you work in an office which is to be moved from one part of the building to another. Your boss, Mr James, calls you in to brief you on this, and says to you:

'Right; I've talked to each of the others about the move and now I'd like to tell you how you can help to make sure it all goes smoothly. I want you to pack the contents of all the drawers of your desk, but make sure you have a bit of a tidy-up first—there's no point in carting a whole load of useless paper and things over there. We might as well start fresh. I want you to be responsible for all the box files as well—that'll mean counting them and putting them somewhere at the other end. I've forgotten where just at the minute because someone's borrowed my plan, but ask me tomorrow so you know before we get there. You don't have to carry them over yourself. Get a tea chest for them and your desk contents—no, better get two tea chests from Harry. You'll need to look after the stationery cupboard too. We've been letting that run down for the last little while so there's not much in it. Check to see if there's anything loose in it and find some boxes for small items. Then I suppose you'll need another tea chest from Harry for that. Oh yes, and on the box files, don't forget we'll need to put them out in the same order at the other end, so better make a note of how they are now—it's not quite alphabetical, is it? Now the other thing is labels for everything. You'll need to get enough sticky labels from Harry for all the tea chests we're taking, so you had better check how many that'll be and issue the labels to everyone. Get big enough ones to write the contents on, and the initials of the person looking after the chest. Oh yes, the other thing is, we want to leave this place reasonably tidy as the Purchasing Department want to get in by the end of the week. Get some sacks from Harry to put all your rubbish in and give one to each of the others too.'

Make notes of the main points of Mr James's instructions, and prepare a list of 'matters arising', indicating what action is needed, and by whom and when it must be taken.

Unit Three

A training session regarding the use of the telephone is to be held for junior and new members of staff in the sales department. You have been asked to assist with this session and have recorded the conversation below for staff to listen to and then discuss. You have been asked to carry out the following preliminary work in readiness for this discussion:

(a) Prepare a corrected version of Miss A's part in the conversation.

(b) List the reasons you will give for Miss A's responses during the conversation being classed as poor telephone technique.

Miss A Hello.

Client Is that the sales department?

Miss A Yes.

Client I'd like to speak to Mr Ryder, please.

Miss A Hang on, I'll see if he's here ...

No, sorry, he's not here, at least I can't find him, perhaps he's gone out. Come to think of it, he did say he might pop out to see the people at that new camping shop in West Street.

Client Well, can you tell me when I can contact him?

Miss A Oh, I don't really know.

Client Perhaps you would give him a message from me ...

Miss A Just a tick while I get paper and pencil.

Client Ask him to telephone Mr Jeff White, please. I shall be in my office until 6.00 p.m.

Miss A OK. Goodbye.

[*RSA, Office Practice II (case study)*]

Unit Four

Display the following information, using a bar graph with scales of 20 mm = £1 000:

Sales figures:

	Sep	Oct	Nov	Dec	Jan	Feb	Mar
	£	£	£	£	£	£	£
Mr X	1 500	2 000	2 000	2 500	3 000	3 500	3 400
Mr Y	1 200	2 300	2 000	2 400	2 800	2 500	2 000
Mr Z	2 000	3 000	1 800	3 000	3 500	4 000	4 000

From the graph you have constructed give the following information:

(a) In which month were Mr Z's sales double those of Mr Y?

(b) In which month of the year were combined sales at their maximum?

(c) In which month of the year were combined sales below £5 000?

Unit Five

Spend half an hour 'hazard-spotting'—that is, exploring your workplace, college or home to see how many potential causes of fire or of damage to people or property you can find. Prepare a list of these hazards; explain why you think each is dangerous and say what should be done about it.

Unit Six

Your office manager has asked you to examine some new systems of filing and recording information, with the twin aims of saving storage space and increasing efficiency. Prepare notes for a brief report on any three storage methods which you feel might be appropriate.

Unit Seven

Part 1
Work through your local telephone directory, writing down names, addresses and telephone numbers at random from each alphabetical section (that is, four beginning with 'A', four with 'B', and so on). Write each name and address on a separate card or slip of paper.

(*a*) Arrange the cards in sets, one for each postal area. In London, for example, you might have cards from NW1, SW19, SE9 and so on. In other areas, use the names of villages or towns as your indexing units.

(*b*) Arrange each set of cards into alphabetical order, using the telephone subscribers' names as your indexing units.

(*c*) Put the sets together according to the alphabetical/alpha-numeric order of districts.

Part 2
Now rearrange the cards or slips prepared in Part 1 in numerical order, according to telephone numbers. (Omit the dialling code—01-942, for instance—if this is given, and use only the subscriber's personal number, that is, the last group of numbers that appears in the directory.)

Type or write out an index of numbers and names, starting with the lowest number and working upwards, for example:

Number	Name
6521	Hardcastle, J. R.
6728	Blythe, T. P.

Unit Eight

The recent introduction of centralized filing to a company has not been without initial difficulties. Write a report for the office manager explaining procedures which, if adopted, would alleviate the following problems:

(*a*) the difficulty the filing clerk has of remembering who has borrowed a particular file when another department also requests it;

(*b*) files frequently being kept beyond the date specified for their return as the borrower may have forgotten that a file is still in his possession;

(*c*) the difficulty of locating current files because cabinets are becoming full with files of completed contracts which have to be retained for several years.

[*RSA, Office Practice II (case study)*]

Unit Nine

Your office manager, Mr Turnbull, is considering whether the purchase of a plain-paper copier is likely to be worth while, given that both an ink and a spirit duplicator are already in the office. Prepare a tabulated statement, making comparisons of the three machines under the following headings:

(*a*) Duplicating process (state the materials you would use)
(*b*) Applications, that is, its suitability for the production of:
   (i)   black typewritten work
   (ii) coloured typewritten work
   (iii) handwriting/drawing
   (iv) photographs
(*c*) Quantities produced
(*d*) Type of paper employed for copies
(*e*) Other remarks.

Unit Ten

(*This Assignment has been designed as a group activity, but if you are working alone you will find it easy to adapt for individual study. You will need access to some form of reprographic equipment.*)

The principal of your college has asked the office practice class to put together a document, which will be presented to the college governors, to provide some examples of the kind of work you do on your course.

Working as a group (of not more than five), decide what you would like to include. Each member of the group should then be responsible for typing (or writing out neatly) at least one page of the document. One member of the group should then produce a 'Contents' page. You should then:

(*a*) write a brief introduction to the document;
(*b*) decide what method of reprography will be most appropriate to produce ten copies suitable for presentation to the governors;
(*c*) ask each member of the group to produce ten copies of his or her own page or pages;
(*d*) collate the copies;
(*e*) bind the pages (if facilities are available) in a form suitable for presentation to the college governors.

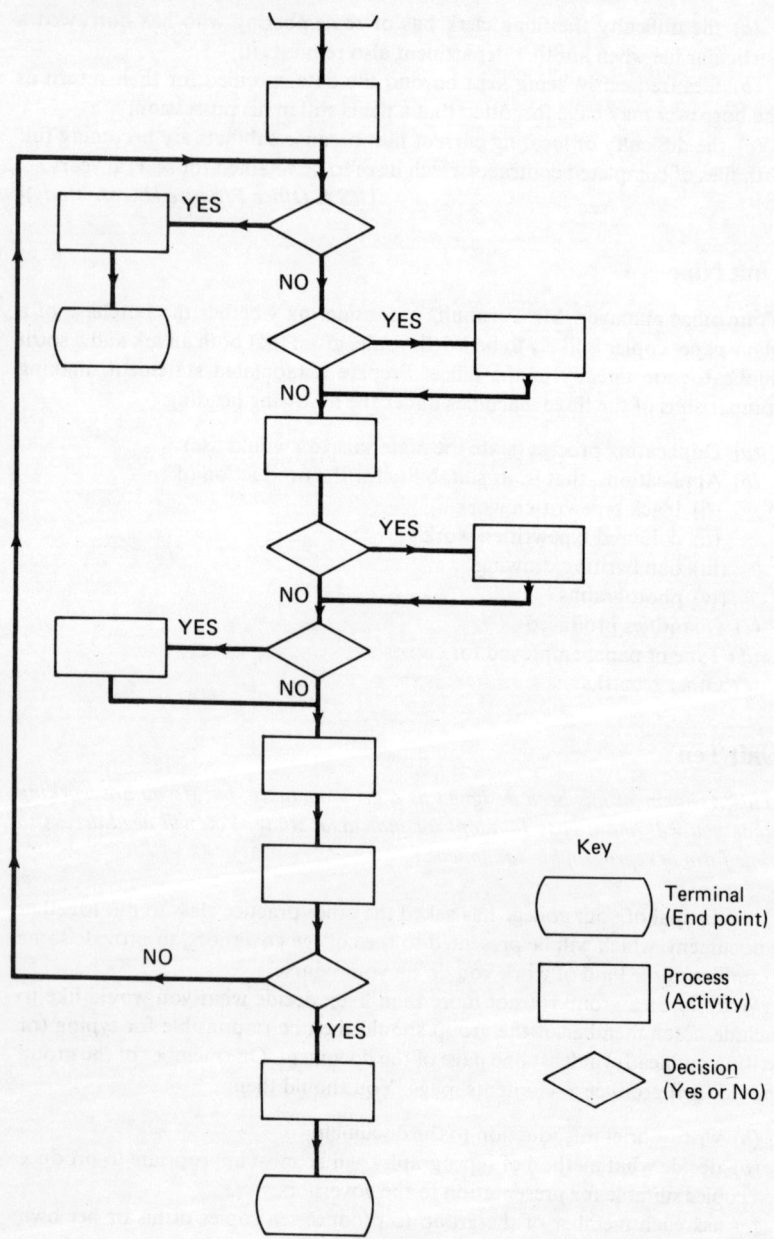

Key

Terminal (End point)

Process (Activity)

Decision (Yes or No)

Fig. A11.1 Incoming mail procedure: complete this chart using the headings in Fig. A11.2

Unit Eleven

(*For the second part of this assignment you will need access to an electronic scanner and either an ink duplicator or an offset litho machine.*)
You are employed in the Reprographic Department, Saltscar Group, Redcar, Cleveland.

Mr J. Nicholson (mail room) requires copies of the attached flow chart (Fig. A11.1) showing the procedure for sorting incoming mail which mail room staff will complete during their training period. Copy and fill in the blank flow chart to show the correct procedure for sorting mail, in order to produce an answer key for Mr Nicholson. A list of relevant headings is attached to assist you (Fig. A11.2).

Remittance enclosed?
Date stamp
Collection tray
Stop
Sort mail
Record
Enclosure?
Last letter?
Start
Deliver unopened
Open mail
Check and record remittance
Registered or recorded delivery?
Attach enclosure
Remittance to cashier
Private or confidential?

Fig. A11.2   Incoming mail procedure

Please produce a stencil on the electronic scanner and duplicate ten A4 copies on the ink duplicator or offset litho. See that safety regulations are observed. Clean the duplicator after use, and store material. File one copy.

[*BTEC General, Use of Office Machines and Equipment*]

Unit Twelve

1. (*a*) The following items have to be posted. Use the current *Postage Rates Compendium* to calculate how much should be charged for each item:

   (i) letter weighing 249 g—second class;
   (ii) letter weighing 138 g valued at £230—registered post;
   (iii) parcel weighing $4\frac{1}{2}$ kg—area rate;

(iv) compensation fee parcel weighing 3½ kg, valued at £20 via national rate;

(v) letter weighing 85 g, first class—recorded delivery.

(b) State two differences between each of the following:

(i) registered and recorded delivery;

(ii) business reply and Freepost services.

(c) Describe briefly three ways in which a large company can save money on postage, without reducing the amount of mail sent.

(d) Name two items of information on a franking slip.

[*RSA, Office Practice I*]

Unit Thirteen

1. Draw up a blank petty cash voucher, using Fig. 13.1 (page 155) as a guide. Make six copies. (These may be carbon copies if you do not have access to reprographic equipment.) Number your vouchers from 001 to 006, and make them out as follows:

Number	Date	Item	Amount £ p	Signature	Passed by
001	24 April	Coffee	1 15		B. Harrow
002	25 April	Envelopes	1 00	A. Smart	B. Harrow
003	25 April	Window-cleaner	5 50	C. True	L. Duff
004	26 April	Newspapers	0 75		
		Magazines	1 25		
		String	0 95	A. Smart	B. Harrow
005	27 April	Flowers	2 20	B. Wiggins	L. Duff
006		Brown paper	1 20	L. Case	

2. Draw up a blank petty cash book page, using Fig. 13.2 (page 157) as a guide. £25.00 in cash was received as imprest on 23 April.

3. Check that the petty cash vouchers are in correct sequence and are properly made out. If any are incorrect, draft a short memo to your office manager, Mr Drew, drawing his attention to the errors.

4. Make the appropriate entries on your petty cash book page, and balance the account as at 27 April. Enter the amount that will be required to restore the imprest to the original £25.00.

Unit Fourteen

Draw up a blank paying-in slip, using Fig. 14.4 (page 164) as a guide.

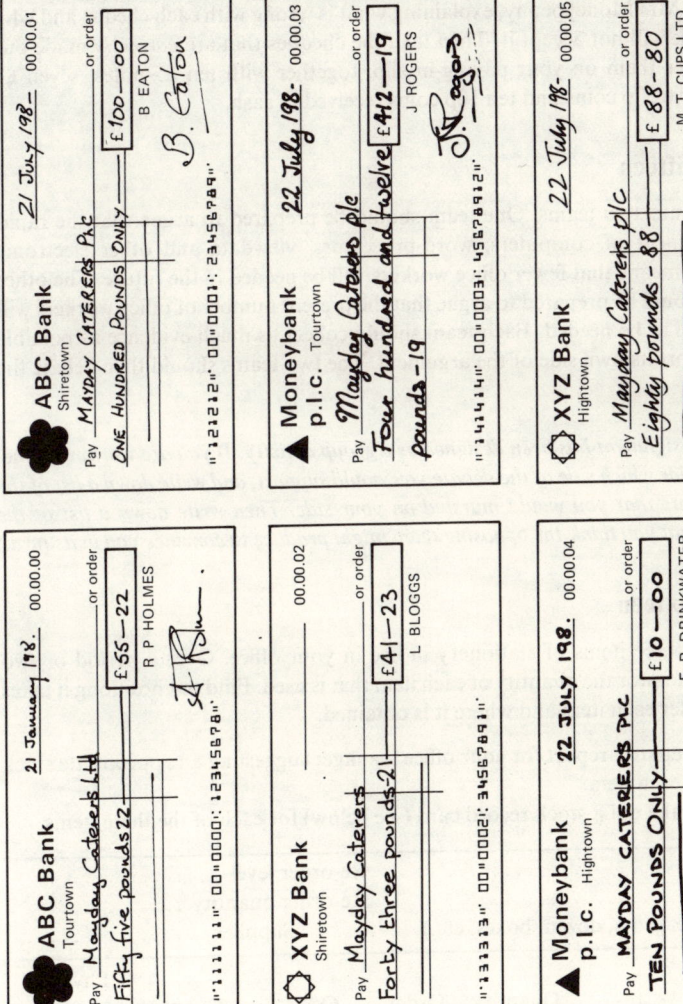

Fig. A14.1

You are employed by Mayday Caterers p.l.c. The cheques shown in Fig. A14.1 have been received today, 23 July. Study the cheques carefully and identify any which are incorrectly completed. Note the drawer's name and the bank and account number of these *incorrect* cheques, and write a short memo to the chief cashier, Mrs Moneypenny, explaining what is wrong with each cheque and why the bank will not accept it. Then take the cheques that are *correctly* made out and enter them on your paying-in slip, together with ten £5 notes, seven £1 coins, five 50p coins and ten 10p coins received in cash.

Unit Fifteen

Divide into two teams. One team should be prepared to argue that the rapid development of computers, word-processors, viewdata and other electronic systems means that fewer office workers will be needed in the future. The other team should be prepared to argue that the present number of office workers will continue to be needed. Each team should collect as much evidence as possible to support its own side of the argument. The two teams should then debate the subject.

(*This Assignment has been designed as a group activity. If you are working alone, first decide which side of the debate you would support, and write down a list of the arguments that you would marshal on your side. Then write down a list of the points that you think the opposing team might produce to convince you in its turn.*)

Unit Sixteen

Choose three items of stationery in use in your office. Over a period of two weeks, monitor the quantity of each item that is used. Find out how long it takes to re-order each item and where it is obtained.

(*a*) Prepare a report for your office manager suggesting an appropriate stock level for each item.

(*b*) Make out a stock record card (see below) for each of the three items.

Item......................   Re-order level ....
Line no. ....   Re-order quantity ....
Units (i.e. gross, dozen, boxes, etc.) ....   Supplier ....

Date	Order no.	Quantity ordered	Order balance	Quantity received	Quantity issued	Physical stock balance

Unit Seventeen

1. Draw up a blank invoice form, using Fig. 17.4 (page 202) as a guide. Make six copies. (These may be carbon copies if you do not have access to reprographic equipment.) Number the invoices 0001 to 0006 and make them out as follows:

Number	Customer	Order no	Product no	Date	Quantity	Description	Unit price
							£ p
0001	Nightrider Ltd	1212K	H12	6 Oct	12	Chairs	26 80
0002	Daytime p.l.c.	49368	F13	6 Oct	20	Stools	15 00
0003	Whispers Ltd	8491B	H12	6 Oct	3	Chairs	26 80
0004	M&J Holdings	65987	H18	6 Oct	6	Tables	130 00
0005	Nightrider Ltd	1214K	H18	8 Oct	5	Tables	130 00
0006	Daytime p.l.c.	49375	H12	8 Oct	6	Chairs	26 80

2. Calculate (using a calculator or adding machine if you have one) and enter the value of goods on each invoice, deducting discount at 40 per cent for all customers purchasing six or more items at once. Calculate and enter VAT at 15 per cent on all goods, and indicate the gross value of each invoice.

Unit Eighteen

Study the order form in Fig. 17.3 (page 201), and if you can also obtain a blank order form from your own purchasing department. Now design an order form for Red Lion Restaurants Ltd of 152 Hill Street, Sutton, Surrey, and write or type it out neatly.

Complete the order for the purchase of 20 tables from Timber Top Tables Ltd, at £30 each, on 20 April this year.

Unit Nineteen

Draw up a blank credit note, using Fig. 17.5 (page 203) as a guide.

(a) On 30 May, Red Lion Restaurants Ltd, 152 Hill Street, Sutton, Surrey returned to Timber Top Tables Ltd, 14 High Street, Preston, the following:

> 3 tables at £30 each
> 5 chairs at £12 each
> 1 bookcase (damaged) at £25
> 4 benches (sent in error) at £15 each

Enter these details on the credit note.

(b) How does this credit note affect the account of Red Lion Restaurants Ltd with Timber Top Tables Ltd?

(c) What effect will this credit note have on Timber Top Tables' sales ledger?

Unit Twenty

(a) Calculate (i) the gross pay and (ii) the net pay for each of the following employees. In your answers, make clear which refer to F. Norton and which to P. Wilson.

Name Hours	Hourly rate	Gross	National Insur- ance	Income tax	Savings	Total deductions	Net pay
F. Norton 49 hr	£2.50		£7.80	£23.90	£4.00		
P. Wilson 41 hr	£2.10		£5.81	£17.75	£2.00		

(b) Draw up an analysis showing the numbers and denominations of notes and coins to pay Mr J. Brown £67.78. Select from the following:

Notes: £10 £5 £1
Coins: 50p 10p 5p 2p 1p

(c) What information is to be found on Form P45 and what happens to each of the three parts?

(d) Briefly describe how National Insurance contributions are calculated and name one cash benefit provided by the NI scheme.

[*RSA, Office Practice I*]

Unit Twenty-one

Your office manager has suggested that you spend some time working in management services, to broaden your understanding of your organization. Write her a memorandum, stating which aspect of management services you would like to be involved in, and why.

Unit Twenty-two

Talk to the receptionist at your college or at the place where you work. Find out how he or she spends the working day, and then prepare a job description, following the headings in Fig. 1.1 (page 5). Now draw up a list of the qualities and experience you think are necessary to do the job well.

Unit Twenty-three

Look through the job advertisements in your local newspaper. Find three jobs for which you think you might be qualified. Draft a separate letter of application for each, highlighting your reasons for wanting the position and why you feel you would be suited for it.

Index